Language Anxiety

From Theory and Research to Classroom Implications

Elaine K. Horwitz
University of Texas
at Austin

Dolly J. Young
University of Tennessee
at Knoxville

Foreword by Robert C. Gardner

PRENTICE HALL, Englewood Cliffs, New Jersey 07632

Library of Congress Cataloging-in-Publication Data

Horwitz, Elaine Kolker
    Language anxiety : from theory and research to classroom implications / Elaine K. Horwitz, Dolly J. Young.
    Includes bibliographical references.
    ISBN 0-13-523796-3 (c) ISBN 0-13-523465-4 (p)
    1. Language and languages—Study and teaching—Psychological aspects.   2. Second language acquisition.   3. Anxiety.   I. Young, Dolly J.   II. Title.
    P 53.7.H67   1991
    401'.93—dc20
                            90-43489
                                CIP

To our children, husbands, parents,
and to present and future
language learners

Acquisitions editor: Steve DeBow
Editorial/production supervision and
interior design: Margaret Lepera and Brian Hatch
Cover design: Marianne Frasco
Prepress buyer: Herb Klein
Manufacturing buyer: David Dickey

© 1991 by Prentice-Hall, Inc.
A Division of Simon & Schuster
Englewood Cliffs, New Jersey 07632

Printed in the United States of America
10 9 8 7 6 5 4 3 2

ISBN 0-13-523796-3 (Case)

ISBN 0-13-523465-4 (Paper)

Prentice-Hall International (UK) Limited, *London*
Prentice-Hall of Australia Pty. Limited, *Sydney*
Prentice-Hall Canada Inc., *Toronto*
Prentice-Hall Hispanoamericana, S.A., *Mexico*
Prentice-Hall of India Private Limited, *New Delhi*
Prentice-Hall of Japan, Inc., *Tokyo*
Simon & Schuster Asia Pte. Ltd., *Singapore*
Editora Prentice-Hall do Brasil, Ltda., *Rio de Janeiro*

Contents

Foreword

I've never written a foreword for a book before, and when invited to do so I accepted the invitation willingly. The topic is one that has interested me for many years and I looked forward to seeing a volume published that dealt with it from many perspectives. When the manuscript arrived, I read it with growing enthusiasm. This book is an interesting mix of theory, empiricism, and advice. It offers to the reader an excellent review of much of the thinking in this fascinating field, and provides an abundance of hypotheses for the researcher, suggestions for the language teacher and advice for the language student (particularly the one troubled by the language learning experience).

I must admit that I have had some difficulty with the concept of language anxiety, not only because I have experienced it myself, but also because I have had problems integrating it into a model of the language learning process. For years, my colleagues and I have included measures of language class anxiety and language use anxiety in many of our studies, but language anxiety has never really been integrated into our socio-educational model of second language acquisition. The socio-educational model focuses on motivation, and proposes that in many cultural contexts such motivation is influenced by attitudes toward the other language community and other ethnic groups in general, and by attitudes toward the language learning context. Language anxiety is considered as another important affective component in the model that is correlated with the various attitudinal and motivational characteristics, but we have yet to determine precisely where it fits into this conceptualization. Reading this book has strengthened my resolve to work harder to determine just where it does fit. Clearly, as well documented throughout this book, language anxiety is a pervasive and prominent force in the language learning context, and any theoretical model that seeks to understand and interpret the language learning process must consider its effect.

I also have some concerns about the measurement of language anxiety. Typically, measures of language anxiety contain statements such as, "It embarrasses me to volunteer answers in my language class." Generally, too, scores on such measures relate negatively to achievement. The favored interpretation is that the anxiety has a detrimental effect on language learning or performance. However, an alternative view is that students who agree with such statements have, for many reasons, not developed proficiency in the language and as a result experience the feelings of anxiety implied in the item, or at least report such feelings in order to explain their difficulties. Resolving these two contrasting interpretations is important if the true role of anxiety in the language learning process is to be understood. This same type of criticism can be, and has been, applied to the interpretation associated with the relation of attitudes and motivation to second language proficiency. In our research, we have been concerned with obtaining data to help clarify the appropriate causal interpretation, but this is a slow and difficult operation. It requires a number of studies (using different designs with different dependent measures), each of which is focused on providing possible interpretations of the process underlying the relationship between attitudinal/motivational attributes and second language proficiency. In my view, similar endeavors are required with the concept of language anxiety, and this book represents a significant first step in this regard.

This book provides a revealing glimpse of the concept of language anxiety from a number of perspectives. As described, such anxiety involves evaluation apprehension, communication anxiety, interpersonal anxiety and the many other concerns that people may experience when placed in a novel situation or in one where an attempt must be made to communicate without the tools necessary to do so. The book discusses research that is throwing light on some of these many aspects and procedures that teachers and students can use to either overcome possible debilitating effects of such anxiety or at least to recognize the symptoms and generality of the phenomenon. Often, too, it is made clear that some obvious solutions will not necessarily work for all individuals. To me, this is an important strength of this book. It offers many suggestions and helpful hints, but never oversimplifies the nature of the phenomenon nor underplays the significance of the anxiety experience for the individuals concerned.

From my own perspective, I kept wondering about the etiology of language anxiety. Does it derive from more general forms of anxiety in that generally anxious individuals have a predisposition to also experience language anxiety, or is it relatively distinct? Does it grow out of experiences directly associated with the language and the learning context, or is it possible that because the other language is a representation of another cultural community, there is a predisposition among some people to experience such anxiety because of their own concerns about ethnicity, foreignness, and the like? Is such anxiety influenced by the nature of the socio-cultural milieu in which the individual lives, or is it equally active in any type of cultural setting? A distinction is often made between second language learning and foreign language learning. The former tends to be used to refer to contexts where the language being learned is a viable one in the immediate environment, whereas the latter refers to language learning in contexts where the other language isn't readily available. Could it be that language anxiety is more relevant in one context than the other?

These are just some of the questions that occurred to me in my first reading of the book, and I anticipate that subsequent readings will suggest not only more questions, but also ways of answering them. Of one thing I am certain: I will be reading this book again. I found it to be stimulating, thought-provoking, and informative, and I know that I will have many occasions to study it again. It is a significant contribution!

Robert C. Gardner
Professor of Psychology
University of Western Ontario
London, Canada

Contributors

Ronald L. Applbaum is president of Westfield State College, Westfield, Massachusetts. He has co-authored seven texts in such wide-ranging areas as public, group, and organizational communications; authored numerous articles in speech communication; and serves as Secretary General of the World Communication Association.

Susan Applbaum has been a high school English teacher for 20 years and is an instructor at the University of Texas–Pan American. At Penn State University she directed a college reticence program designed to help students cope with oral communication anxiety. She has co-authored several articles and book chapters in speech communication.

Bruce L. Brown is professor of psychology at Brigham Young University. He has done theoretical and empirical work on various aspects of the psychology of language and culture. He has also developed a number of multivariate graphical methods for data analysis.

Christine M. Campbell is Test Project Director, Testing Division, The Defense Language Institute. Author of articles on anxiety, critical thinking, and testing in the foreign language classroom, she currently compiles the "In Other Professional Journals" section in *The Modern Language Journal*.

David Crookall is a tenured professor in France and currently teaches in the MA TESOL Program at the University of Alabama. He is co-editor of *Simulation, Gaming, and Language Learning* (Newbury House/Harper & Row) and of

Communication and Simulation (Multilingual Matters), and is editor of *Simulation & Gaming: An International Journal* (Sage Publications).

John Daly is a professor in the College of Communications at the University of Texas at Austin. He is the author of more than 70 scholarly articles and chapters in the fields of communication, psychology, education, English, anthropology, and linguistics, editor of four academic books, and former editor of the journal *Communication Education.*

Karen A. Foss is professor of speech communication and Program Leader of Women's Studies at Humboldt State University. She publishes in the areas of rhetorical theory and criticism, communication and gender, and communication apprehension.

Robert C. Gardner is professor of psychology at the University of Western Ontario, London, Canada. He has written books and articles on the role of attitudes and motivation on second language learning and articles on ethnic stereotypes, psycholinguistics, and statistics.

Elaine K. Horwitz is associate professor of curriculum and instruction at the University of Texas at Austin where she teaches courses in second language acquisition and second language methodology. She has published widely in the areas of individual differences and communicative approaches to language and teaching. Her current research centers on language anxiety and student beliefs about language learning.

Michael B. Horwitz is a psychologist in private practice in Austin, Texas. His research and publications center primarily on the therapeutic relationship, anxiety management, and smoking cessation. He is the author of *The Guide to Smoke-Free Dining.*

Randal L. Jones is a professor of German and former director of the Humanities Research Center at Brigham Young University. He has published widely in the areas of second language testing and technological applications to second language learning and research.

April S. Koch is a Spanish lecturer and first-year Spanish coordinator at Penn State University. She has previously taught Spanish at the University of California at Irvine and Orange Coast College. She recently published an article concerning creative and communicative homework in *Hispania.*

Peter MacIntyre is currently completing his doctoral studies at the University of Western Ontario. He was graduated from the University College of Cape Breton with an undergraduate degree in psychology and speech communication. His interests include second language learning and communication, specifically the role of anxiety in language learning.

Harold S. Madsen is a professor at Brigham Young University where he is Linguistics Chair. He has advised various overseas ministries of education on testing and chaired the TOEFL Committee of Examiners. His research interests range from IRT test applications to test affect. He is the author of *Techniques in Testing* and *Computer: ESL.*

Hugo A. Mejías is an associate professor at the University of Texas–Pan American. A native of Chile, he was graduated from and taught at the University of Chile for several years. His fields of interest and publications are Spanish-language dialectology and sociolinguistics.

José A. Ortiz is a member of the faculty, Department of Spanish, The Defense Language Institute. He has published on foreign language anxiety and is currently working with Christine Campbell on a textbook for college Spanish.

Rebecca Oxford is coordinator of the Foreign Language Education Program at the University of Alabama, having previously worked at the Center for Applied Linguistics (Washington, D.C.). She is the author of *Learning Strategies: What Every Teacher Should Know* and co-editor of *Simulation, Gaming, and Language Learning* (both published by Newbury House).

Jo Ann Cope Powell is currently a doctoral candidate in counseling psychology at the University of Texas. She has worked as a Learning Specialist at the University of Texas since 1971 and has taught college English. She is married and has two stepsons.

Mary Lou Price is currently an education research specialist for the Texas Education Agency. She received a Master of Arts in French Literature from the University of North Carolina at Chapel Hill and a Ph.D. in French Linguistics from the University of Texas at Austin.

Armeda C. Reiztel is associate professor of speech communication, linguistics, and TESL at Humboldt State University. Her areas of research include intercultural communication and communication education. She has taught ESL in the United States and Mexico.

Thomas Scovel is professor of English at San Francisco State University. His research areas include psycholinguistics and adult second language acquisition. He is the author of *A Time to Speak,* a book on the critical period.

Tracy Terrell is professor of linguistics at the University of California at San Diego and Director of the Language Program. He has published widely in second language acquisition and methodology and is the originator of the Natural Approach Method. He is the author of *Dos Mundos, Deux Mondes, and Kontakte* (published by McGraw-Hill).

Robert T. Trotter II is professor and chair of the Anthropology Department at Northern Arizona University. His primary research interests are cross-cultural health care, multi-cultural education, special interest in health beliefs, alcohol studies, cognition, and communication. He is past-president of the National Association for the Practice of Anthropology.

Dolly J. Young is assistant professor of Spanish at the University of Tennessee at Knoxville where she coordinates the first-year language program and teaches graduate courses in methodology and second language acquisition. Her areas of interest and publication are language anxiety and second language reading. She is co-author of *Esquemas; Estratégias para leer.*

Preface

Sometimes when I speak English in class, I am so afraid I feel like hiding behind my chair.

I feel so dumb in my German class. I want to sit in the back of the room so maybe I won't get called on to speak. When I know I am going to have to say something, I spend what seems like eternity thinking of how it should be said and when I say it, it still doesn't come out right.

I put off taking French because I knew it was going to be hard for me. It is the most difficult course I am taking. I don't sound like I think I am supposed to and I make so many mistakes it's not even funny. But, I study a lot for this class! My family doesn't even see me anymore.

I dread going to Spanish class. My teacher is kind of nice and it can be fun, but I hate it when the teacher calls on me to speak. I freeze up and can't think of what to say or how to say it. And my pronunciation is terrible. Sometimes I think people don't even understand what I am saying.

For the past decade, questions about anxiety and language learning have emerged in virtually every aspect of language instruction: student performance, curriculum planning, grading, placement, teacher expectations, and program organization. Efforts to address these questions have resulted in a new field of research, a field that encompasses not only second language but also foreign language study. Indeed, the entire field of anxiety research, like this volume, is necessarily interdisciplinary. Studies about language anxiety range from investigations of how factors such as instructional organization or students' preconceptions affect learning to examinations of how language anxiety is related to and different from other types of anxiety. The papers included in this volume represent this variety of focus and research approach.

In another sense, the study of language anxiety is not a new field. Language teachers have long been aware of the fact that many of their students experience discomfort in the course of language learning. The academic literature, on the other hand, has offered a somewhat confusing account of language anxiety; researchers have been unable to establish a clear picture of how anxiety affects language learning and performance. While many studies have shown that anxious individuals are less successful at language learning, several studies have found no relationship between anxiety and language learning, and occasionally anxiety has been found to facilitate language learning. At a time when anxiety reactions to science and mathematics study are becoming increasingly well understood, we are only beginning to define language anxiety and identify its effects in susceptible individuals.

This collection of essays attempts to bridge the gap between learners' and teachers' intuitive perceptions of the language learning experience and the academic literature on language anxiety. By considering the phenomenon of language anxiety from the perspectives of theorists, researchers, learners, and teachers, we hope to describe language anxiety more clearly and, ultimately, offer guidance for its reduction. The volume is directed both at practitioners who encounter anxious learners and scholars who seek to refine our understanding of the role of anxiety in language learning. Teachers and program directors will be sensitized to the characteristics of anxious students and find many concrete suggestions for decreasing anxiety, as will counselors and other professionals who treat students with language learning problems.

The text is organized into six parts and an afterword, each part offering insight into a different dimension or aspect of language anxiety. The chapters consider a range of topics: definitions of language anxiety; how anxiety functions in language learning; the relationship between language anxiety and others types of anxiety; the effects of anxiety on language performance; the emotional experience of the anxious language learner; and the relationship of instructional practice and program organization to learner anxiety.

Most of the chapters have been written specifically for this volume, but several are classic treatments of anxiety that have appeared elsewhere.[1] Each section includes a preview highlighting important issues to help synthesize and apply theoretical perspectives and empirical findings to classroom practice. The term *language anxiety* rather than *foreign language anxiety* or *second language anxiety* was deliberately chosen. We believe that both foreign and second language learners experience anxiety and that a comparison of learning contexts is useful in determining the role of culture and learning environment in anxiety reactions. Each chapter may emphasize second or foreign language learning depending on the background and outlook of the author.

Finally, a word about the ultimate concern of this text, namely language learners. In our study of language anxiety we have been truly surprised at the number of students who experience anxiety and distress in their language classes. Although this book is addressed to language teaching professionals, reducing the anxiety associated with language learning will require the cooperative efforts of both teachers and students. We must help students understand why they become anxious and offer them strategies for coping with anxiety. As a first step, we must acknowledge students' feelings of insecurity and let them know that their discomfort is not only shared by other language learners but also recognized by their instructors. Above all, we must listen to our students when they offer their reactions to language learning. It is, therefore, our sincere hope that this volume will initiate a dialogue about language anxiety between second language teachers and their students. We believe these discussions will offer insights and accommodations that will help turn all language classrooms into more supportive learning environments. (Editors contributed equally to this volume, and are listed alphabetically.)

Elaine K. Horwitz
Dolly J. Young

1. In some cases, reference styles have been changed to make the volume consistent.

Acknowledgments

We wish to thank the numerous people involved in the many phases of this book. Heartfelt thanks go to Drs. Janet Swaffar, Katie Arens, Mary Traschel, Timothy Joseph, and Michael Horwitz for their insightful comments and invaluable suggestions concerning the conception and realization of this work. We also wish to thank our editor, Steve DeBow, for his enthusiasm and support throughout the project. Special thanks go to Merry Wolf for her meticulous work in formatting this volume and Byung-Kyoo Ahn for his help in gathering examples of anxious language learners abroad. Finally, our sincere gratitude to the contributors of this volume and to the journals that granted permission to reprint classic articles. Without these contributions, this work would not be possible. Specifically, we acknowledge:

Young, Dolly J. (1986, October). The relationship between anxiety and foreign language oral proficiency ratings. *Foreign Language Annals, 12,* 439–448. Reprinted with permission from the American Council on the Teaching of Foreign Languages, publishers of *Foreign Language Annals.*

Scovel, Thomas. (1978, June). The effect of affect: A review of the anxiety literature. *Language Learning, 28,* 129–142.

Horwitz, Elaine K. (1986, September). Preliminary evidence for the reliability and validity of a foreign language anxiety scale. *TESOL Quarterly, 20,* 559–562. Copyright 1986 by *TESOL Quarterly.* Reprinted by permission.

Foss, Karen A., & Reitzel, Armeda C. (1988, September). A relational model for managing second language anxiety. *TESOL Quarterly, 22,* 427–454. Copyright 1988 by *TESOL Quarterly.* Reprinted by permission.

Horwitz, Elaine K., Horwitz, Michael B., & Cope, Jo Ann. (1986, summer). Foreign language classroom anxiety. *The Modern Language Journal, 70,* 125–132.

MacIntyre, P. D., & Gardner, R. C. (1989). Anxiety and second language learning: Toward a theoretical clarification. *Language Learning, 39,* 251–275.

Part One

Anxiety and Language Learning

Language anxiety is only one of several types of anxiety that have been identified by psychologists. Most teachers are familiar with test anxiety or public-speaking anxiety. In addition, certain individuals seem to be generally anxious as a part of their personality. In the first two sections of this volume we consider basic questions such as: What kind of anxiety is language anxiety? What behaviors are associated with it? How does language anxiety affect language learning?

In general, there are two approaches to the description of language anxiety: (1) Language anxiety may be viewed as a manifestation of other more general types of anxiety. For example, test-anxious people may feel anxious when learning a language because they feel constantly tested, or shy people may feel uncomfortable because of the demands of communicating publicly. Or (2) Language anxiety may be seen as a distinctive form of anxiety expressed in response to language learning. That is, something unique to the language-learning experience makes some individuals nervous.

The two contributions presented in this section represent the former perspective; that is, they consider many types of anxiety—for example, test anxiety, anxiety as a stable personality trait, and communication apprehension—and how they relate to second-language learning. In the opening chapter, Daly discusses reactions to second language learning from the perspective of first language communication apprehension. As communication apprehension refers to the anxiety experienced by many people when communicating in their first language, it would seem to have many logical ties to second language anxiety. Daly presents an overview of how first language researchers have approached the description, measurement, and treatment of anxiety and offers suggestions for their application to second language learning. Thus, his paper offers a rich program of how the second language literature might approach the exploration of language anxiety.

1

Scovel's (1978) hallmark paper reviews the wide range of anxiety theories and measures that have been discussed in the academic discourse on language anxiety. For the nonspecialist, Scovel's paper offers an especially lucid description of the types of anxiety that have been studied in connection with language learning. Scovel is credited with synthesizing the then available literature on language anxiety and for recognizing its confused state. Specifically, he concludes that it is difficult to determine the effect of anxiety in language learning because of (1) the inconsistency of anxiety instruments used to assess language anxiety, and (2) the complex and intricate hierarchy of variables that may intervene in the language-learning process. Thus, his paper highlights the importance of having a clear conception of language anxiety before one can document the effects of anxiety on language learning. It also focuses attention on learner variables that may serve to increase or limit learner anxiety.

While Daly makes a cogent case for the application of communication apprehension to language learning and performance, Scovel predicts the trend we shall see in the papers contained in the following section of this volume, namely the identification of an anxiety form unique to language learning. While the jury is still out on both of these perspectives, they imply different approaches to the description and measurement of language anxiety, and the reader should begin to consider the implications of each.

Chapter One

Understanding Communication Apprehension: An Introduction for Language Educators

John Daly   The University of Texas at Austin

INTRODUCTION

One of the most studied topics in the field of speech communication is the tendency on the part of some people to avoid, and even fear, communicating orally. Working under a variety of rubrics such as *stage fright, speech anxiety, communication apprehension, reticence,* and *social anxiety,* scholars have spent considerable time and effort describing the phenomena as well as developing means for its assessment. Much attention has also been directed toward identifying correlates and consequences of communication apprehension and refining ways of alleviating the anxiety. My purpose in this chapter is not to discuss any one aspect of this research thoroughly, but rather to offer a brief overview of theory and research on the topic that will provide a map for interested readers to frame their own interests so they may later delve more deeply into the literature.

It is also important to note that this chapter is written from the perspective of a person whose intellectual home is the field of communication, not language education. It is clear, though, that many of the major conceptual, as well as practical, concerns of second language scholars interested in anxiety are similar to those long considered in the domain of communication. As such, reasoning from the analogy of first language anxiety may offer insights that will aid educators in coping with language anxiety.

One final word about definitions is necessary. Communication apprehension is the fear or anxiety an individual feels about orally communicating. It is important to note that there are a number of other related constructs not directly tied to orality, but which nonetheless emphasize people's anxieties about communication. For instance, there is a good deal of research in the area of writing apprehension—the fear or anxiety an individual may feel about the act of composing written materials (Daly, 1985). There is some research on touch avoidance—the anxiety a person may feel about touching and being touched (Andersen & Leibowitz, 1978). There is also some scholarship on receiver apprehension—an anxiety some people may experience when listening or receiving information (Wheeless, 1975). Finally, a limited amount of work has addressed people's anxieties about singing—singing apprehension (Andersen, Andersen, & Garrison, 1978). Each of these constructs may have some interesting relationships to language anxieties, but they appear to be less directly related than communication apprehension. Thus we limit the discussion in this chapter to that construct. I also enter with the understanding that other chapters in this volume will highlight research on language anxiety and also the cross-cultural aspects of communication apprehension. Consequently, these topics are left largely unexplored in this chapter. Here we will briefly examine the measurement of communication apprehension, theories of its development, various consequences and correlates of it, major strategies for alleviating the anxiety, and characteristics associated with situation-based apprehension. The chapter concludes with a short discussion of a special sort of communication apprehension that is of direct relevance to language instructors: public-speaking anxiety or stage fright.

MEASURING THE ANXIETY

In order to work with a psychological construct there must be some way to measure it. More practically, if teachers want to assess the impact of their instructional activities on some belief, attitude, or anxiety, they must have a means for assessing it. There are three major ways communication apprehension has been measured: *behavioral observation or ratings, physiological assessments,* and *self-reports.* Each has a history of research associated with it and, interestingly, the three are relatively uncorrelated (Clevenger, 1959). The low correlations among the three may be explained by the differing domains of interest they are tapping. Behavioral observations are typically sensitive to visible signs of nervousness or fear in a speaker (for example, fidgeting, reduced gaze, stuttering and stammering), while physiological measures tap less visible, and more momentary, reactions by a speaker such as blood pressure, heart rate, galvanic skin response, and temperature. Both observational techniques and physiological assessments tend to be poor measures of the dispositional apprehension since any number of reasons, aside from apprehension, may exist for a particular behavior or physiological reaction.

The most common method used in measuring communication apprehension is through the use of self-reports. There are at least 50 different self-report measures in the literature ranging from single-item questions to extensive, well-developed, multifactor measures. In the field of communication, the most commonly used measure is one devised by McCroskey (1984a). Labeled the "Personal Report of Communication Apprehension" (PRCA), it is composed of 24 items that can be divided into four subscales tapping communication apprehension in four contexts (public speaking, meetings, groups, and dyadic exchanges). The PRCA has well-established validity and excellent reliability.

DEVELOPMENT OF COMMUNICATION APPREHENSION

The development of communication apprehension is probably the least researched and understood issue in the scholarly literature. Yet understanding it is critical to a thorough appreciation of the apprehension construct as well as to its remediation. To date, five explanations for the development of the anxiety have been offered. While they don't contradict each other, they do highlight different contributory variables. In all likelihood no single explanation accounts for the etiology of the apprehension. However, these five perspectives offer a good sense of possible routes to apprehension (for a more thorough review, see Van Kleeck & Daly, 1982).

The first explanation rests in the realm of genetic predisposition. Early research on fraternal and identical twins, later research on twins raised apart, and, most recently, studies of adopted children consistently indicate that one's genetic legacy may be a substantial contributor to one's apprehension. The research hasn't actually looked at communication apprehension per se. Instead, research has focused on the hereditary basis of various temperament characteristics such as sociability and activity (Buss, 1988), which represent core underlying dimensions of communication apprehension. The proliferation of evidence justifying a conclusion that genetics may be a major contributor presents a knotty problem for people who have to deal with apprehensive communicators. What can one do if genetics is the cause? The answer lies in the variation left unexplained by genetics. Clearly, apprehension has no single causative agent. Rather, one's genetics establishes a predisposition that is either ameliorated or exacerbated by other environmental factors.

One's history of reinforcements and punishments related to the act of communicating may also play a central role in the development of communication apprehension. Individuals who, from early childhood, find that their attempts to communicate are greeted with negative reactions by significant others will quickly learn that staying quiet is more highly rewarded than talking. A consistent history of punishments for communication attempts may easily create an apprehensive individual. With respect to foreign language learning, a number of scenarios are possible. Imagine this scene: A young child is watching a foreign language television program and repeating some of the words. After uttering the words a number of times, the child proudly rushes to her parents and repeats the words with glee. Were the parents to respond encouragingly with supportive and positive remarks, bets are that the child would continue practicing the language. But what would happen if the parent were to react angrily, "Mary, stop talking like some foreigner and just learn your own language!" If this incident represented a pattern of responses to the child, over time she would probably come to avoid learning, and especially speaking, a foreign language.

Tied closely to a reinforcement and punishment view of communication apprehension is an explanation resurrected from early research in the area of learned helplessness. Work on learned helplessness stressed the importance of consistency in rewards and punishments. Random and inconsistent patterns of rewards, punishments, and nonresponses for engaging in the same activity were hypothesized to lead to behavioral withdrawal. Applied to communication apprehension (see McCroskey, 1987), this explanation suggests that individuals become apprehensive when they receive random and unpredictable patterns of rewards and punishments for engaging in the same verbal activity. The unpredictability of others' responses to a person's communication attempts leads him or her to become apprehensive about communicating.

Another explanation for the development of communication apprehension focuses on the adequacy of people's early communication skills acquisition. Children who are not provided with the opportunity to garner good communication skills early in life are more likely to be apprehensive than those who receive a wealth of early experience in communication. Although the evidence for this explanation is indirect at best, there does seem to be some justification for believing that skill development is related to the development of apprehension. It may well be that the critical issue is when skills develop. Children who have a head start from early training in communication may become less apprehensive than children who receive the same sorts of training later.

The final perspective (among the predominant ones) emphasizes the role of appropriate models of communicating. Specifically, it is thought that children who have adequate communication models are generally less apprehensive than children who have been exposed to inadequate models. The research basis for this explanation stems primarily from studies of social withdrawal among young children. Researchers have found that by exposing socially withdrawn youngsters to films where other children engage in appropriate social-interactive activities, their level of withdrawal decreases significantly. The view rests on the presumption that individuals garner some of their communication skills by observing others engaged in communicating.

These latter two perspectives interact with the reinforcement and learned helplessness views in an interesting, cyclical way. Individuals who feel anxious about communicating often avoid opportunities to enhance their communication skills (that is, practice). After much avoidance, when these individuals find themselves in situations where communication is required they are likely to do less well than their more skilled counterparts. This negative judgment (offered by oneself or others) of performance is likely to confirm the expectation of a poor performance and contribute to even greater anxiety and, as a consequence, lead to avoidance of settings where communication skills might be enhanced. Over time, this vicious cycle ensures that an apprehensive individual is likely to stay apprehensive.

What Is Associated with Communication Apprehension?

Probably the most thoroughly examined area in the literature on communication apprehension concerns its relationships to other behaviors and its impact on people. What happens to individuals who are apprehensive about communicating? In discussing communication apprehension it is important to remember that the apprehension, while perhaps reflected in a number of behaviors that together signal reduced communication activity, is not the sole cause of reduced social activity. People don't talk, and fear talking, for any number of reasons, only one of which may be communication anxiety. In the typical classroom, students might avoid talking because they are unprepared, uninterested, unwilling to disclose, alienated from the class, lacking confidence in their competence, or because they fear communicating. (A much more thorough description of this idea can be found in McCroskey [1987]). Only the last reason is within the realm of communication apprehension. I point this out because too often, after reading a discussion of communication apprehension, people tend to believe that apprehension is the only reason individuals are unwilling to talk. That is not so.

With this in mind, let us examine some of the major variables associated with apprehension. This review is at best cursory. A more comprehensive survey can be found in Daly and Stafford (1984). The bulk of the literature has focused on four areas: classroom, work, social settings, and personality variables associated with apprehension.

Classroom. From the start of a person's schooling, willingness to communicate plays an important role in how well one performs and how positively one is perceived. In early studies, scholars found that teachers have a positive bias toward talkative children in their classrooms. When presented with descriptions of students that varied only in the purported degree of apprehension each child had, teachers were much more favorably disposed toward the nonapprehensive student (McCroskey & Daly, 1976). Later research validated this finding with actual students (Powers & Smythe, 1980). This bias is reflected in the policy of many teachers to include classroom participation in grade calculations. Within the classroom, nonapprehensive students are more verbally participative (Richmond, 1984), choose courses and majors that require more communication (Daly & Shamo, 1977), select seats that are in high interaction zones, participate in more activities, and are perceived by both teacher and peers as more friendly and intelligent than their more anxious counterparts (McCroskey, 1977a; Richmond, 1984; Richmond & McCroskey, 1988). While there is consistent research demonstrating no difference in intelligence between high and low apprehensive students, there is considerable evidence suggesting that by the time students leave high school, low apprehensives are better prepared academically. They do better on standardized measures of academic achievement (McCroskey & Andersen, 1976) and, in college, have higher overall grade point averages. Indeed, some recent research suggests that highly apprehensive students are more likely to drop out of college than are low apprehensive ones.

We live in an educational world where orality is seen as a necessary, positive personal characteristic. Apprehensive students, through years of veiled discrimination, must feel the impact of this bias in a series of significant, long-lasting consequences. Over time, the system they are part of regularly discriminates against them. Interestingly, the impact of communication apprehension in the educational setting is not limited to the student. Teachers' levels of apprehension also impact on what happens in the school. For instance, apprehensive teachers are far more likely to be found at the lower levels of grade school or at the college level (McCroskey, Andersen, Richmond, & Wheeless, 1981). They also generally receive less positive evaluations from their students (Richmond & McCroskey, 1988).

Work and occupations. One of the critical prerequisites for success in virtually any occupation is a person's ability (and willingness) to communicate. In initial employment interviews, some evidence suggests that highly apprehensive applicants fare less well. They are perceived less positively and are offered significantly lower starting salaries (Daly, Richmond, & Leth, 1979). In selecting positions, highly apprehensive individuals choose occupations which they perceive to have lower communication associated with them (and which, parenthetically, are usually of lower status) (Daly & McCroskey, 1975). Evidence also suggests that, once in a job, highly apprehensive individuals are generally less satisfied in their work and less successful. For instance, they move less quickly up the organizational ladder. Why? In part because higher-tier jobs demand great amounts of communication; in part because the person must be good at communication-related skills such as networking, meetings, and presentations in order to climb the organizational ladder successfully (Richmond & McCroskey, 1988). In meetings, highly apprehensive people, in general, participate less, and when they do offer good suggestions or ideas, the credit is often attributed to the more talkative individuals who take up the idea and extend it. Highly apprehensive people are perceived to have less of the qualities demanded in leadership roles (Daly, McCroskey, & Richmond, 1977).

Social. Highly apprehensive individuals live in very different social worlds from their low apprehensive counterparts (see reviews by Daly & Stafford, 1984; McCroskey, 1977c; Richmond & McCroskey, 1988). In particular, apprehensive individuals are perceived less positively in terms of social attractiveness and general competence than are nonapprehensive individuals. High apprehensives also tend to have fewer friends, and more often than not those friends are family members. They tend to interact less often with strangers, are less willing to engage in assertive social behaviors, are less innovative, tend to take on few, if any, leadership roles in their communities, are often socially isolated, and, nonverbally, engage in a variety of withdrawn behaviors (for example, lower gaze, more anxiety cues, more fidgeting, greater personal space).

Concerning intimate relationships, evidence suggests that high apprehensives are less likely to "date around," more likely to date a single person to the exclusion of others, and less likely to accept blind dates. When actual verbal behaviors are examined, the results are predictable: Apprehensive individuals tend to talk less, are less able to interrupt successfully, engage in more speech disfluencies and rhetorical interrogatives, have longer latencies of verbal responses, make more negative and fewer positive self-statements, exhibit more submissiveness, and remember less about their conversations than low apprehensives. Useful future research may relate this to language learning and use. Might apprehensives be less likely to interact in a second language? Might they be less willing to talk with strangers they meet in other societies?

Personality characteristics.   Virtually any one personality characteristic directly or indirectly affected by social interaction has been found to be correlated with apprehension. More than a hundred significant personality correlates have been reported in research dating from the mid-1950s (see review by Daly & Stafford, 1984). Probably the single strongest and most consistent correlate of oral communication apprehension has been self-esteem. Highly apprehensive people have lower self-esteem than do less apprehensive individuals. Apprehension is also inversely related to the tendency of a person to self-disclose, be dominant, assertive, argumentative, and involved in social interactions. Apprehension is positively related to loneliness, general anxiety, test anxiety, intolerance for ambiguity, and touch avoidance. When all the personality characteristics are considered together the image they paint is not a positive one for the apprehensive individual. Most socially valued personality characteristics are seldom found in highly communicative-apprehensive people.

TREATMENT OF COMMUNICATION APPREHENSION

When scholars have explored means for reducing communication apprehension, attention has focused on two primary strands of research. The first emphasizes skill development. This approach assumes that the major problem involved in apprehension is the person's limited knowledge about, or ability in, communication. Thus, if a person's skill at communicating is enhanced, his or her apprehension would be alleviated. In a rough sense that is the basis of most communication classes. When people get more experience in actually talking, they will feel more comfortable about it. Regrettably, the weight of evidence does not support this reasoning. Some studies suggest that for highly apprehensive people a class that attempts to teach skills can actually boomerang—making them even more apprehensive (Richmond, 1984; Richmond & McCroskey, 1988), a finding reminiscent of the vicious circle mentioned in the section on the development of the apprehension. Moreover, evidence also suggests that by the time people reach college the actual skill levels of high and low apprehensive individuals may not really be that different. What is different (in terms of magnitude) is the belief, on the part of the high apprehensive, that his or her skills are substantially less than average.

The second research approach has a more clinical orientation. The most common behavioral therapy used on communication apprehension is systematic desensitization, a therapy that attempts to teach the anxious individual to link relaxation cues to images of communication events (Friedrich & Goss, 1984). This therapy has a long history of success with apprehension. There is also good data to suggest that it can be administered by people with relatively little training and can result in substantial changes after only five or six treatment sessions (many universities and colleges have ongoing systematic desensitization programs). Another therapeutic approach is cognitive restructuring (Fremouw, 1984). The therapy challenges "irrational beliefs" held by an apprehensive individual about communication and attempts to replace them with self-statements that permit the individual to better cope with communication. For example, highly apprehensive public speakers generally believe that audiences, after hearing them speak, think poorly of them as speakers. Even in the face of empirical evidence that an audience liked their speeches, apprehensive speakers persevere in their belief that the speech was poorly received.

The best therapeutic approach would seem to be a combination of the two strands. Behavioral therapies alone are not sufficient nor are ones solely based on skill development. Why? Because each, by itself, only does half the job. Simply making people comfortable with speaking or eliminating their irrational beliefs about the activity does not ensure that when they attempt to communicate they will perform successfully. If they fail in their first attempts after therapy they may retreat to their former apprehension. What is needed is some additional skills training. Similarly, if you simply try to change skills, you don't affect people's willingness to communicate. If people don't want to talk, they won't. What is called for is more work on the beliefs and anxieties of the individuals affected. Together, though, the techniques have been quite successful in alleviating apprehension.

SITUATIONAL APPREHENSION

The vast majority of work on communication apprehension has focused on the disposition of communication apprehension. In this strand of research, scholars assume that people differ, in consistent and enduring ways, in their fear or anxiety about communicating (Daly, 1987). An approach focusing on the disposition assumes that apprehension is a personality trait. More recently, some scholars have begun to consider the nature of situation-based apprehension. That is, they have started to examine what it is about situations that make people more or less anxious about communicating regardless of their dispositional apprehension. For the most part, research on this topic is preliminary; in many cases, what has been done is mostly theoretical. However, several characteristics of anxiety-provoking situations have been identified (Daly & Buss, 1984; Richmond & McCroskey, 1988):

1. *Evaluation.* The greater the degree of evaluation perceived in a setting, the greater the situational apprehension. The job interview is a good example. Although most conversations between two people are not typically that difficult (for example, an initial conversation at a cocktail party), the added dimension that your conversation partner is also judging your suitability for a job can lead to increased anxiety. The degree of perceived evaluation likely plays a substantial role in language anxiety. People may be comfortable speaking the language until they become conscious that someone may be judging their performance. Then they start getting nervous. This may explain why some students report being able to converse easily at home but when they get into a classroom they find themselves tongue-tied.

2. *Novelty.* The less familiar the situation and the people involved, the greater the situational apprehension. Whenever individuals encounter new situations or unfamiliar problems, the tendency initially is to withdraw or remain quiet. On the other hand, people tend to be more comfortable and less anxious in familiar settings. Findings indicate that

the behavioral manifestations (lower interaction, less positive perceptions) of communication apprehension do not arise when the highly apprehensive individual is with close friends. This finding is somewhat comforting because it implies that it is not simply the act of communication that is anxiety inducing. In language study, much of the nervousness associated with taking a language could be due to the novelty. When people conquer the sense that the language they are learning is new and become familiar with its culture, people, and literature, anxiety is likely to decrease.

3. *Ambiguity.* Closely related to novelty is ambiguity. As might be expected, the more ambiguous the situation, the greater the situational apprehension. When people don't know what they are being judged on, or what is going to happen, they are likely to become more reticent than in the opposite sort of setting. People get nervous when they feel unsure, when they don't know what they are supposed to do. In second language learning this often happens, leading, in turn, to greater anxiety. When people first enter a new culture the ambiguity of much of the vocabulary, and especially of the social norms, will make them more anxious about communicating.

4. *Conspicuousness.* The more conspicuousness the person feels, the more apprehension he or she will typically experience. Imagine walking into a party and having everyone turn to stare at you. That experience alone is likely to make you more anxious. People generally prefer not to be the focus of attention especially when they feel they are engaging in an activity where their competence is low. This has several possible implications for language learning. For example, when people are learning a language it may be better to have them perform without many other people around. Standing in front of or even sitting at a desk in a classroom of peers while reciting in an unfamiliar language is likely to make almost anyone anxious. The sense of conspicuousness is heightened when people feel they are making mistakes—a likely event as one struggles through the pronunciation, grammar, and vocabulary of a new language. A recent conversation with a student who had just finished her third year of Russian highlights the negative influence of conspicuousness. During her first visit to Moscow she felt totally incompetent communicating until one day when she found herself getting angry at a clerk. The angrier she got the more fluent her Russian became. When she stopped thinking about how she sounded and how others were reacting to her, her sense of conspicuousness disappeared as did her anxiety.

5. *Prior History.* The extent to which the situation has, in the past, created anxiety and fear in the person is highly correlated with the amount of situational apprehension the person feels. If your experience in a particular setting has always been negative or your contacts with a particular person have always been anxiety creating, it is likely that the same setting with the same individual will make you anxious on future occasions. The application to second language learning is straightforward. People who previously have had positive experiences learning languages are, in all likelihood, less anxious about conquering another one than are those who recollect nothing but fear, anxiety, and failure from prior attempts.

Classroom strategies.   In classroom settings, there are some very simple ways teachers can reduce the amount of situational apprehension a student feels. While probably quite obvious to the reader, the following four suggestions highlight some of the critical issues involved in creating a more supportive atmosphere for the apprehensive student. In many cases, the techniques have direct applicability to language education.

1. *Do not seat students alphabetically.* If students are seated alphabetically it is quite likely that some apprehensive students will be placed toward the front and some nonapprehensive students toward the rear. Such a seating arrangement can bring panic to the appre-

hensive student who would prefer not to be noticed and envious anguish to the nonapprehensive student who would much prefer sitting in front where interaction is high. As students generally sit in the same location day after day once they have chosen a spot, if desired the instructor can create a seating chart after the students have established their own seating arrangement.

2. *Don't require oral performances.* In most cases, and in most subject fields, teachers often confound what a student knows with how well he or she can orally communicate that information. Required oral presentations, oral book reports, oral reading, and oral descriptions of math problem solving and the like can be traumatic for communicatively anxious individuals. In most cases, what a student actually knows about the material may not be evident from how he or she discusses it. One clear exception is language classes where a strong speaking requirement component is necessary. In these cases, it is important for teachers to remember that what one hears aloud from students, and especially from apprehensive students, may not be a good sampling of their knowledge of the written portion of a language. It is quite possible for a highly apprehensive student to be highly competent in understanding the grammar, syntax, and vocabulary of a language and yet appear very incompetent when asked to speak the language aloud.

3. *Don't call on students randomly.* In many classrooms, teachers call on students in a random fashion trying, perhaps, to keep them alert or monitor their preparation. This random questioning creates, for the highly apprehensive student, great anxiety—far greater anxiety than that experienced by the low apprehensive one. Why? Because the performance being sought is a verbal one, and any failure in an oral activity represents, in the words of one apprehensive individual, a "nightmare experience." Even if the apprehensive student is prepared, the randomness of the questioning and thus the unpredictability of the talk makes him or her more nervous, thus exacerbating any performance fears. Letting students volunteer to participate or providing predictable participation patterns (calling on people row-by-row, seat-by-seat) is the wiser strategy.

4. *Don't punish classroom talk.* Too often teachers assume that any talk that is not directly tied to a student-teacher interaction is bad. Students whispering to each other, students talking out of turn, and students talking loudly in group meetings often receive punishments for their "outbursts." The apprehensive student sees the punishment and infers that talking is not something desired in that classroom; that if one talks, he or she will be punished. A better strategy is to reward appropriate talk and when punishing any sort of talk publicly tell the class that talking is more than acceptable when it is task relevant. Remember, as well, that in many cases, talk that seems off-task to a teacher is not necessarily off-task to students. For instance, students will often turn to a peer for clarification of something a teacher is discussing or share an example with another student about a principle being discussed by a teacher. Those sorts of exchanges may appear to the teacher to be whispers between friends. They are, but they are also relevant to the learning experience.

An Application: Public-Speaking Anxiety (Stage Fright)

Research on communication apprehension, and its variants, is broad in its coverage of topics. Interest ranges from various social anxieties (for example, heterosexual social anxiety—dating anxiety, in short) to subject-specific anxieties (writing apprehension, touch avoidance, singing apprehension, etc.). One topic that has been examined for many years, and which is undoubtedly of great importance to second language educators, is public-speaking anxiety.

The fear of giving a public speech is the single biggest fear of the American population (Bruskin, 1973) exceeding such phobias as fear of snakes, heights, and elevators. Interestingly, in that survey, public speaking was a major fear of only those earning less than what today would be about $70,000. For those in higher-income brackets, public speaking was seldom a fear.

What makes someone experience stage fright? Many of the same situational characteristics described above (evaluation, novelty, ambiguity, conspicuousness, prior history) also contribute to public-speaking anxiety. For instance, evidence suggests that people who experience stage fright tend to become highly self-focused as a function of feeling conspicuous. Increased self-focus leads to reduced attention on the audience and the environment, leading, in turn, to poorer speech performances. In addition to the factors described above, several others have been cited in the literature on public-speaking anxiety.

One is *rule rigidity*. Rose (1985), in a discussion of "writer's block," argues that one characteristic of people who experience blocking is a tendency to become stuck on some rule about what good writing is. They believe, for instance, that one must have a perfect opening sentence in a composition. And until they write that perfect first sentence they can't go further into the essay. People who aren't blocked may have the same belief but don't apply the rule as rigidly. Instead, they continue writing, knowing that later on they can go back and rewrite the first sentence. In short, people with writer's block let the rules run them; people who get over blocks run the rules. The same phenomena can be seen in public speaking. Many people who experience stage fright do so because they have very fixed rules about what a presentation ought to look like. "It must have an interesting opening, three points, and a dynamite conclusion" is a rule you might hear an anxious speaker utter. Now clearly the rule is reasonable but the critical issue is how rigidly it is applied. While for most speeches such a structure might be preferred, it is not a must. Some speeches don't need three points, some don't have great introductions, and some need no conclusion. The same goes with nonverbal behaviors and pronunciation issues. Certainly one's behaviors when speaking are important, but a good speaker can get away with virtually anything if he or she is competent enough. Extreme stage fright is often accompanied with rule rigidity. In language anxiety, the same rigidity very likely will appear among the anxious. While the nonanxious student may blissfully mispronounce some words, skip over others, and change the structure and even meaning of some materials, the anxious student may focus too much on what "should" be done. These "shoulds" may, in the end, get in the way of becoming conversational in a language.

A second factor may be the labels people apply to the arousal they experience when speaking. Individuals who experience stage fright will often talk of the butterflies in their stomachs, the sweating palms, the racing heartbeat, the shaking hands. Although anxious people associate these manifestations with fear and anxiety, they might also be labeled "excitement." The arousal could be relabeled from fear to fun, from nervousness about failure to excitement about coming success. The actual physiological characteristics associated with fear and excitement are not that different. The critical issue is the label that one applies.

A third factor in understanding stage fright is the audience. In conversations, meetings, and groups, audience characteristics play some role but certainly not as powerful a role as they do in public-speaking situations. In public speaking one is addressing an audience, and it can be difficult to adapt one's message properly to the audience. But certain characteristics of the audience can make it doubly difficult. For instance, the greater the heterogeneity of the audience the more anxious that speakers tend to be. If audience members all have one level of knowledge about the topic, if all are from the same demographic group, all are of about the same age, all have the same interests, and so on, then it is much easier to talk to them than if they differ on these characteristics. Thus, the greater the heterogeneity of the audience, the greater the speaker's stage fright. The heterogeneity of the audience may be a particular problem in English classes for foreign students where many countries and cultures are represented.

SUMMARY

This admittedly brief foray into the literature on communication apprehension can best be seen as an introduction to the growing disciplinary concern. There is no topic in the field of communication that has received as much attention in the past thirty years as communication apprehension. The reason is simple—it clearly affects, in significant ways, a sizable portion of the population. This chapter will be successful if it accomplishes two things. First, readers will have gained some familiarity with the construct and will be prompted to read further. Second, readers will find immediate and useful applications of this literature to the study of language anxiety. Fields of inquiry often develop through analogy and metaphor—finding in one discipline ideas, methods, constructs, and theories that can be transplanted to another field. The underlying contention of this chapter is that for the scholar interested in language anxiety there is much that is useful in the field of communication apprehension. Certainly the opposite is also true. But that awaits another time and another chapter.

Chapter Two

The Effect of Affect on Foreign Language Learning: A Review of the Anxiety Research

Thomas Scovel   San Francisco State University

AFFECTIVE VARIABLES

One does not have to delve deeply into the literature on the relationship between affective variables and second language learning to discover that "affect" is a cover term under which is swept a wide range of disparate constructs and behaviors. Included under the rubric of affective variables are such various categories as: "cognitive style" (Brown, 1973), "ego boundaries" (Taylor, 1974), "reserved vs. outgoing personality" (Chastain, 1975), and "adventuresome" (Tucker, Hamayan, & Genesee, 1976). Perhaps the most peculiar candidate of all for an affective construct, and, at the same time, the most indicative of the need for a more precise definition of affect in second language acquisition, is the variable "conformist Protestant ethic" suggested by Scoon (1971). Affective variables have often been defined as the converse of cognitive variables; that is, they are everything which impinges on language learning which is unrelated to cognition. Although half a definition is better than none at all, this interpretation is imprecise; furthermore, it forces us to accomplish an even more formidable task —to define cognitive variables! As Lamendella (1977) has wryly observed, there are two kinds of researchers who deal with cognition, those who define it erroneously and those who don't define it at all. In the interests of avoiding such a nihilistic approach to the definition of affective variables, a necessary prelude to the investigation into their relationship with second language learning is to attempt to place affect in a proper perspective—as a subset, along with cognition, whatever it may be (if it is at all!), of a larger set of variables, a class that would include as separate subsets many of the constructs found in the literature to date, including the examples cited above.

Several investigators have suggested a broad, classificatory term for this large set of variables of which affect could be considered an appropriate subset, among them being: "initiating factors" (Schumann, 1976a), "perseverance factors" (Swain & Naiman, 1976), and "personality characteristics" (Swain & Burnaby, 1976), but perhaps the most direct and simplest is "learner variables" (Swain, 1977). After reviewing Schwartz's classification of motivational factors in learning, Chastain (1976) suggests that there appear to be two different types of factors which influence the learner; in other words, "learner variables" can be divided into two subcategories: intrinsic learner variables and extrinsic ones.

> Some students are generally motivated intrinsically; others extrinsically. Schwartz (1972) lists the intrinsic motivators as anxiety, need to achieve, self-concepts, and aspirations; and the extrinsic motivators as sociocultural influences and social reinforcers. (p. 73)

It can be seen, therefore, that most of the constructs and behaviors which have been misclassified as affective factors in the literature can be subsumed under the category "learner variables," either intrinsic or extrinsic to the learner, but affect, if we adhere to its traditional definition in psychology, is itself only one variable within intrinsic learner variables, and, therefore, if we are to proceed with an examination of the relationship of anxiety to foreign language learning, we must first of all realize that we are talking about only one affective variable among many intrinsic learner variables.

Another way of viewing this set of factors which comprise the personality of the language learner is to adopt a classificatory scheme from a source quite alien to the traditional literature of applied linguistics and applied psychology. The advantage of going so far afield is twofold: it provides us with a fresh perspective of the variables which we in language learning research have become so accustomed to, and it serves to reinforce the point of view that is central to the position of this article, that affect (feeling) is but one ingredient in the complex and marvelous chemistry that creates the personality. The model I am thinking of is adopted from the rich tradition of Buddhist philosophy. Like all major religious literature, Buddhist texts have dealt with the essential nature of man and the make-up of human personality. Thus, it is not surprising to discover that the personality has been thoroughly investigated, and, according to Buddhist belief, it is classified into five *skandhas* or "mind-body complexes" (Conze, 1967, p. 107).

> As the stars in a constellation do not really belong together, but it is we who have arranged them into an arbitrary unit, so also our "personality" is a mere conventional grouping of disparate elements, all of which belong to one of the five groups, known as the skandhas.

Table 1 categorizes intrinsic learner variables into the five skandhas of Buddhist philosophy, citing an example from language learning research for each of the personality characteristics (learner variables) which relate to language acquisition. Under this scheme, affective variables, if they are to be viewed correctly, are those factors which deal with *vedanā* (feelings), the emotions of pleasure and displeasure that surround the enterprise of a task such as second language learning.

It should be clear from this introductory discussion that affective factors are those that deal with the emotional reactions and motivations of the learner; they signal the arousal of the limbic system and its direct intervention in the task of learning. Having made this point, we may now proceed to an examination of one of the most important affective variables identified in learning tasks—anxiety.

Table 1

SOME INTRINSIC LEARNER VARIABLES: CLASSIFIED AS *SKANDHAS,* THE FIVE
COMPONENTS OF THE MIND-BODY ACCORDING TO BUDDHIST PHILOSOPHY

Skandhas	English Term	Example of Research on this Variable
rūpa	body	lateralization and the critical period for language learning
samskārā	impulses	integrative vs. instrumental motivation
samjñā	perceptions and cognition	the conscious use of the "monitor" by adult language learners
vijñāna	consciousness or soul	empathy
vedanā	feelings or affective variables	anxiety

ANXIETY AND FOREIGN LANGUAGE LEARNING

The research into the relationship of anxiety to foreign language learning has provided mixed and confusing results, immediately suggesting that anxiety itself is neither a simple nor well-understood psychological construct and that it is perhaps premature to attempt to relate it to the global and comprehensive task of language acquisition. Some studies have revealed incomplete correlations between anxiety and measures of language proficiency; Swain and Burnaby (1976), for example, in their study of English-speaking French immersion children found a negative correlation between anxiety and one measure of the children's proficiency in French, but, at the same time, found no other significant correlations, either negative or positive, with any other proficiency measures. Tucker et al. also found that anxiety (in this case, one of a cluster of variables in a factor analysis) correlated again with one measure of French proficiency, but not with any of the three other criterion measures of language proficiency which they examined. It is perplexing to find anxiety implicated with one skill at one level, but never with other skills at different levels. Other studies have revealed complete correlations, that is, there is a consistent relationship between the academic performance of a language student in the classroom and an anxiety measure, but these correlations directly contradict the results obtained with other students or other languages. Backman (1976) found that the two worst English-learning Spanish speakers in her study scored the highest and the lowest on the anxiety measure she utilized. In a larger study, Chastain (1975) found a negative correlation between French audio-lingual method student scores on tests and anxiety, but, in contradiction, he discovered a positive correlation between anxiety and the scores of German and Spanish students using the traditional method. Chastain accurately identifies the crux of the problem in these anxiety studies when he states that: "perhaps some concern about a test is a plus while too much anxiety can produce negative results" (p. 160).

If Chastain's paper indicates the direction toward which anxiety/language studies should move, it is an article by Kleinmann (1977) which actually takes a step in the right direction, first by defining two different types of anxiety, and then seeking to discover a correlation between these two different constructs and measures of second language learning behavior. Kleinmann was interested in examining the relationship between the syntactic structures in English that are avoided by foreign students and syntactic structures of the students' native languages—the hypothesis being that the English structures which contrasted most markedly with the native language of the student would be avoided most frequently. After examining the English output of Arabic and Spanish students using a variety of tests, Kleinmann was able to confirm his hypothesis. Of secondary interest to him was the relationship between the avoidance behavior of the subjects and anxiety, the assumption being that "facilitating anxiety" would encourage learners to employ the very English structures that their native language group would tend to avoid. Table 2 summarizes some of the results obtained by Kleinmann and indicates that, in general, facilitating anxiety does function in the predicted manner. Apparently, the Spanish students who scored high on facilitating anxiety measures (e.g., "Nervousness while using English helps me do better") frequently used infinitive complements and direct object pronouns in English, structures that were avoided because of their difficulty by the other Spanish-speaking students. In the same manner, Arabic students who scored high on facilitating anxiety measures tended to use the passive (the present progressive proved to be an exception) more frequently than their Arabic-speaking peers, who usually avoided this structure because of its divergence from Arabic syntax. Kleinmann summarizes his conclusions about the relationship between this affective variable and language acquisition behavior with the following important statement.

> The findings suggest avoidance operating as a group phenomenon, but within the particular avoiding group, use of the generally avoided structure is a function of facilitating anxiety levels of the group's members. This finding is not inconsistent with a study conducted by Chastain (1975), who found a significant negative correlation between test anxiety and final course grade in a university audio-lingual French-as-a-foreign-language class. Obviously, the anxiety there had a debilitating influence. But Chastain also implied a facilitating influence of anxiety based on his findings that anxiety was a significant predictor of success in learning Spanish as a foreign language. The evidence, therefore, seems to support the notion that certain affective measures influence learner behavior in a foreign language. (p. 105)

The studies by Kleinmann and Chastain indicate the manner in which an affective variable, in this case, anxiety, can be appropriately investigated, but it behooves us to examine other ways in which anxiety can be viewed, not as a simple, unitary construct, but as a cluster of affective states, influenced by factors which are intrinsic and extrinsic to the foreign language learner. For this multidimensional perspective of anxiety, we must turn from language learning research and direct our attention on some of the work that has been done on anxiety in applied psychology.

ANXIETY RESEARCH IN APPLIED PSYCHOLOGY

Anxiety is commonly described by psychologists as a state of apprehension, a vague fear that is only indirectly associated with an object (Hilgard, Atkinson, & Atkinson, 1971). Because anxiety is clearly an emotional state, it is generated through the arousal of the limbic system, the primitive, subcortical "chasis" of the cerebrum, which plays an important, though indirect, role in many kinds of human enterprises, including communication (Lamendella, 1977). Anxiety is usually measured in one of three ways: by behavioral tests, where the actions of a subject are observed (floor pacing by a father in a maternity waiting room); by the subject's self-report of internal feelings and reactions ("I feel uneasy when awaiting the delivery of my first child"); or by physiological tests, where measures of heart rate, blood pressure, or pal-

Table 2

CORRELATIONS BETWEEN TWO MEASURES OF ANXIETY AND TENDENCY TO USE ENGLISH STRUCTURES NORMALLY AVOIDED BY NATIVE LANGUAGE GROUP (ADAPTED FROM KLEINMANN, 1977)

		Use of English structures normally avoided by Spanish *speaking EFL students*		*Use of English structures normally avoided by* Arabic *speaking EFL students*	
		infinitive complement	*direct object pron.*	*passive*	*present progressive*
Spanish speaking students	high facilitating anxiety	sig. cor. ($p < .01$)	sig. cor. ($p < .01$)	—	—
	high debilitating anxiety	—	—	—	—
Arabic speaking students	high facilitating anxiety	—	—	sig. cor. ($p < .05$)	#
	high debilitating anxiety	—	—	—	—

— no significant correlation obtained, as predicted
no significant correlation obtained, despite prediction

mar sweating are taken and these are assumed to be correlated to the subject's emotional state.

Because the limbic system can trigger a variety of physiological responses through the autonomic nervous system, physiological measures have long been used as an easily quantifiable indicator of a subject's emotional state. A study by Schaffer (1947) undertaken on combat aviators over three decades ago indicated that physiological reactions associated with anxiety varied from rapid pulse rate (most common) to soiling pants (least common)! Despite the illusion of empirical objectivity conveyed by the physiological experimentation, there is enormous individual variation in the physiological reactions of subjects under different states of emotional arousal. Schnore (1959), for example, discovered that patterns of physiological responses varied considerably among individuals (e.g., one subject might exhibit a lower heart rate than another during a "high arousal" task, but, at the same time, a higher degree of forearm tension than the other subject). The most promising avenue of research into the correlation of physiological measures of emotional states to human behavior seems to lead to the athletic arena, where quality of performance is measured almost entirely by active physical behavior. It is common, therefore, to encounter studies such as that undertaken by Nideffer and Yock (1976), which measured the relationship between amount of sweating during pre-race warmups and success in actual races by competitive swimmers. It was found that the higher the arousal level of the swimmers during the pre-race periods, as measured by increased palmar sweating, the poorer their results in actual races. If palmar sweating is an accurate measure of affective arousal, and if this emotional state is akin to anxiety, then it appears that increased emotional activity has an adverse effect on the ability to perform demanding physical activities at optimal levels of success. Even though language learning is largely a cerebral, rather than a physical endeavor, it is related in many ways to the acquisition of athletic skills, especially the neuromuscular task of speaking (Scovel, 1973), and it might be worthwhile to investigate the possible relationship between physiological measures of emotional arousal and success in foreign language performance, especially in articulatory tasks.

The other two measures of affective arousal, paper and pencil tests of behavior and self-reports, are not as easily quantifiable as the physiological tests, but they do have an advantage in that they are much more precise in focusing in on a specific affective construct, say anxiety, than the physical measures which can only assume to be related to affective involvement; in addition, these behavioral measures are easy to administer to large groups of subjects. For these reasons, they have been used more abundantly in applied psychology than the physiological tests. These behavioral tests are numerous and include, among others, the following: the Achievement Anxiety Test (AAT), the Taylor Manifest Anxiety Scale (MAS), the Yale Test Anxiety Scales (TAS), the State/Trait Anxiety Inventory (STAI), the Test Anxiety Scale for Children (TASC), the Children's Manifest Anxiety Scale (CMAS), and the Digit Span Test. Unfortunately, as Beeman, Martin, and Meyers (1972) point out, the reliability between these behavioral measures of anxiety and the physiological measures remains unsubstantiated.

> The relationship between paper and pencil measures of anxiety and physiological measures have been studied for years and contradictory evidence is the rule . . . Generally, there is a low correlation between clinically rated anxiety, self-rated anxiety, and psychometric anxiety. (p. 427)

There has been a large amount of research undertaken in educational psychology which attempts to assess the impact of anxiety, as measured by these many behavioral tests, on academic performance. As might be expected, the more that researchers have investigated the topic, the more complex the relationship between anxiety and classroom performance has grown, and the models first constructed to account for affect in learning have been encumbered with increasing numbers of intervening variables. Among the most important of these are: the subject studied or tested at school, the children's level of intelligence, the difficulty of the learning skill under investigation, and the degree of familiarity the children have with the learning task. It has been discovered, for example, that higher states of anxiety facilitate learning at upper levels of intelligence whereas they are associated with poorer performance at lower IQ levels, ceteris paribus (Verma & Nijhawan, 1976); furthermore, increased anxiety is likely to improve performance at later stages in a learning activity, but conversely hinders academic performance at earlier stages of the same activity (Beeman, Martin, & Meyers, 1972). Based on an earlier model of emotional drive by Taylor (1956) and Spence (1958), which claimed that high emotional drive facilitates performance when correct response reinforcement is stronger than competing response reinforcement (usually occurring at initial stages of learning), Spielberger (1966a) has presented an elaborate model which effectively integrates intelligence, stage of learning, and difficulty of task into an examination of the impact of anxiety on learning performance. In brief, the model claims that high anxiety (HA) facilitates learning when the task is relatively easy but leads to decrements in performance when the task becomes more difficult. This means that for low IQ students with HA motivation, simple tasks will be learned well with little or no initial exposure, intermediate tasks will be learned well after increased exposure, and that difficult tasks will probably be learned poorly, if at all, even after periods of long exposure. For high IQ students with HA drive, simple and intermediate tasks will be learned well irrespective of exposure, and for difficult tasks, although there might be a decrement in performance at the initial stages of the task, HA will eventually facilitate high levels of performance after a period of increased exposure. Consequently, Spielberger's model suggests that whereas HA will eventually provide positive motivation for high IQ students learning a difficult skill, it will provide negative reinforcement to the low IQ student, even under continued exposure to the activity to be acquired.

In an investigation of 7th grade children studying a variety of subjects in 12 different Australian schools, Gaudry and Fitzgerald (1971) confirmed the hypotheses proposed by Spielberger and implicated a cognitive factor (IQ) as an intervening variable in any consideration of the affective construct, anxiety. This led them to conclude:

> ... while high anxiety was associated with slightly higher performance for the most able children, it was associated with lower performance at all other levels except the centre group where the mean scores were identical. (p. 161)

Aside from the above-mentioned factors which seem to regulate the effect of affect on academic performance, be they non-affective intrinsic factors such as intelligence, or extrinsic factors such as level of difficulty of the material learned, another important fact to be taken into account is the point considered earlier in the discussion of Kleinmann's study, where it was emphasized that anxiety itself is not a simple, unitary construct that can be comfortably quantified into either "high" or "low" amounts. On the one hand, some researchers feel that momentary anxiety should be distinguished from a more permanent predisposition to be anxious, and that this dichotomy would help to account for some of the conflicting results of previous anxiety studies. This sentiment led Spielberger, Gorsuch, and Lushene (1970) to develop a measure which distinguishes between state anxiety (SA) and trait anxiety (TA), a distinction which appears to resolve some of the discrepancies of earlier studies which failed to consider this parameter of subject behavior (Hodges & Spielberger, 1969). On the other hand, some researchers have felt it important to define anxiety in terms of the potential effect it has on performance; hence, Alpert and Haber (1960) developed the Achievement Anxiety Test to identify the amount of facilitating and/or debilitating anxiety a subject possesses. The authors of this instrument are quick to point out that these constructs are not extremes on a continuum, but are independent of each other:

> In fact, these two constructs of debilitating and facilitating anxiety may be uncorrelated. Thus, an individual may possess a large amount of both anxieties, or of one, but not the other, or of none of either. The nature of this correlation can be determined empirically following the construction of two such independent measures of anxiety . . . (p. 213)

ANXIETY MOTIVATION IN FOREIGN LANGUAGE LEARNING

The facilitating/debilitating measure constructed by Alpert and Haber presents an attractive path down which future research on the effects of anxiety on foreign language acquisition might proceed, providing that a sincere attempt is made by language researchers to control or account for the many intervening variables that have already been mentioned. Indeed, there are several current trends in EFL which suggest that the field in which applied linguists labor is fertile for research on affect to take root and blossom—especially research on anxiety, as long as it is well-designed, empirical, and, if the pun can be forgiven, well-grounded.

The attractiveness of this binary approach to anxiety lies in its common sense viewpoint that learning, whatever the activity might be, is enhanced by both positive and negative motivation. A good performance, in music, in sports, or in language learning, especially the overt social act of speaking, depends on enough anxiety to arouse the neuromuscular system to optimal levels of performance, but, at the same time, not so much that the complex neuromuscular systems underlying these skills are disrupted. In this sense, these two aspects of anxiety fulfill a similar function to that of the two complementary components of the autonomic nervous system, the sympathetic and the parasympathetic; one arouses, the other depresses—each working together and in balance to keep the organism in tune with its ever-changing environment. So it is with facilitating and debilitating anxiety in the normal learner—each working in tandem, serving simultaneously to motivate and to warn, as the individual gropes to learn an ever-changing sequence of new facts about the environment. It is not at all remarkable that these two aspects of anxiety are so directly linked to the limbic system, the source of all affective arousal, because they appear to be emotional correlates of two of the four basic drives which are generated by this primitive portion of the human brain. Facilitating anxiety motivates the learner to "fight" the new learning task; it gears the learner emotionally for approach behavior. Debilitating anxiety, in contrast, motivates the learner to "flee" the new learning task; it stimulates the individual emotionally to adopt avoidance behavior. Kleinmann's work is a good example of the interplay between these two basic drives of the limbic system as manifested by the cooperative functioning of two different types of anxiety in a language learning task. Although the difference between the students' native language and the target language encouraged them to avoid (to "flee" from) the English structures which were different, those students who scored high on facilitative anxiety were emotionally equipped to approach (to "fight" in primitive terms) the very structures that their peers tended to avoid.

Another consideration that should be incorporated into the affective research is the Monitor Model for adult language acquisition. Krashen (1976) has sought to distinguish between two different types of activity in which adults engage when they attempt to master a new language. Adult learners can pick up a language informally and unconsciously, in a manner similar to children. This process, called *language acquisition,* contrasts with *language learning,* the formal, conscious study of a language more commonly undertaken by adults than by children. It is Krashen's contention that in this latter sphere of endeavor, adults have an opportunity to *monitor* their language output, using the rules and patterns they have been formally taught, to edit their target language production. Krashen's model presents yet another variable to be accounted for in our investigation of the effect of anxiety on language learning performance. Regardless of what specific measures of affect are used, I would imagine that anxiety is more directly implicated in the formal activity of language learning than in the informal enterprise of language acquisition. Be that as it may, the monitor theory should be incorporated into any model concerning the effect of affect on foreign language learning, for it deals with the intrinsic learner variables that are part and parcel of the learner's personality, and, as such, have a bearing on the individual's affective motivation.

Currently, there is great interest in the psychological motivation of adult foreign language learners, especially in terms of the students' relationship to their teachers and their learning environment. This interest has encouraged the development of several new methods: among them, the Silent Way (Gattegno, 1972), Counseling-Learning (Curran,

1976), and Suggestopedia (Lozanov, 1973). As Stevick (1976) has pointed out, these methods are to be commended in that they recognize the importance of affective motivation in the task of foreign language learning. It is fair to claim that all of these methods are interested in controlling and regulating affective motivation, in particular, anxiety, and in a vague way, proponents of these methods are making claims that are supported by Kleinmann's anxiety results. Blatchford (1976), for example, in a discussion of the Silent Way, refers to the negative effects of "tenseness" (debilitating anxiety?) but to the salubrious benefits of "tension" (facilitating anxiety?) in the EFL classroom. I would like to emphasize, however, that the results of the anxiety research in applied psychology do not provide a ringing endorsement of these new methodologies; rather, the results indicate what language teachers have known all along, that students learn better in a supportive, nonthreatening environment. As Brown (1977) has pointed out in his fair but forthright review of Counseling Learning, the enormous magnitude and variety of affective and cognitive variables that intervene at both the individual and the cultural level in language learning, make it difficult, if not impossible, to prescribe one single method as the most congruent with the emotional and intellectual needs of the majority of students.

The conclusion might read like a good news–bad news joke, and if that is so, I trust that the news is not so much amusing as it is informative. The good news is that we are able to isolate affective variables in our research into the psychology of language acquisition; this is illustrated by Kleinmann's study, which measured the effects of anxiety on language learning performance in a well-circumscribed experiment. The bad news is that the deeper we delve into the phenomenon of language learning, the more complex the identification of particular variables becomes. As this paper has suggested, before we begin to measure anxiety, we must become more cognizant of the intricate hierarchy of learner variables that intervene: the intrinsic/extrinsic factors, the affective/cognitive variables, and then the various measures of anxiety and their relationship to these other factors. But the overwhelming intricacy of these intertwining systems should not deter us from the task of trying to discover natural patterns and continuities, for, at the very least, we will realize even more profoundly and with even deeper respect than before, the marvelous act that our students so subtly perform in front of us day by day, the act of inheriting someone else's language and culture.

Part Two

Language Anxiety: Conceptualizations and Research Paradigms

While the papers in the first section consider the role of many types of anxiety in language learning, the papers in this second section seek to define language anxiety as a specific type of anxiety and offer suggestions for the exploration of the phenomenon of language anxiety. They pose questions such as "How is language anxiety related to and different from other types of anxiety? Is it unidimensional or made up of several components? Do different aspects of language anxiety affect language learning in different ways?"

After examining the role of related types of anxiety in language learning—specifically communication apprehension, fear of negative evaluation, and test anxiety—Horwitz, Horwitz, and Cope conclude that language anxiety is a type of anxiety unique to second-language learning; that is, they conceive of language anxiety as something more than the sum of its component parts. In the second article in this section, Horwitz offers a construct validation study of a foreign language anxiety scale as further evidence for the existence of a specific anxiety reaction to language learning. Importantly, she found that anxious students receive lower grades in their foreign language class. On the other hand, MacIntyre and Gardner, in the third article in this section, test Horwitz, Horwitz, and Cope's original three-part model of language anxiety (communication apprehension, fear of negative evaluation, and test anxiety) and conclude that all three have an important role in language anxiety. Thus, they lend support to the view that language anxiety is a composite of other types of anxiety.

While a discussion of the nature of language anxiety might appear somewhat removed from the problems of an anxious learner in a particular classroom, we must not forget Scovel's caution that different conceptions of anxiety imply different research and measurement modalities. Horwitz, Horwitz, and Cope base their instrument for anxiety measurement on their conception of language anxiety. How language anxiety is perceived has profound implications for the direction of future research efforts.

Chapter Three

Foreign Language Classroom Anxiety

Elaine K. Horwitz   The University of Texas at Austin
Michael B. Horwitz   Austin, Texas
Jo Ann Cope   The University of Texas at Austin

"I just know I have some kind of disability: I can't learn a foreign language no matter how hard I try."

"When I'm in my Spanish class I just freeze! I can't think of a thing when my teacher calls on me. My mind goes blank."

"I feel like my French teacher is some kind of Martian death ray: I never know when he'll point at me!"

"It's about time someone studied why some people can't learn languages."[1]

Such statements are all too familiar to teachers of foreign languages. Many people claim to have a mental block against learning a foreign language, although these same people may be good learners in other situations, strongly motivated, and have a sincere liking for speakers of the target language. What, then, prevents them from achieving their desired goal? In many cases, they may have an anxiety reaction which impedes their ability to perform successfully in a foreign language class. Anxiety is the subjective feeling of tension, apprehension, nervousness, and worry associated with an arousal of the autonomic nervous system (Spielberger, 1983). Just as anxiety prevents some people from performing successfully in science or mathematics, many people find foreign language learning, especially in classroom situations, particularly stressful.

When anxiety is limited to the language learning situation, it falls into the category of specific anxiety reactions. Psychologists use the term specific anxiety reaction to differentiate people who are generally anxious in a variety of situations from those who are anxious only in specific situations. Researchers have identified several specific anxieties associated with school tasks such as test-taking and with academic subjects such as mathematics or science (Tobias, 1978; Mallow, 1981).

Second language researchers and theorists have long been aware that anxiety is often associated with language learning. Teachers and students generally feel strongly that anxiety is a major obstacle to be overcome in learning to speak another language, and several recent approaches to foreign language teaching, such as community language learning and suggestopedia, are explicitly directed at reducing learner anxiety. However, second language research has neither adequately defined foreign language anxiety nor described its specific effects on foreign language learning. This paper attempts to fill this gap by identifying foreign language anxiety as a conceptually distinct variable in foreign language learning and interpreting it within the context of existing theoretical and empirical work on specific anxiety reactions. The symptoms and consequences of foreign language anxiety should thus become readily identifiable to those concerned with language learning and teaching.

EFFECTS OF ANXIETY ON LANGUAGE LEARNING

Second language studies.   For many years, scholars have considered the anxiety-provoking potential of learning a foreign language. Curran (1976) and Stevick (1980) discuss in detail the defensive position imposed on the learner by most language teaching methods; Guiora (1983) argues that language learning itself is "a profoundly unsettling psychological proposition" because it directly threatens an individual's self-concept and worldview. More recently researchers have attempted to quantify the effects of anxiety on foreign language learning, but these efforts have met with mixed results. While the pertinent studies have differed in the measures employed, they can generally be characterized by their comparison of students' self-reports of anxiety with their language proficiency ratings, obtained through a discrete skills task or a global measure such as final course grade. In his 1978 (this volume) review of research, Scovel argues that scholars have been unable to establish a clear-cut relationship between anxiety and overall foreign language achievement; he attributes the discrepant findings at least in part to the inconsistency of anxiety measures used and concludes: "It is perhaps premature to relate it [anxiety] to the global and comprehensive task of language acquisition."

Studies seeking more specific effects of anxiety on language learning have been more revealing. Kleinmann (1977) found that ESL students with high levels of debilitating anxiety attempted different types of grammatical constructions than did less anxious ESL students; and Steinberg and Horwitz (1986) found that students experiencing an anxiety-producing condition attempted less interpretive (more concrete) messages than those experiencing a relaxed condition. These studies indicate that anxiety can affect the communication strategies students employ in language class. That is, the more anxious student tends to avoid attempting difficult or personal messages in the target language. These findings are also consistent with research on other types of specific communication anxiety. Researchers studying writing in a native language have found that students with higher levels of writing anxiety write shorter compositions and qualify their writing less than their calmer counterparts do (Daly & Miller, 1975; Daly, 1977).

A review of the literature found only one instrument specifically designed to measure foreign language anxiety. Gardner, Clement, Smythe, and Smythe (1979) developed five items to measure French class anxiety as part of their test battery on attitudes and motivation. Gardner, Smythe, Clement, and Gliksman (1976) found small negative correlations (ranging from $r = -.13$ to $r = -.43$) between this scale and four measures of achievement (aural comprehension, speaking, final grade, and a composite of three sub-scales of the Canadian Achievement Test in French).

This brief review suggests two reasons for the dearth of conclusions concerning anxiety and second language achievement. First, the anxiety measures typically have not been specific to foreign language learning. Only the research by Gardner utilized a measure relevant to language anxiety, and it was restricted to French classroom anxiety. Second, few achievement studies have looked at the subtle effects of anxiety on foreign language learning. Although research has not clearly demonstrated the effect of anxiety on language learning, practitioners have had ample experience with anxious learners.

Clinical experience. The subjective feelings, psycho-physiological symptoms, and behavioral responses of the anxious foreign language learner are essentially the same as for any specific anxiety. They experience apprehension, worry, even dread. They have difficulty concentrating, become forgetful, sweat, and have palpitations. They exhibit avoidance behavior such as missing class and postponing homework. Clinical experience with foreign language students in university classes and at the Learning Skills Center (LSC) at the University of Texas also suggests several discrete problems caused by anxiety and illustrates poignantly how these problems can interfere with language learning. Principally, counselors find that anxiety centers on the two basic task requirements of foreign language learning: listening and speaking. Difficulty in speaking in class is probably the most frequently cited concern of the anxious foreign language students seeking help at the LSC. Students often report that they feel fairly comfortable responding to a drill or delivering prepared speeches in their foreign language class but tend to "freeze" in a role-play situation. A female student speaks of the evenings in her dorm room spent rehearsing what she should have said in class the day before. Anxious language learners also complain of difficulties discriminating the sounds and structures of a target language message. One male student claims to hear only a loud buzz whenever his teacher speaks the foreign language. Anxious students may also have difficulty grasping the content of a target language message. Many LSC clients claim that they have little or no idea of what the teacher is saying in extended target language utterances.

Foreign language anxiety frequently shows up in testing situations. Students commonly report to counselors that they "know" a certain grammar point but "forget" it during a test or an oral exercise when many grammar points must be remembered and coordinated simultaneously. The problem can also be isolated in persistent "careless" errors in spelling or syntax. The student realizes, usually some time after the test, that he or she knew the correct answer but put down the wrong one due to nervousness. If the student realizes he or she is making preventable errors during the test, anxiety—and errors—may escalate.

Overstudying is a related phenomenon. Students who are overly concerned about their performance may become so anxious when they make errors, they may attempt to compensate by studying even more. Their frustration is understandable when their compulsive effort does not lead to improved grades. One bright woman who had lived in Mexico spent eight hours a day preparing for a beginning Spanish class—and still did poorly. The reverse behavior is also possible. Anxious students may avoid studying and in some cases skip class entirely in an effort to alleviate their anxiety.

Certain beliefs about language learning also contribute to the student's tension and frustration in the classroom. We note that a number of students believe nothing should be said in the foreign language until it can be said correctly and that it is not okay to guess an unknown foreign language word (Horwitz, 1984). Beliefs such as these must produce anxiety since students are expected to communicate in the second tongue before fluency is attained and even excellent language students make mistakes or forget words and need to guess more than occasionally.

In light of current theory and research in second language acquisition, the problem of anxiety and the accompanying erroneous beliefs about language learning discussed here represent serious impediments to the development of second language fluency as well as to performance. Savignon (1972) stresses the vital role of spontaneous conversational interactions in the development of communicative competence, while Krashen (1980) argues that the extraction of meaning from second language messages (second language acquisition in his terminology) is the primary process in the development of a second language. Anxiety contributes to an affective filter, according to Krashen, which makes the individual unreceptive to language input; thus, the learner fails to "take in" the available target language messages and language acquisition does not progress. The anxious student is also inhibited when attempting to utilize any second language fluency he or she has managed to acquire. The resulting poor test performance and inability to perform in class can contribute to a teacher's inaccurate assessment that the student lacks either some necessary aptitude for learning a language or sufficient motivation to do the necessary work for a good performance.

FOREIGN LANGUAGE ANXIETY: CONCEPTUAL FOUNDATIONS

Because foreign language anxiety concerns performance evaluation within an academic and social context, it is useful to draw parallels between it and three related performance anxieties: (1) communication apprehension; (2) test anxiety; and (3) fear of negative evaluation. Due to its emphasis on interpersonal interactions, the construct of communication apprehension is quite relevant to the conceptualization of foreign language anxiety (McCroskey, 1977). Communication apprehension is a type of shyness characterized by fear of or anxiety about communicating with people. Difficulty in speaking in dyads or groups (oral communication anxiety) or in public ("stage fright"), or in listening to or learning a spoken message (receiver anxiety) are all manifestations of communication apprehension. Communication apprehension or some similar reaction obviously plays a large role in foreign language anxiety. People who typically have trouble speaking in groups are likely to experience even greater difficulty speaking in a foreign language class where they have little control of the communicative situation and their performance is constantly monitored. Moreover, in addition to all the usual concerns about oral communication, the foreign language class requires the student to communicate via a medium in which only limited facility is possessed. The special communication apprehension permeating foreign language learning derives from the personal knowledge that one will almost certainly have difficulty understanding others and making oneself understood. Possibly because of this knowledge, many otherwise talkative people are silent in a foreign language class. And yet, the converse also seems to be true. Ordinarily self-conscious and inhibited speakers may find that communicating in a foreign language makes them feel as if someone else is speaking and they therefore feel less anxious.[2] This phenomenon may be similar to stutterers who are sometimes able to enunciate normally when singing or acting.

Since performance evaluation is an ongoing feature of most foreign language classes, test anxiety is also relevant to a discussion of foreign language anxiety. Test anxiety refers to a type of performance anxiety stemming from a fear of failure (Gordon & Sarason, 1955; Sarason, 1980). Test-anxious students often put unrealistic demands on themselves and feel that anything less than a perfect test performance is a failure. Students who are test-anxious in foreign language class probably experience considerable difficulty since tests and quizzes are frequent and even the brightest and most prepared students often make errors. Oral tests have the potential of provoking both test and oral communication anxiety simultaneously in susceptible students.

Fear of negative evaluation, defined as "apprehension about others' evaluations, avoidance of evaluative situations, and the expectation that others would evaluate oneself negatively," is a third anxiety related to foreign language learning (Watson & Friend, 1969). Although similar to test anxiety, fear of negative evaluation is broader in scope because it is not limited to test-taking situations; rather, it may occur in any social, evaluative situation such as interviewing for a job or speaking in foreign language class. Unique among academic subject matters, foreign languages require continual evaluation by the only fluent speaker in the class, the teacher. Students may also be acutely sensitive to the evaluations—real or imagined—of their peers.

Although communication apprehension, test anxiety, and fear of negative evaluation provide useful conceptual building blocks for a description of foreign language anxiety, we propose that foreign language anxiety is not simply the combination of these fears transferred to foreign language learning. Rather, we conceive foreign language anxiety as a distinct complex of self-perceptions, beliefs, feelings, and behaviors related to classroom language learning arising from the uniqueness of the language learning process.

Adults typically perceive themselves as reasonably intelligent, socially adept individuals, sensitive to different sociocultural mores. These assumptions are rarely challenged when communicating in a native language as it is usually not difficult to understand others or to make oneself understood. However, the situation when learning a foreign language stands in marked contrast. Because individual communication attempts will be evaluated according to uncertain or even unknown linguistic and sociocultural standards, second language communication entails risk taking and is necessarily problematic. Because complex and nonspontaneous mental operations are required in order to communicate at all, any performance in the L2 is likely to challenge an individual's self-concept as a competent communicator and lead to reticence, self-consciousness, fear, or even panic.

Authentic communication also becomes problematic in the second language because of the immature command of the second language relative to the first. Thus, adult language learners' self-perceptions of genuineness in presenting themselves to others may be threatened by the limited range of meaning and affect that can be deliberately communicated. In sum, the language learner's self-esteem is vulnerable to the awareness that the range of communicative choices and authenticity is restricted. The importance of the disparity between the "true" self as known to the language learner and the more limited self as can be presented at any given moment in the foreign language would seem to distinguish foreign language anxiety from other academic anxieties such as those associated with mathematics or science. Probably no other field of study implicates self-concept and self-expression to the degree that language study does.

IDENTIFYING FOREIGN LANGUAGE ANXIETY

Since anxiety can have profound effects on many aspects of foreign language learning, it is important to be able to identify those students who are particularly anxious in foreign language class. During the summer of 1983, students in beginning language classes at the University of Texas were invited to participate in a "Support Group for Foreign Language Learning." Of the 225 students informed of the support groups, 78, over one-third, were concerned enough about their foreign language class to indicate that they would like to join such a group. Due to time and space limitations, participation had to be limited to two groups of fifteen students each. Group meetings consisted of student discussion of concerns and difficulties in language learning, didactic presentations on effective language learning strategies, and anxiety management exercises. The difficulties these students related were compelling.

They spoke of "freezing" in class, standing outside the door trying to summon up enough courage to enter, and going blank prior to tests. They also reported many of the psychophysiological symptoms commonly associated with anxiety (tenseness, trembling, perspiring, palpitations, and sleep disturbances).

The experiences related in the support groups contributed to the development of the Foreign Language Classroom Anxiety Scale (FLCAS) (Horwitz, 1983). The scale has demonstrated internal reliability, achieving an alpha coefficient of .93 with all items producing significant corrected item-total scale correlations. Test-retest reliability over eight weeks yielded an $r = .83$ ($p < .001$). A construct validation study is currently underway to establish foreign language anxiety as a phenomenon related to but distinguishable from other specific anxieties (Horwitz, 1986, this volume).

Pilot testing with the FLCAS affords an opportunity to examine the scope and severity of foreign language anxiety. To date, the results demonstrate that students with debilitating anxiety in the foreign language classroom setting can be identified and that they share a number of characteristics in common. The responses of 75 university students (39 males and 36 females ranging in age from 18 to 27) from four intact introductory Spanish classes are reported here. The FLCAS was administered to the students during their scheduled language class the third week of the semester.

The items presented are reflective of communication apprehension, test anxiety, and fear of negative evaluation in the foreign language classroom. Responses to all FLCAS items are reported in Table 1. All percentages refer to the number of students who agreed or strongly agreed (or disagreed and strongly disagreed) with statements indicative of foreign language anxiety. (Percentages are rounded to the nearest whole number.)

Students who test high on anxiety report that they are afraid to speak in the foreign

Table 1

FLCAS ITEMS WITH PERCENTAGES OF STUDENTS SELECTING EACH ALTERNATIVE

	SA*	A	N	D	SD
1. I never feel quite sure of myself when I am speaking in my foreign language class.					
	11**	51	17	20	1
2. I *don't* worry about making mistakes in language class.					
	11	23	1	53	12
3. I tremble when I know that I'm going to be called on in language class.					
	5	16	31	29	19
4. It frightens me when I don't understand what the teacher is saying in the foreign language.					
	8	27	29	20	16
5. It wouldn't bother me at all to take more foreign language classes.					
	15	47	12	16	11
6. During language class, I find myself thinking about things that have nothing to do with the course.					
	7	19	31	32	12
7. I keep thinking that the other students are better at languages than I am.					
	13	25	20	28	13
8. I am usually at ease during tests in my language class.					
	5	35	19	20	21
9. I start to panic when I have to speak without preparation in language class.					
	12	37	19	28	4
10. I worry about the consequences of failing my foreign language class.					
	25	17	12	29	16

Table 1 (continued)

	SA*	A	N	D	SD

11. I don't understand why some people get so upset over foreign language classes.
 5   17   36   37   4

12. In language class, I can get so nervous I forget things I know.
 9   48   11   25   7

13. It embarrasses me to volunteer answers in my language class.
 0   9   19   57   15

14. I would *not* be nervous speaking the foreign language with native speakers.
 5   12   17   51   15

15. I get upset when I don't understand what the teacher is correcting.
 1   31   28   37   3

16. Even if I am well prepared for language class, I feel anxious about it.
 5   37   17   24   16

17. I often feel like not going to my language class.
 19   28   19   23   12

18. I feel confident when I speak in foreign language class.
 1   28   24   43   4

19. I am afraid that my language teacher is ready to correct every mistake I make.
 0   15   31   40   15

20. I can feel my heart pounding when I'm going to be called on in language class.
 5   27   19   37   12

21. The more I study for a language test, the more confused I get.
 4   12   8   48   28

22. I *don't* feel pressure to prepare very well for language class.
 3   12   19   44   23

23. I always feel that the other students speak the foreign language better than I do.
 12   19   25   31   13

24. I feel very self-conscious about speaking the foreign language in front of other students.
 3   25   19   47   7

25. Language class moves so quickly I worry about getting left behind.
 16   43   11   28   3

26. I feel more tense and nervous in my language class than in my other classes.
 13   25   19   31   12

27. I get nervous and confused when I am speaking in my language class.
 5   28   28   31   8

28. When I'm on my way to language class, I feel very sure and relaxed.
 5   27   40   24   4

29. I get nervous when I don't understand every word the language teacher says.
 3   24   24   43   7

30. I feel overwhelmed by the number of rules you have to learn to speak a foreign language.
 9   25   32   32   1

31. I am afraid that the other students will laugh at me when I speak the foreign language.
 3   7   20   53   17

32. I would probably feel comfortable around native speakers of the foreign language.
 5   23   20   41   11

33. I get nervous when the language teacher asks questions which I haven't prepared in advance.
 5   44   17   31   3

---

* SA = strongly agree; A = agree; N = neither agree nor disagree; D = disagree; SD = strongly disagree.

** Data in this table are rounded to the nearest whole number. Percentages may not add to 100 due to rounding.

language. They endorse FLCAS items indicative of speech anxiety such as "I start to panic when I have to speak without preparation in language class" (49%); "I get nervous and confused when I am speaking in my language class" (33%); "I feel very self-conscious about speaking the foreign language in front of other students" (28%). They also reject statements like "I feel confident when I speak in foreign language class" (47%). Anxious students feel a deep self-consciousness when asked to risk revealing themselves by speaking the foreign language in the presence of other people.

The fact that anxious students fear they will not understand *all* language input is also consistent with communication apprehension. Students endorse statements like "it frightens me when I don't understand what the teacher is saying in the foreign language" (35%); "I get nervous when I don't understand every word the language teacher says" (27%). They believe that in order to have any chance of comprehending the target language message they must understand every word that is spoken.

Anxious students also fear being less competent than other students or being negatively evaluated by them. They report: "I keep thinking that other students are better at languages than I am" (38%); "I always feel that the other students speak the foreign language better than I do" (31%); "language class moves so quickly, I worry about getting left behind" (59%); "it embarrasses me to volunteer answers in my language class" (9%); "I am afraid that the other students will laugh at me when I speak the foreign language" (10%). Thus, they may skip class, overstudy, or seek refuge in the last row in an effort to avoid the humiliation or embarrassment of being called on to speak.

Anxious students are afraid to make mistakes in the foreign language. They endorse the statement "I am afraid that my language teacher is ready to correct every mistake I make" (15%), while disagreeing with "I *don't* worry about making mistakes in language class" (65%). These students seem to feel constantly tested and to perceive every correction as a failure.

Student responses to two FLCAS items—"I feel overwhelmed by the number of rules you have to learn to speak a foreign language" (34%) and "I feel more tense and nervous in my language class than in my other classes" (38%)—lend further support to the view that foreign language anxiety is a distinct set of beliefs, perceptions, and feelings in response to foreign language learning in the classroom and not merely a composite of other anxieties. The latter item was found to be the single best discriminator of anxiety on the FLCAS as measured by its correlation with the total score. These results suggest that anxious students feel uniquely unable to deal with the task of language learning.

Our findings suggest that significant foreign language anxiety is experienced by many students in response to at least some aspects of foreign language learning. A majority of the statements reflective of foreign language anxiety (19 of 33 items) were supported by a third or more of the students surveyed, and seven statements were supported by over half the students. Although at this point we can only speculate as to how many people experience severe reactions to foreign language learning, these results (considered in light of the number of students who expressed a need for a student language-support group) imply that anxious students are common in foreign language classrooms (at least in beginning classes on the university level).

PEDAGOGICAL IMPLICATIONS

In general, educators have two options when dealing with anxious students: (1) they can help them learn to cope with the existing anxiety-provoking situation; or (2) they can make the learning context less stressful. But before either option is viable, the teacher must first acknowledge the existence of foreign language anxiety. Teachers probably have seen in their students many or all of the negative effects of anxiety discussed in this article; extremely anxious students are highly motivated to avoid engaging in the classroom activities they fear most. They may appear simply unprepared or indifferent. Therefore, teachers should always consider the possibility that anxiety is responsible for the student behaviors discussed here before attributing poor student performance solely to lack of ability, inadequate background, or poor motivation. Specific techniques which teachers may use to allay students' anxiety include relaxation exercises, advice on effective language learning strategies, behavioral contracting, and journal keeping.[3] But language teachers have neither sufficient time nor adequate expertise to deal with severe anxiety reactions. Such students, when identified, should probably be referred for specialized help to outside counselors or learning specialists.[4] Therapists employing behavior modification techniques, such as systematic desensitization, have successfully treated a variety of specific anxieties related to learning, and these techniques should prove equally useful in the case of foreign language anxiety.

Reducing stress by changing the context of foreign language learning is the more important and considerably more difficult task. As long as foreign language learning takes place in a formal school setting where evaluation is inextricably tied to performance, anxiety is likely to continue to flourish. Teachers might create student support systems and closely monitor the classroom climate to identify specific sources of student anxiety. As students appear to be acutely sensitive to target language corrections, the selection of error correction techniques should be based on instructional philosophy and on reducing defensive reactions in students. The impact of these (or any) corrective practices on foreign language anxiety and ultimate foreign language achievement must, of course, be studied in the classroom. How much current teaching practices contribute to foreign language anxiety and how much is due to the intrinsic nature of language learning are important issues to be addressed before firm conclusions regarding optimal interventions can be reached.

CONCLUSIONS

Scholars are only beginning to understand the role of anxiety in foreign language learning; we do not yet know how pervasive foreign language anxiety is nor do we comprehend its precise repercussions in the classroom. We do know that individual reactions can vary widely. Some students may experience an anxious reaction of such intensity that they postpone required foreign language courses until the last possible moment or change their major to avoid foreign language study. Students who experience moderate anxiety may simply procrastinate in doing homework, avoid speaking in class, or crouch in the last row. Other students seldom, if ever, experience anxiety or tension in a foreign language class.

The effects of anxiety can extend beyond the classroom. Just as math anxiety serves as a critical job filter, channeling some women and some members of other minority groups away from high-paying, high-demand math and engineering careers, foreign language anxiety, too, may play a role in students' selections of courses, majors, and ultimately, careers (Richardson & Woolfolk, 1981). Foreign language anxiety may also be a factor in student objections to foreign language requirements.

In recent years there have been signs of a revival of interest in foreign language study both as an applied skill in conjunction with business study, for example, and for its intrinsic humanistic value as an essential part of a traditional liberal education. With an increasing number of schools establishing or reestablishing foreign language requirements, teachers will likely encounter an even greater percentage of students vulnerable to foreign language anxiety. The rise of foreign language requirements is occurring in conjunction with an increased emphasis on spontaneous speaking in the foreign language class. Since speaking in the target language seems to be the most threatening aspect of foreign language learning, the current emphasis on the development of communicative competence poses particularly great difficulties for the anxious student.

Foreign language anxiety can probably be alleviated, at least to an extent, by a supportive teacher who will acknowledge students' feelings of isolation and helplessness and offer concrete suggestions for attaining foreign language confidence. But if we are to improve foreign language teaching at all levels of education, we must recognize, cope with, and eventually overcome, debilitating foreign language anxiety as a factor shaping students' experiences in foreign language learning.

NOTES

1. These quotations have been collected by counselors at the Learning Skills Center at the University of Texas at Austin.

2. The practice in suggestopedia of providing students new target language identities may also capitalize on this phenomenon.

3. See McCoy (1979) for a discussion of dealing with student anxieties in the foreign language classroom. Techniques for teaching relaxation are included in Benson (1973) and Jacobson (1938). Behavioral contracting is an anxiety reduction method for students having difficulty attending to the learning task. The student agrees to spend a specific amount of time on a task, such as going to the language lab, and then reports back to the teacher on her or his success.

4. When an anxiety reaction is both specific and severe, psychologists typically use the term "phobia."

Chapter Four

Preliminary Evidence for the Reliability and Validity of a Foreign Language Anxiety Scale

Elaine K. Horwitz   The University of Texas at Austin

Research on the relationship of anxiety to achievement in a second language has been hampered by the absence of a validated measure of anxiety specific to language learning. Although teachers and students generally feel that anxiety is an obstacle to be overcome in learning a second language, the empirical literature does not substantiate a clear-cut relationship between anxiety and second language achievement or performance (see Scovel [this volume] and Horwitz, Horwitz, & Cope [this volume], for a fuller discussion). One likely explanation for discrepant findings is that existing measures of anxiety do not test an individual's response to the specific stimulus of language learning. The Foreign Language Classroom Anxiety Scale (FLCAS) has been developed to provide investigators with a standard instrument for this purpose.

This self-report measure assesses the degree of anxiety, as evidenced by negative performance expectancies and social comparisons, psychophysiological symptoms, and avoidance behaviors. Sample items are as follows: "I never feel quite sure of myself when speaking in my foreign language class"; "I keep thinking that the other students are better at languages than I am"; and "I am afraid that my language teacher is ready to correct every mistake I make." Items were developed from student self-reports, clinical experience, and a review of related instruments. Specifically:

1. Two groups of anxious foreign language students were recruited to participate in a "Support Group for Foreign Language Learning." These first-semester language students met twice weekly and discussed difficulties and concerns with their foreign language classes. (Of the 225 students informed of the support groups, 78–over one-third–were concerned enough about their foreign language class to indicate that they would like to join such a group.) Scale items were developed to reflect these students' experiences in their own language classes.

2. Counselors at the Learning Skills Center at the University of Texas at Austin were interviewed about their experiences with anxious language learners, and relevant items were developed.

3. The author's experience with anxious students in her own foreign language classes also served as a basis for scale items.

4. The literature on anxiety revealed instruments for several related types of anxiety. Measures of test anxiety (Sarason, 1978), speech anxiety (Paul, 1966), and communication apprehension (McCroskey, 1970) were reviewed to identify relevant items.

5. The five items from the French Class Anxiety Scale (Gardner, Clement, Smythe, & Smythe, 1979) were made generic and added to the item pool.

The 33 items in the FLCAS have significant part-whole correlations with the total scale, are balanced for wording to reduce the effects of acquiescent and negative response sets, and address conceptually and clinically important aspects of anxiety. The FLCAS has been scored on a 5-point Likert Scale, ranging from *strongly agree* to *strongly disagree*, but alternative scaling methods, including true/false and frequency ratings (e.g., "very often," "never"), are currently being studied.

To date, the FLCAS has been administered, in a number of separate studies, to approximately 300 students in introductory undergraduate foreign language classes at the University of Texas at Austin and has demonstrated satisfactory reliability with this population. Possible scores on the FLCAS range from 33 to 165. In one sample of 108 students, scores ranged from 45 to 147 ($M = 94.5$, $Mdn = 95.0$, $SD = 21.4$). Internal consistency, as measured by Cronbach's alpha coefficient, was .93, and test-retest reliability over 8 weeks was $r = .83$, $p = .001$, $n = 78$.[1]

Criterion-related studies that bear on the construct validity of the scale have also been conducted. Correlation of the FLCAS with the Trait scale of the State-Trait Anxiety Inventory (Spielberger, 1983) obtained $r = .29$, $p = .002$, $n = 108$; with the Personal Report of Communication Apprehension (McCroskey, 1970), $r = .28$, $p = .063$, $n = 44$; with the Fear of Negative Evaluation Scale (Watson & Friend, 1969), $r = .36$, $p = .007$, $n = 56$; and with the Test Anxiety Scale (Sarason, 1978), $r = .53$, $p = .001$, $n = 60$. These results suggest that foreign language anxiety can be discriminated from these related constructs, although it appears that foreign language classroom anxiety is moderately associated with test anxiety. Scores on the FLCAS have also been associated with expected grade in the foreign language course, $r = -.52$, $p = .001$, $n = 108$, and with the item, "Rate your anxiety level concerning foreign language class," $r = .77$, $p = .001$, $n = 108$.

Correlations between the FLCAS and actual final grade were very similar to the one with expected grade. The correlation between the FLCAS and final grade was $r = -.49$, $p = .003$, $n = 35$, for two intact beginning Spanish classes, and $r = -.54$, $p = .001$, $n = 32$, for two beginning French classes. Thus, higher levels of anxiety, as measured by the FLCAS, are associated with lower final grades. On the other hand, the relationship between test anxiety (Sarason, 1978) and final grade was not significant in the French classes; $r = -.16$, $p = .391$, $n = 32$. (Data on test anxiety were not available for the Spanish classes.)

Since test anxiety had achieved the highest correlation with foreign language anxiety, a partial correlation coefficient was computed to determine the relationship between the FLCAS and final grade, with test anxiety statistically controlled. The resulting partial correlation was significant ($r = -.53$, $p = .002$, $n = 29$), suggesting that the relationship between

---

[1] All significance tests reported are two tailed.

foreign language anxiety and overall classroom achievement is independent of the confounding effects of test anxiety. These results indicate that anxiety specifically related to foreign language class accounts for approximately 25% of the variance in final grades. It seems reasonable to assume that foreign language anxiety would correlate even more strongly with a measure of language proficiency.

Results to date suggest that foreign language anxiety can be reliably and validly measured and that it plays an important role in language learning. Further research with the FLCAS could improve our understanding of the effect of anxiety on language learning as well as the impact of different instructional methods or teaching styles on the learner. It is also hoped that the FLCAS will facilitate the identification of students experiencing debilitating anxiety so that appropriate classroom and individual interventions may be offered.

Chapter Five

Anxiety and Second Language Learning: Toward a Theoretical Clarification

P. D. MacIntyre and R. C. Gardner   The University of Western Ontario

INTRODUCTION

In his review of the literature on the role of anxiety in second language learning, Scovel (1978, this volume) discusses four studies, each of which had somewhat inconsistent results. He points out, for example, that Swain and Burnaby (1976) found a negative correlation between language class anxiety and one measure of children's ability to speak French but no significant correlations with other measures of proficiency. Similarly, Tucker, Hamayan, and Genesee (1976) found one index of performance to be significantly negatively related to French class anxiety, but reported three other indices that were not correlated significantly with this type of anxiety. Also, while Chastain (1975) found that test anxiety correlated negatively with proficiency in an audio-lingual French course it showed no relationship to proficiency in regular French or German courses. Further complicating the issue was the positive correlation between test anxiety and grades in Spanish and the lack of any relationship between manifest anxiety and grades in any of the courses. The final study cited by Scovel (Kleinmann, 1977) considered two types of anxiety, facilitating and debilitating (see Alpert & Haber, 1960). Facilitating anxiety is considered to be an asset to performance and showed the predicted positive correlations with Arabic students' willingness to attempt difficult linguistic structures in English. Debilitating anxiety, which is the more common interpretation of "anxiety," is considered to be detrimental to performance, but did not show the expected negative correlations with performance. In summary, Scovel (1978, this volume) stated that foreign language anxiety research suffered from several ambiguities.

Horwitz, Horwitz, and Cope (1986, this volume) make a similar statement almost a decade after Scovel's review. As a remedy, they outline a theoretical framework from which to begin. Horwitz, Horwitz, and Cope (1986, this volume) describe three components of foreign language anxiety. The first is communication apprehension. They propose that the language student has mature thoughts and ideas but an immature second language vocabulary with which to express them. The inability either to express oneself or to comprehend another person leads to frustration and apprehension. The second component, closely related to the first, is fear of negative social evaluation. Because students are unsure of themselves and what they are saying, they may feel that they are not able to make the proper social impression. The third component is test anxiety, viz., apprehension over academic evaluation. The pedagogical requirements of the school and teacher require that the student continually be assessed on aspects of proficiency while it is being acquired. These three components then, communication apprehension, fear of social evaluation, and test anxiety, are viewed by Horwitz and colleagues to have a deleterious effect on second language acquisition.

The concept of second language anxiety has also been investigated in the context of attitudes and motivation and their relationship to proficiency. Because the primary focus is on attitudes and motivation, detailed information is not always given about the relationship of anxiety to proficiency. The Attitudes and Motivation Test Battery (AMTB) contains the French Class Anxiety Scale (Gardner, 1985). This scale measures the degree to which students report feeling embarrassed or anxious in language class. It has shown strong reliability (Gardner, Smythe, & Lalonde, 1984) but the role assigned it in the language acquisition process has been debated (Lalonde & Gardner, 1984). The concern of most studies that use the AMTB has been with larger issues of attitudes and motivation, rather than the more specific role of any single construct such as anxiety. However, both the global and the specific issues deserve attention, and it is worthwhile to look more closely at the results of some of these studies to gain some insight into the specific role of foreign language anxiety in the language-learning process.

When the above studies and others (see MacIntyre & Gardner, 1988) are examined in detail, the consistency of the findings is noteworthy. Studies have reported significant correlations of French class anxiety with course grades (see for example, Gardner, Lalonde, Moorcroft, & Evers, 1987). One large study of over 1,000 students in grades 7 through 11 (Gardner, Smythe, Clement, & Gliksman, 1976) found that French class anxiety correlated more strongly with proficiency as the students entered higher grade levels. In fact, the highest single correlation between any AMTB scale and proficiency in grade 11 was the anxiety measure ($r = -.43, p < .001$). Also, factor analyses consistently report loadings of French class anxiety on a proficiency factor (Clément, 1987; Clément & Kruidenier, 1985; Gardner, Moorcroft, & MacIntyre, 1987). Using regression procedures, both Gliksman (1981) and Trylong (1987) found that the addition of French class anxiety scores to an equation already containing attitude and motivation indices resulted in a significant improvement in prediction. Trylong (1987) concluded that aptitude, attitudes, and anxiety "interact in unique and powerful ways as they relate to achievement" (p. 65).

While the results of these latter studies in particular show that foreign language anxiety is a predictor of success in language class, the problems noted by Scovel (1978, this volume) and Horwitz and colleagues (1986, this volume) cannot be ignored. The difficulty may be traced to the instruments chosen to measure anxiety in some of the studies. Relevant to this point is Endler's (1980) argument for a multidimensional view of anxiety. He proposes that to study anxiety is to study the interaction of the person in the situation producing that anxiety. Some situations arouse anxiety while others do not, so both the individual and the context must be taken into consideration. Instruments such as the Taylor (1953) Manifest Anxiety Scale or Spielberger's (1983) State-Trait Anxiety Inventory attempt to define a personality trait of anxiety applicable across several situations, but this may not be the best way to measure anxiety in a language-learning context. Gardner (1985) has proposed that scales directly concerned with foreign language anxiety are more appropriate for studying language anxiety than are general anxiety scales.

While the instruments used to measure language anxiety should be specific to the language area, theoretical links to the more general anxiety literature can be strengthened. For example, Tobias (1979, 1980, 1986) has proposed a model of the effects of anxiety on learning from instruction. She suggests that anxious persons tend to engage in self-directed, derogatory cognition rather than focusing on the task itself. These task-irrelevant thoughts compete with task-relevant ones for limited cognitive resources. Nonanxious individuals tend not to engage in such self-preoccupations, giving them an advantage when the task at hand is taxing. This theory helps explain the often-cited finding of an interaction among anxiety, task difficulty, and ability (Hunsley, 1985; Sarason, 1986; Spielberger, 1983).

According to Tobias (1986), interference may occur at three levels: input, processing, and output. During input, anxiety may cause attention deficits and poor initial processing of information. In short, not as much information is registered. For example, people with higher anxiety seem easily distracted from the task because time is divided between the processing of emotion-related and task-related cognition. At the processing stage, if the task is relatively simple, anxiety may have little effect. However, as the task becomes more difficult, relative to ability, anxiety shows greater impact on processing. Interference with the rehearsal of new information would be an example of this type of effect. At the output stage, anxiety may interfere with the retrieval of previously learned information. The experience of "freezing" on a test can be attributed to the influence of anxiety at the time of retrieval.

The present study has two major goals. First, the Horwitz, Horwitz and Cope (1986, this volume) theory will be evaluated as a theoretical framework from which foreign language anxiety research can proceed. Several relevant anxiety scales will be factor-analyzed to determine the dimensionality that underlies them. Second, the theory of Tobias (1986) will be used to propose the mechanism by which foreign language anxiety may operate. A suggestion for explaining the initial development of such apprehension will be offered. In order to examine such relationships, the present study employed a paired associate task in which subjects were taught the English equivalents of 38 French nouns. In addition, three measures of vocabulary production were taken and the level of anxiety experienced during production was manipulated by placing time limits on the interval between responses. The relationship between the dimensions of anxiety and the various measures of learning and production was then examined.

METHOD

This study involved three phases. In the first phase, a questionnaire containing a series of anxiety scales was administered. In the second part, subjects were given four trials to learn 38 English-French pairs administered by computer and were tested prior to each trial. Spielberger's (1983) State anxiety scale was administered after three of these tests. The final phase involved French vocabulary production and free recall of the paired associates.

Subjects

Fifty-two male and 52 female subjects were tested individually during sessions lasting approximately one hour. All subjects were introductory psychology students who received course credit in exchange for their participation. Only individuals between the ages of 18 and 25, with English as their native language, were recruited.

Materials

Nine anxiety scales were administered to all participants. Each of these measures is described below. Item keying was balanced between positively and negatively worded items in all cases except the Test anxiety scale, which contains only items indicative of anxiety. Cronbach's alpha reliability coefficients (α) for the present sample are presented with each scale, along with a sample item.

Scales were grouped by response format with items from each scale mixed together randomly. Section 1 contained the French class anxiety, English class anxiety, and Mathematics class anxiety scales, which were answered on 6-point Likert scales. Section 2 contained the French use anxiety, Trait anxiety, and Computer anxiety scales also using a 6-point Likert response format. In section 3 were the measures of Test anxiety and Audience anxiety, which required true/false responses.

Classroom anxieties. This scale was administered such that each item appeared above three separate 6-point Likert response scales corresponding to French ($\alpha = .90$), Mathematics ($\alpha = .89$), and English ($\alpha = .87$) classes. Eight items were adapted from Gardner's (1985) French class anxiety scale to assess anxiety experienced in any classroom. The items were presented such that anxiety in each class was assessed separately. A sample item is "I was generally tense whenever participating in 'French class'; 'Math class'; 'English class'."

French use anxiety ($\alpha = .86$). This scale contains the same eight items used by Gliksman (1981) and was designed to measure the amount of anxiety experienced when using French in interpersonal situations. A sample item is "It would bother me if I had to speak French on the telephone."

Trait anxiety ($\alpha = .68$). A general measure of anxiety was obtained using 10 items chosen from the 20-item scale contained in the Jackson Personality Inventory (Jackson, 1978). A sample item is "I sometimes feel jittery."

Computer anxiety ($\alpha = .89$). This 8-item scale was developed to assess the impact of a respondent's reaction to the use of a computer. A sample item is "It bothers me to have anything to do with a computer." The scale items are contained in MacIntyre (1988).

Test anxiety ($\alpha = .65$). This scale contains 10 of the items used by Sarason & Mandler (1956) to assess the degree to which the respondent feels anxious in formal testing situations. A sample item is "I dread courses where the instructor has the habit of giving 'pop' quizzes."

Audience sensitivity ($\alpha = .72$). Ten items were chosen from the scale developed by Paivio (1965) to measure the degree of apprehension experienced in situations where the respondent encounters a group of people. A sample item is "If I came late to a meeting, I'd rather stand than take a front seat."

State anxiety. Spielberger's (1983) 20-item scale was used as a measure of anxiety at the particular moment when the computer tests were being completed. It was administered three times during the learning phase, following the first ($\alpha_1 = .91$), third ($\alpha_2 = .92$), and fifth ($\alpha_3 = .91$) test trials. A sample item is "I feel calm."

Paired associates.   In addition to these anxiety scales, subjects were also presented with a paired-associates learning task. Thirty-eight French–English noun pairs were administered by computer. These pairs were considered equivalent in image-evoking potential. The mean translation probability reported by Desrochers (1980) for this group of pairs is 0.02, with a median of zero. An example of a pair is "Le phare = headlight."

Vocabulary test.   Subjects were also given a vocabulary production test. Six items were administered orally by the experimenter in a random order. Three of the items required the subject to respond orally and three required written responses. For each subject, it was randomly determined which of the six items would be answered orally and which answered in writing. Each item required a list of single-word responses appropriate to a given category. An example from this test is: "List, in French, all the items that would be put in a refrigerator."

Procedure

Upon arrival at the testing room, each subject was presented with a questionnaire requesting information on the number of years the person had studied French in school, the number of years since the person's last French course, the title of the last course, and the final mark in that course. The remainder of the questionnaire contained the anxiety scales as described above.

Subjects then began the learning task. To establish a base level, subjects were presented first with a 38-item multiple-choice test containing the pairs to be learned. In this test, a French noun, with article, was presented on the screen along with five randomly chosen and numbered English alternatives. Subjects indicated their response by typing the number corresponding to their choice. Each subject was given a unique random order of the French nouns. Additionally, the correct English noun was randomly positioned among the alternatives. The 37 remaining English nouns each had an equal probability of being selected as an incorrect alternative for each of the 38 French nouns for each trial. No English word was presented twice within the same set of options.

Following this first test, subjects were presented with a learning trial in which the 38 paired associates were presented one at a time. Each pair was presented for 2.5 seconds and consisted of the French noun and article, an equals sign (" = "), and the English translation. The presentation of the 38 pairs was followed by another test phase, and another learning phase, etc., until five tests and four learning trials had been completed. Subjects were presented with the State anxiety scale immediately after the first, third, and fifth tests.

Following the learning phase, each subject's knowledge of previous vocabulary was tested. It was randomly predetermined that the first three questions from the vocabulary test would be answered in either the oral or written mode and subjects were given the appropriate materials. At this point, they were also randomly assigned to either a *High Pressure* or *Low Pressure* condition. All subjects were given two minutes to give as many responses as possible; however, subjects in the High Pressure condition were told that if they stopped speaking or writing for more than 15 seconds at a time they would be given the next item. When switching response modalities the experimenter reminded the subject that the next three questions were similar to the ones just answered and that the same time limits applied. Following this, the experimenter administered the Free Recall test. Subjects were asked to recall orally the pairs they had learned previously. A maximum of four minutes was allotted with a 15-second time limit between responses for those in the High Pressure condition.

RESULTS

The results of this study fall into two general categories. The first deals with the relationships among the anxiety measures and is primarily concerned with the underlying dimensionality. The second set of analyses examines the relationship between anxiety and both the learning and production of French vocabulary.

A preliminary analysis of variance was performed to determine whether subjects report experiencing different levels of anxiety in French, Mathematics, and English classes. A significant effect was obtained ($F(2,206) = 9.79$, $p < .001$) and post hoc comparisons of the means showed that the mean French class anxiety score ($\overline{X} = 17.79$) was significantly higher than the mean for both the English class ($\overline{X} = 12.58$) and Mathematics class ($\overline{X} = 13.90$) anxiety, which did not differ significantly between themselves. This analysis indicates that the French class is the most anxiety-provoking of the three examined.

Dimensionality of Anxiety

In order to determine the dimensionality underlying the various measures of anxiety, the intercorrelations of all of the anxiety scales were subjected to a Principal Components analysis and Varimax rotation. Three factors were obtained with eigenvalues greater than 1.0. However, application of the screen test (Cattell, 1966) indicated that a two-factor solution was most appropriate. The two extracted factors (see Table 1) accounted for 48% of the total variance.

Factor I obtained high (greater than $\pm .50$) loadings from seven measures and appears to define a dimension of *General Anxiety*. The Trait anxiety scale, all three of the administrations of the Spielberger State anxiety scale, the Test anxiety scale, the Computer anxiety scale, and the Mathematics class anxiety scale produced appreciable factor loadings. Because of the wide range and generic nature of situations referred to in the scales defining this factor, it seems best identified as a *General Anxiety* factor.

Factor II appears to identify a dimension of *Communicative Anxiety*. This factor obtained appreciable loadings from French class anxiety, French use anxiety, English class anxiety, and the Audience sensitivity scale. This factor will be referred to as *Communicative Anxiety*, since each of these measures involve, to some extent, anxiety reactions in oral communication situations.

Anxiety and Learning

In order to control the Type I error rate, Hummel and Sligo's (1971) recommendations were followed and the initial analysis was conducted using a $2 \times 2 \times 5$ split plot factorial design MANOVA. The number of pairs correctly identified per learning trial and the latency of each trial were entered as dependent variables with General Anxiety (high versus low), Communicative Anxiety (high versus low), and Trials (one through five) as the factors. The General Anxiety and Communicative Anxiety groups were defined in terms of a median split of factor scores based on the preceding Principal Components analysis. Significant multivariate effects were found for Communicative Anxiety (Wilks' lambda = .828, $p < .001$), Trials (Wilks' lambda = .112, $p < .001$), and for the Communicative Anxiety by Trials interaction (Wilks'

Table 1
VARIMAX ROTATED FACTOR MATRIX

	FACTOR I	*FACTOR II*
	General Anxiety	*Communicative Anxiety*
French Class	−.02	.78
French Use	.01	.64
English Class	.09	.58
Audience	.25	.60
Math Class	.63	−.12
Computer	.59	−.23
Trait	.51	.28
Test	.75	.08
State 1	.68	.30
State 2	.70	.29
State 3	.60	.37

lambda $= .956$, $p < .05$). Following the suggestion of Hummel and Sligo (1971), attention is directed to significant univariate tests for these factors. Significant effects were obtained for Communicative Anxiety ($F (1,100) = 19.15, p < .001$), Trials ($F (4,400) = 673.02, p < .001$) and the Communicative Anxiety by Trials interaction ($F (4,400) = 2.49, p < .05$) for the number correct. In the case of latency, only the univariate effect for Trials was significant ($F (4,400) = 224.36, p < .001$).

The significant main effects found for Trials simply indicate that learning had taken place and that responses were made increasingly rapidly, as expected. The Communicative Anxiety by Trials interaction is presented in Figure 1. As can be seen, the difference between the Communicative Anxiety groups widened for the second, third, and fourth trials as compared to the first and last trials indicating that the low Communicative Anxiety group was learning more rapidly between the second and fourth trials. Inspection of the means and standard deviations suggests that a ceiling effect was responsible for the narrowing of the gap between groups for the fifth trial.

Since subjects had varying degrees of prior experience with French, several analyses of covariance were performed in order to control for the effects of the initial differences among subjects. For the first analysis, the number correct on the first trial was entered as a covariate for each of the other four trials. Analyses of covariance were also performed removing the effects of years of study and marks in French. All three of these analyses show results that are equivalent to the analysis just presented. Inspection of the adjusted means showed that, as in the above analysis, the significant Communicative Anxiety by Trials interaction was accounted for by the narrowing of the gap between the high and low anxiety groups on the fifth trial.

Table 2 presents the correlations between each of the anxiety scales and the Number Correct and Latency for each trial. In order to reduce the experiment-wise Type I error rate, only those with a Type I probability level less than (.01) are reported. Only four correlations between anxiety and latency are significant, two involving State anxiety and two involving French class anxiety. These correlations show that high scores on these measures tend to be associated with longer latencies only on the later trials.

In terms of learning, French class anxiety was significantly negatively correlated with

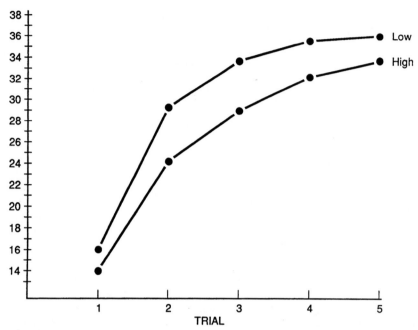

FIGURE 1   Communicative anxiety by trials interaction.

Number Correct over all five trials, while French use anxiety correlated significantly with the Number Correct for the first three trials. The only other scale to be associated with vocabulary acquisition was Spielberger's State anxiety scale. As can be seen in Table 2, State anxiety correlates significantly negatively with Number Correct only on those trials that precede its administration.

Two cross-lagged panel analyses (Kenney, 1975) of the correlations between State anxiety and proficiency were performed to evaluate the direction of "causation" between anxiety and performance on the learning task. For the first analysis, Time 1 includes the Number Correct on the second trial paired with the first State scale and Time 2 is Number Correct on the third trial paired with the second State scale. Using the formula presented by Marascuilo and Levin (1983, p. 71) to test for the difference between correlated correlations, a significant Z score indicates that one of the diagonal correlations is greater than the other. The diagonal paths for this analysis are significantly different ($Z = 3.59, p < .001$) indicating that the correlation between Number Correct at Trial 2 and State anxiety 2 ($r = -.33$) is significantly greater than the correlation between State anxiety 1 and Number Correct at Trial 3 ($r = -.05$). A similar analysis was conducted in which Time 1 represents Number Correct on Trial 4 and the second State anxiety, Time 2 represents Number Correct on Trial 5 and the third State anxiety scale. This analysis also indicates ($Z = 3.23, p < .001$) that the correlation between Number Correct at Trial 4 and State anxiety 3 ($r = -.26$) is stronger than the correlation between State anxiety 2 with Number Correct at Trial 5 ($r = -.07$). Both tests suggest that it is more likely that poor performance leads to State anxiety than it is that State anxiety leads to poor performance.

Table 2

RELATIONSHIP OF INDIVIDUAL ANXIETY SCALES TO THE NUMBER OF CORRECTLY IDENTIFIED PAIRS AND LATENCY PER TRIAL

	Trial 1	Trial 2	Trial 3	Trial 4	Trial 5
French Class					
No. Correct	−.30*	−.37**	−.37**	−.42**	−.34**
Time	.05	.12	.22	.28*	.25*
French Use					
No. Correct	−.50**	−.42**	−.32**	−.22	−.19
Time	.10	.10	.14	.16	.13
English Class					
No. Correct	.00	−.15	−.09	−.21	−.14
Time	.02	.03	.06	.07	.11
Math Class					
No. Correct	.12	.22	.12	.09	.09
Time	.01	−.02	−.11	−.09	−.10
Trait					
No. Correct	−.09	−.03	.01	.00	.00
Time	.04	.00	−.02	.05	.00
Audience					
No. Correct	.05	−.02	−.04	−.15	−.14
Time	−.22	−.16	−.20	−.12	−.05
Test					
No. Correct	−.03	−.20	−.14	−.02	−.04
Time	.16	.21	.20	.23	.16
Computer					
No. Correct	.00	.07	.06	−.02	.00
Time	.08	.06	−.02	.01	.00
State 1					
No. Correct	−.16	−.16	−.05	.02	.06
Time	.20	.24	.19	.18	.09
State 2					
No. Correct	−.17	−.33**	−.28*	−.16	−.07
Time	.03	.20	.28*	.29*	.21
State 3					
No. Correct	−.10	−.24	−.26*	−.26*	−.19
Time	−.11	.00	.11	.18	.17

* $= p < .01$.
** $= p < .001$ (2-tailed).

Recall of the Pairs

A $2 \times 2 \times 2$ analysis of variance was performed to compare the effects of General Anxiety, Communicative Anxiety, and Pressure Condition on the free recall of the pairs. Significant main effects were found for Communicative Anxiety ($F(1,96) = 9.58, p < .01$) and Pressure Condition ($F(1,96) = 6.29, p < .01$). Those with high Communicative Anxiety tended to have lower scores ($\overline{X} = 31.87$) than their less anxious counterparts ($\overline{X} = 44.65$). Also, the High Pressure condition seems to have restricted the scores of those in that group ($\overline{X} =$

32.87) as compared to the subjects under Low Pressure ($\overline{X}$ = 43.65). None of the interactions were significant.

When all of the 11 correlations between the anxiety scale scores and the free recall scores are examined, only two coefficients were significant at the .01 level; French class anxiety ($r = -.30$) and the second administration of the State anxiety scale ($r = -.28$).

Vocabulary Tasks

A 2 × 2 × 2 MANOVA was performed using the Oral and Written Proficiency scores as the dependent measures with General Anxiety, Communicative Anxiety, and Pressure Condition as the independent variables. Significant multivariate effects were obtained only for Communicative Anxiety (Wilks's lambda = .79, $p < .001$) and this was reflected in the significant univariate effects for both oral and written scores. Those subjects with high Communicative Anxiety had lower scores on both the oral ($\overline{X}$ = 15.06) and written ($\overline{X}$ = 17.40) measures than did those in the low Communicative Anxiety group ($\overline{X}$ = 27.04 and $\overline{X}$ = 23.81, respectively).

When the correlations of the individual anxiety scales with the Written Proficiency scores are examined, only French class anxiety ($r = -.34$, $p < .001$) and French use anxiety ($r = -.42$, $p < .001$) display a significant relationship to proficiency. Similar results are obtained for the Oral Proficiency scores. Again, only French class anxiety ($r = -.40$, $p < .001$) and French use anxiety ($r = -.54$, $p < .001$) are significantly related to oral proficiency scores.

DISCUSSION

Two orthogonal factors were extracted from the intercorrelations of the 11 anxiety scales. The first factor, *General Anxiety*, was largely based on the loadings of Trait and the three State anxiety scales. Although some authors argue that the distinction between State and Trait anxiety is meaningful (Spielberger, 1983), there is evidence that these concepts are not qualitatively different (Endler, 1980; Chrisjohn, 1981). The results of this investigation would fall into the latter category. Each of the three administrations of the State anxiety scale loaded on the same factor as Trait anxiety. In past studies, State anxiety has been correlated significantly with language proficiency in some investigations (e.g., Young, 1986, this volume) but not in others (e.g., Gardner et al., 1987). This pattern is similar to that shown by general trait anxiety measures and test anxiety measures (e.g., Chastain, 1975). The conclusion may be reached that this dimension of general anxiety and those scales that comprise it are not related to language behavior in a reliable manner.

The second factor, *Communicative Anxiety*, is independent of the first and was defined by French class anxiety, French use anxiety, English class anxiety, and Audience sensitivity. Clearly the first three are language-related anxieties with Audience sensitivity suggesting that this dimension reflects the communicative aspects of language. The Communicative Anxiety construct, as defined by the scales used here, has a distinct foreign language component. Because the factors are independent of each other, they can be considered as two separate traits.

Horwitz, Horwitz, and Cope, (1986, this volume) list communication apprehension, social-evaluative anxiety, and test anxiety as the three elements of foreign language classroom anxiety. The Communicative Anxiety dimension generated by the preceding analysis bears an obvious relationship to the communication apprehension component proposed by Horwitz and colleagues. Communicative Anxiety is also conceptually related to social-evaluative anxiety as each involves apprehension surrounding social perceptions and self-consciousness when speaking or participating in a social context. The results of this study do not, however, support the generalization made by Horwitz and colleagues concerning test anxiety since the Test anxiety scale contributes to the *General Anxiety* factor and not to the *Communicative Anxiety* one. This suggests that test anxiety is a general problem and not one specific to the language classroom. In addition, test anxiety has been shown to influence language course grades both positively and negatively (Chastain, 1975; Horwitz, 1986, this volume) and therefore a closer examination of the role of test anxiety in the foreign language classroom seems warranted.

The second focus of this study was on the relationship between anxiety and both the learning and production of French vocabulary. Tobias (1979, 1986) has postulated three levels at which anxiety might influence learning: input, processing, and output. Each of the dependent measures can be related to one or more levels of this model, as each is primarily dependent on one phase of memory. In Tobias's formulation, anxiety-prone people engage in self-related cognition about their reaction to a task rather than concentrating on the task at hand. The division of cognitive resources between task-irrelevant and task-relevant thoughts produces deficits in the performance of highly anxious individuals.

It is possible to evaluate the results of this study in terms of the predictions that would be generated by the Tobias model for each stage of processing. First, anxiety would likely have a relatively stable influence on the learning of the pairs, regardless of the stage of learning or the mode of production. According to Tobias (1986), in order for highly anxious subjects to improve, relative to those low in anxiety, they should be given the opportunity to compensate for their misdirected attention by reviewing the material to be learned. This was prohibited in the present study. A second prediction would be that those high in anxiety should require more time to respond if they were able to compensate for their anxiety. This would imply that an effect would be observed either in the number of words correctly recognized or in the latency of responses, but not both. A third prediction is that long-term memory retrieval will suffer from the division of cognitive resources and that the vocabulary production scores will be lower for those high in anxiety.

The presence of a difference between the Communicative Anxiety groups on performance throughout the five trials indicates that anxiety has an impact on learning. The presence of this effect even after controlling for scores on the first trial, for reported marks in French, and for years of study is evidence in favor of the stable, negative influence of this type of anxiety. Since scores on the scales that comprise this dimension could not have been influenced by performance on the learning task, it is reasonable to suggest that high Communicative Anxiety "caused" performance deficits. More specifically, both of the French anxiety scales correlate with learning, suggesting that it is French-related anxiety that causes poor performance on the test of French vocabulary learning.

Generally speaking, few of the anxiety measures correlate with latency, with the exception of French class anxiety and State anxiety. The State anxiety scale shows an inconsistent pattern of correlations. The second administration correlated with the latency of both the trial preceding it and the following trial. However, neither of the other two administrations show a similar pattern, neither State-1 nor State-3 correlate with the latency of any trial. This pattern is difficult to interpret and is analogous to the type of ambiguous result found when past studies have employed state-trait anxiety constructs. The French class anxiety scale correlated significantly with the final two trials, possibly indicating that the subjects became more reminiscent of their French classroom experiences and those with higher French class anxiety took longer to respond because of their self-concerns. In summary, the correlations of anxiety with trial latencies are weak and occur for later trials. This set of results is consistent with the predictions generated by the Tobias model.

In terms of the output side of Tobias's model, the oral proficiency and written proficiency tasks relied on long-term memory. Only French class and French use anxiety correlated significantly with scores on these measures. It can be assumed that respondents knew many more vocabulary items than were produced and that more effective retrieval would have increased their scores. The task then becomes a matter of locating appropriate items in memory. The significant effect for Communicative Anxiety can be taken as evidence that this anxiety interferes with the retrieval of these items.

While the production tasks showed the expected effects, the anticipated difference between the two pressure conditions did not fully emerge. It was expected that subjects with high anxiety would perform poorly on all three tasks (oral, written, and recall) in the High Pressure condition, relative to those under low pressure. However, there was a significant effect for pressure only for the free recall task. After the fact, it would seem that this may be related to the type of memory search required. For the oral and written vocabulary tests, the subjects were required to search through long-term, distant memory for appropriate responses. After the first 15-second lapse in responding, subjects in the High Pressure condition were stopped. The lapse would likely occur when the subject had "run out" of retrieval cues. For this reason, extending the time limit to the full two minutes did not result in significantly more responses. On the other hand, the free recall task required a search through much more recent memory. The contextual cues available during learning were still available during recall. In short, a 15-second lapse did not indicate that retrieval cues had been completely exhausted and subjects given the full two minutes were able to remember significantly more items.

Model of Causality

The results presented above tend to indicate that anxiety leads to deficits in learning and performance. The cross-lagged panel analyses show that State anxiety is more likely to be a product than a predictor of the number of pairs being learned. It appears that the emotional state of the respondent is most closely associated with performance on the preceding test rather than on a following test. These results point to the impact of performance on State anxiety while the previous results point to the effects of anxiety on performance. Although not a point addressed by Tobias, the potential for some kind of circularity of effect has been suggested (Levitt, 1980).

While Communicative Anxiety has an impact on learning and performance, performance can influence State anxiety. These two perspectives on the direction of causality are not mutually exclusive, and, in fact, can be combined into a single framework. The key is to note that each one of the above interpretations concentrates on a different type of anxiety, the first on foreign language anxiety and the second on State anxiety. The model to be suggested is that foreign language anxiety causes poor performance in the foreign language that produces elevations in State anxiety. This mechanism can account for the findings related to the Communicative Anxiety dimension, as well as the individual correlations of the French class, French use, and State anxieties with performance.

This interpretation might indicate that when a student experiences repeated episodes of State anxiety within language contexts, it solidifies into a situation-specific anxiety, such as French class anxiety, for example. This anxiety is maintained and strengthened by the same sequence of poor performance leading to anxiety that created the French class anxiety in the first place. Presumably, a differentiation between State anxiety and French anxiety develops since State anxiety and foreign language anxiety are associated with two different factors. This would happen as the student comes to associate anxiety with French class, as opposed to Mathematics class, for example. Discrimination between the different types of anxiety develops and determines the source to which the anxiety is attributed.

GENERAL CONCLUSIONS

The inconsistencies of past work in the area of foreign language anxiety are likely attributable to an inappropriate level of instrument specificity. This study has shown a relationship between foreign language anxiety and foreign language vocabulary learning and production. The orthogonal factors generated in the analysis of the anxiety scales indicate that foreign language anxiety is distinct from general anxiety, which possibly accounts for the poor relationship of general anxiety and second language proficiency. The factor analysis suggests that foreign language anxiety may be part of a larger construct that could be labeled Communicative Anxiety.

Both the theories of Horwitz, Horwitz, and Cope (1986, this volume) and Tobias (1986) were supported by the results of this study. Horwitz et al. (1986, this volume) proposed a tripartite description of foreign language anxiety with communication apprehension, fear of social evaluation, and test anxiety as the components. Only Test anxiety did not emerge as an important factor in the present study. Tobias's (1986) model of learning from instruction also received support. Clearly anxiety was shown to influence both the learning (input/processing) and the production (output) of French vocabulary.

The model of the development of foreign language anxiety that has been suggested here requires further testing; however, such a model is able to accommodate not only the results of the present study but also explain the inconsistent findings observed in past studies. Additional research is obviously needed, but this model would seem to have promise for interpreting previous ambiguities and promoting a clearer understanding of the role of anxiety in both second language learning and production.

NOTES

This research was supported, in part, by a grant (No. 410–85–190) from the Social Science and Humanities Research Council of Canada to the second author for research on the topic "The role of individual difference variables in second-language acquisition and retention." The authors would like to express their thanks to A. Young and R. Moorcroft for their assistance in scoring the French production tasks and to the reviewers of this manuscript for their suggestions.

Part Three

Empirical Findings: How Language Anxiety Affects Student Performance

This section is composed of research studies examining the specific effects of language anxiety. Do different language tasks elicit different levels of anxiety? In what way does anxiety interfere with the development and production of a second language? Is there a relationship between anxiety and student ability? This section is especially important because it alerts teachers to ways in which second language performance can be hampered by anxiety.

In considering these papers, the reader should keep in mind a distinction between language learning and language performance. Poor performance on language tests or classroom tasks could be indicative of inadequate knowledge or skill (learning) or temporary dysfluency (performance). This distinction is especially important in light of the new trend toward oral proficiency testing where questions of general communication apprehension are raised. Linguistic avoidance must also be considered. Kleinmann (1977) and Steinberg and Horwitz (1986) found that anxious learners tended to avoid certain linguistic structures and certain kinds of topics. When examining students' performance in a second language, many factors come into play.

The first papers in this section are devoted to the issue of anxiety and specific language testing conditions. Young looks at the relationship of anxiety to student performance on an oral proficiency interview and raises the possibility that the effects of anxiety on oral performance may be moderated by the student's actual ability in the language.

In the second article, Madsen, Brown, and Jones investigate students' anxiety in the face of different categories of foreign language test items and find that different types of tests evoke different levels of anxiety. Amounts of anxiety also varied by class level (beginning vs. intermediate) and, consistently with Young, by student ability level ("*A*" vs. "*C*"). Interestingly, students' anxiety levels do not seem to be directly related to the perceived difficulty of the exam. Although language anxiety is often associated with oral performance, Madsen, Brown, and Jones find that many types of language learning can be anxiety-provoking.

In the final article, Mejias, Applbaum, Applbaum, and Trotter examine language use outside of the classroom and find higher levels of communication apprehension in Mexican-American high school and college students than in Anglo students at a similar level. Importantly, subjects report higher levels of anxiety in their nondominant language.

In the case of these minority students, we need to be concerned with the consequences of language anxiety beyond the personal trauma of anxiety reactions. As Daly pointed out, anxiety associated with language use can affect the academic success of students. When language anxiety is found to be prevalent in a specific student population, whole groups of students may be achieving below their potential.

These articles suggest that anxiety about speaking a language can affect the quality of oral language production, making individuals appear less fluent than they really area. Lack of ability or perceived lack of ability can, in turn, have consequences for an individual's success in school. On the other hand, all language anxiety does not emanate from oral performance. In the section following, students offer their own experiences with language anxiety. While oral performance is often a concern, the reader should be alert to other aspects of language learning that can be anxiety-provoking.

Chapter Six

The Relationship Between Anxiety and Foreign Language Oral Proficiency Ratings

Dolly J. Young   University of Tennessee at Knoxville

THE PROBLEM

Competency testing as a requirement for teacher certification is a much discussed issue nowadays, and many states have already imposed competency requirements in various fields. The American Council on the Teaching of Foreign Languages (ACTFL) has developed the Oral Proficiency Interview (OPI), designed to assess an individual's oral proficiency on the basis of a face-to-face structured conversation. Professionals in foreign language education, however, have serious concerns about the OPI test (Lantolf & Frawley, 1985; Savignon, 1985). Among these is the desire to understand the role of anxiety in an individual's performance during the interview. Because major decisions about one's career presumably rest on this OPI performance, anxiety might reasonably be suspected of having some influence on the results.

Existing research on text anxiety shows that anxiety can affect an individual's performance both positively and negatively (Alpert & Haber, 1960; Benton, Hartman, & Sarason, 1955; Daly & Stafford, 1984; McCroskey, 1984a; Pimsleur, Mosberg, & Morrison, 1962; Sarason, 1978, 1980a, 1980b, 1983; Schwarzer, van der Ploeg, & Spielberger, 1982; Spielberger, 1972; Spielberger, Gonzalez, Taylor, Algaze, & Anton, 1978; Verma & Nijhawan, 1976). Some research on test anxiety indicates that an individual's objectively measured ability to perform the task at hand can determine the effect of anxiety on performance (Spielberger, 1966a; Verma, & Nijhawan, 1976). One study investigated the effects of anxiety, reinforcement, and intelligence on the learning of a difficult task and found that anxiety and reinforcement do not have any effect on performance when the individual has "adequate capacity to perform the task" (Spielberger, 1966, p. 306). With subjects of low ability, however, anxiety interferes with learning under all reinforcement conditions. Most test anxiety researchers would agree that test anxiety is a complex construct; because a variety of test anxiety theories exist, the type of anxiety measured should be kept in mind when attempting to interpret research results.

Research in speech communication also suggests anxiety can affect an individual's performance. Anxiety, for example, may affect the quality of an individual's communication or willingness to communicate (Daly & Stafford, 1984; McCroskey, 1978, 1984a). McCroskey has labeled this anxiety over speaking as "communication apprehension," which he defines as "an individual's level of fear or anxiety associated with either real or anticipated oral communication with another person or persons" (1984a, p. 192). Speech communication is not the only communication field to recognize that anxiety can have negative effects on students. Daly and Miller's (1975b) work on writing apprehension suggests that anxiety "may not only produce less adept writing; it may be reflected in career choice and other far-reaching consequences" (p. 242).

Anxiety and Second Language Learning/Performance

Researchers in second language learning or performance have recognized the potentially negative effect of anxiety on language learning—witness the emergence of teaching methodologies such as the Natural Approach, Counseling-Learning and Suggestopedia. Research on anxiety as an affective variable in language performance or language development has also been carried out, but with mixed results (Backman, 1976; Brewster, 1971; Chastain, 1975; Dunkel, 1947; Gardner, Smythe, Clément, & Gliksman, 1976; Guiora, Beit-Hallahmi, Brannon, Dull, & Scovel, 1972; Kleinmann, 1977; Pimsleur, Mosberg & Morrison, 1962; Steinberg, 1982; Swain & Burnaby, 1976; Tucker, Hamayan & Genesee, 1976; Westcott, 1973; Wittenborn, Larsen, & Mogil, 1945). Scovel (1978, this volume), in a review of these studies, concluded that "the research into the relationship of anxiety to foreign language learning has provided mixed and confusing results, immediately suggesting that anxiety itself is neither a simple nor well-understood psychological construct" (p. 132).

Although much research has been done on test anxiety and communication apprehension and some on anxiety and second language learning, there is little research available specifically on the relationship between anxiety and oral performance in a foreign language testing situation. The exceptions are Kleinmann (1977) and Steinberg (1982).

Kleinmann (1977) studied avoidance behavior in the context of second language learning. On the basis of contrastive analysis, native Spanish, Arabic, and Portuguese speakers have been predicted to avoid difficult language structures in English. Kleinmann, however, found that some of these structures were actually produced depending on the affective state of the learner. The affective state of the learner was determined by Alpert and Haber's Facilitating/Debilitating Anxiety Scale. Facilitating anxiety is an increase in drive level which results in improved performance while debilitating anxiety is an increase in arousal or drive level which leads to poor performance. Kleinmann's findings suggest that avoidance operates "as a group phenomenon, but within the particular avoiding group, use of the generally avoided structures is a function of the facilitating anxiety levels of the group's members" (1977, p. 105).

Steinberg (1982) studied the role of anxiety on second language oral performance by inducing anxiety in half of her subjects and comparing oral performance by groups—the anxiety-induced group with that of the group with no induced anxiety. She found that her more anxious individuals tended to be less subjective and more objective in their oral responses than the less anxious individuals.

The results of these two studies, which dealt specifically with the effects of anxiety on second language oral production, suggest that anxiety could materially affect an individual's avoidance behavior and the quality of language input.

In a recent study on classroom anxiety, Horwitz, Horwitz, and Cope (1986, this volume) attempted to identify foreign language classroom anxiety. Using a measure designed to tap anxiety specific to foreign language learning and production, the researchers conclude that "significant foreign language anxiety is experienced by many students in response to at least some aspects of foreign language learning" (1986, p. 19) and that "speaking in the target language seems to be the most threatening aspect of foreign language learning" (1986, p. 23). In light of this, and bearing in mind the importance oral testing will have in the near future, the relationship between anxiety and oral test performance merits examination.

RESEARCH METHODOLOGY

Subjects

Sixty university-level majors or prospective teachers of French, German, or Spanish participated in the study. Twenty-three percent of the subjects were French majors/prospective French teachers, 38% Spanish, and 38% German. Subjects volunteered to take the Oral Proficiency Interview, which was administered in their respective languages by ACTFL interviewers-in-training. Several months later, 32 of these 60 subjects took a follow-up dictation test.

Instruments

The purpose of this study was to investigate the relationship between anxiety and foreign language oral performance, but to determine this relationship accurately, language ability had to be taken into account. This was done through two independent instruments, a Self-Appraisal of Speaking Proficiency and a dictation test. To insure an accurate assessment of anxiety, four separate anxiety instruments were employed.*

Proficiency measures. The Oral Proficiency Interview is derived from the Foreign Service Institute (FSI) Oral Interview test and is designed to assess oral performance in a foreign language on the basis of a face-to-face structured conversation. Since the FSI test was developed out of the need to assess the language skills of foreign service officers, changes were made by the Educational Testing Service, the Interagency Language Roundtable, and ACTFL to adapt it to meet the "needs and purposes of the academic community" (Omaggio, 1986, p. 12).

A dictation test was used to assess subjects' global language proficiency. Research indicates that there is a high correlation between dictation test results and language proficiency (Bacheller, 1980; Croft, 1980; Cziko, 1980; Oller & Streiff, 1975; Savignon, 1982; Stansfield, 1985). The dictation paragraphs were written at three different levels: intermediate, advanced, and superior. In composing these paragraphs, ACTFL provisional proficiency guidelines for listening, speaking, and writing were kept in mind. For each language, at least two paragraphs per level were sent off to two ACTFL-trained OPI interviewer/raters; each rater assigned an independent ACTFL rating to each paragraph. Only paragraphs which were rated similarly by both ACTFL raters were used in the dictation; for example, when two raters assigned a rating of intermediate to the same paragraph, that paragraph was selected as the intermediate-level dictation paragraph. In the final analysis of the data, however, level of difficulty did not become a variable because a comparison of means across passages for the French and Spanish passages indicated that the passages were not discriminating level of difficulty. In other words, the Spanish passage labeled "superior" proved to be easier than the passage labeled "advanced," and the French passage identified as "advanced" proved to be harder than the passage identified as "superior." For this reason, a mean score for each scoring method across passages was derived. Means of replicate dictation scores were then normalized to percent.

The dictation passages were tape recorded by native speakers of each language and then administered to several other native speakers. Native speakers were given the dictations to check for tape quality, speed of dictation, and voice clarity. All native speakers scored 98–100% on the dictation test. Savignon's (1982) scoring method of Exact Word (EW), Phonetic Similarity (PS), and Conveyance of Meaning (CM) was used to score the dictation passages. Before formal scoring of the tests, a training session was held on scoring procedures, and intra- and inter-rater reliabilities were checked by scoring method: Inter-rater reliabilities were .99 (EW), .93 (PS) and .98 (CM). Intra-rater reliabilities were .98 (EW), .94 (PS), and .98 (CM).

An adapted version of Wild's (1975) Self-Appraisal of Speaking Proficiency (SASP) was used in this study to measure the subjects' self-appraisal of their foreign language oral proficiency. The statements in this questionnaire were grouped hierarchically on a 7-point scale from 0 to 5 according to FSI Oral Language Proficiency Guidelines.

Anxiety measures.   The State Anxiety Inventory assessed subjects' level of anxiety prior to taking the OPI. Spielberger (1983) distinguishes between "state anxiety" and "trait anxiety." Whereas state anxiety reflects an "unpleasant emotional state or condition," trait anxiety is regarded as a "relatively stable individual difference in anxiety-proneness as a personality trait" (1983, p. 1). State anxiety is marked by subjective feelings of worry, apprehension, nervousness, and tension and by activation of the individual's nervous system. It is transitory; that is, it is not a long-lasting personality feature but a feature that surfaces in response to a particular situation. The study reported here focused on the role of state anxiety as generated by the OPI.

The Cognitive Interference Questionnaire attempted to sample subjects' thoughts during the OPI and dictation tests. A cognitive interpretation of test anxiety maintains that the discrepancy in performance between high test-anxious and low test-anxious individuals arises from the "differential attention focuses of high and low test-anxious persons in evaluative conditions, with the test-anxious individual dividing attention between self-preoccupied worry and task cues and the less anxious person focusing more fully on task-relevant variables (Wine, 1980, p. 355).

A Self-Report of Anxiety was constructed to assess anxiety directly. Subjects were asked to rate their own anxiety on a scale where 1 indicated "no anxiety" and 7 indicated "high anxiety."

The Foreign Language Anxiety Scale of Reactions approached anxiety indirectly by probing subjects' general attitudes toward speaking in a foreign language. This scale consists of several sample items taken from Horwitz's Scale of Reactions to Foreign Language Class in addition to several items specifically constructed for this study.

Procedure

In May of 1984, the OPI was administered at the University of Texas at Austin, Southwest Texas State University at San Marcos, and the University of Texas at El Paso. The Self-Appraisal of Speaking Proficiency and the State Anxiety Inventory were given before the OPI. Then, subjects took the oral interview individually in the interviewers' offices or in a conference room of the appropriate language department. When they finished, the subjects completed the other three anxiety measures: The Cognitive Interference Questionnaire, the Self-Report of Anxiety, and the Foreign Language Anxiety Scale of Reactions.

Two months after the OPI was given, subjects were contacted again, and those still in Texas were given the dictation test. Most subjects took the test at the Foreign Language Education Center at the University of Texas. For three out-of-town subjects, the test was administered at university libraries in their cities (San Antonio, San Marcos, and Denton). For the dictation, subjects were given the same four anxiety tests in the same order as in the oral interview testing situation. Instructions for the dictation test were on the tape, and students were told to write their answers on the form provided and not to stop the tape.

RESULTS

The Relationship Among Proficiency Measures

The OPI ratings were recoded to match the SASP/Interagency Language Roundtable scale. This conversion is justifiable on three grounds: In the first place, these two scales are theoretically parallel. Second, the difference between intermediate-low and intermediate-mid is not as important as the difference between an intermediate-high and an advanced. Third, the interviewers who administered these oral interview tests were in training; therefore, the OPI scores may not be as precise as could be anticipated from certified OPI interviewers/raters.

The mean score for the entire sample was 2.4 on the SASP and 2.1 on the OPI. Subjects apparently appraised their own proficiency slightly higher than did their OPI testers. Even so, for all 60 subjects, OPI and SASP scores correlated significantly ($r = .60, p < .001$) although there was some variation by language (see Table 1).

There were also significant correlations between the SASP and dictation scores. Pearson Correlation Coefficients for the SASP and dictation scores by scoring method indicated that dictation scores produced by all three scoring methods (EW, PS, CM) were significantly correlated to the SASP ($r = .48, .56, .58$, respectively, $p < .005$). As the coefficients indicated, however, this relationship was only moderate. When correlated by language, the relationship

Table 1

CORRELATIONS BETWEEN OPI AND SASP BY LANGUAGE

| | | Correlation Between | |
Language	*n*	*OPI & SASP*	*Significance (p =)*
French	14	.32	.139
Spanish	23	.56	.003
German	23	.81	.001

was mixed: The French and German language group showed strong significant positive correlations between SASP and dictation, (r = .68 to .93,} p < .05), but no significant correlations were found for the Spanish language group, (r > .08, p > .76). Because of the low N for each of these language groups, these differences by language must be viewed with some caution.

Significant correlations were found between the OPI and the EW, PS, CM dictation scoring methods (r = .66, .68, and .70, respectively, p < .001). These correlations were stronger than those between the SASP and dictation. Like the SASP and dictation, the OPI and dictation correlation coefficients varied in significance by language. A strong significant correlation between OPI and dictation scores was found for French and German students (r = .66 to.97, p < .05). For the Spanish language group, a significant correlation was found between dictation and the EW scoring method (r = .53, p < .04), but no significant correlations were found for the PS or CM scoring methods, (r > .47, p > .08).

Because both proficiency measures correlated significantly with the OPI, this suggests that the OPI is indeed assessing foreign language proficiency.

The Relationship Between Anxiety Measures and OPI Scores

Table 2 summarizes the Pearson Correlation Coefficients between the OPI and the anxiety measures. There was a significant negative relationship between the OPI scores and scores on the Self-Report of Anxiety (SRA), the State Anxiety Inventory (SAI), and the Foreign Language Anxiety Scale of Reactions (FLASR). At first glance, this might seem to indicate that as anxiety increases, the quality of oral performance decreases. The correlations, however, were only low to moderate, with FLASR reporting the strongest negative correlation, and a closer look revealed them to be spurious: when the effect of ability was accounted for, no significant correlations were found (see Table 3).

Table 2

CORRELATIONS: OPI AND ANXIETY SCORES

OPI with	Pearson's Coefficient	
	r =	p =
SAI	−.32	.01
CIQ	−.15	.13
SRA	−.32	.01
FLASR	−.38	.01

Table 3

ONE-WAY AND PARTIAL CORRELATIONS: OPI AND ANXIETY SCORES

OPI with	One-way		Four-way	
	r =	p =	r =	p =
SAI	−.02	.45	.25	.12
CIQ	.13	.19	.09	.33
SRA	−.07	.33	.25	.12
FLASR	−.15	.15	−.22	.16

When one-way partial correlations—controlling for SASP scores—and four-way partial correlations—controlling for all ability measures—were performed on OPI and anxiety scores, none of the correlations were significant. In other words, once the effect of an individual's language proficiency was accounted for, oral performance would no longer be expected to decrease as anxiety increased.

DISCUSSION OF FINDINGS

The central question addressed by this study was whether oral interview performance is affected by anxiety. It was found that for three of the four anxiety measures, there was a significant negative correlation between the OPI and anxiety, ostensibly leading to the conclusion that as anxiety increases, oral proficiency decreases. However, when four-way partial correlations were performed to control for proficiency score variances, there were no longer any significant correlations between the OPI and the anxiety measures. In practical terms this indicates that ability, not anxiety, is the more important variable affecting OPI scores, at least under the conditions of an unofficial administration of the OPI. The subjects of this study were not terribly anxious, perhaps because they knew that the OPI results could have no negative repercussions for them. Thus, under these conditions the OPI test may indeed have been solely a measure of the subjects' language proficiency.

Because anxiety could be significantly higher under an official administration of the OPI, this study should be replicated if and when the OPI becomes an official test for prospective language teachers in the state of Texas. If, during an official administration of the OPI, anxiety were to have a significant negative correlation with subjects' oral performance, then we would have evidence to believe that this could be due to *test anxiety* and not necessarily to anxiety from speaking in a foreign language. In other words, subjects in the particular study reported here experienced little test anxiety because they were taking the OPI as practice. However, test anxiety surfaces when an individual perceives a situation as threatening or difficult. In an official administration of the OPI, the seriousness of the results could induce anxiety in the subjects. Test anxiety would most likely affect prospective foreign language teachers with low levels of oral proficiency more than those with high levels of proficiency. If this is true, test anxiety cannot be viewed without examining an individual's proficiency, and future research in this area will have to investigate the interactive, cause/effect aspects of the anxiety/proficiency relationship. For example, is it anxiety which causes low levels of proficiency—as Krashen's Affective Filter concept would suggest (Krashen, 1982)—or do low levels of proficiency result in high levels of anxiety?

CONCLUSION

This study represents an attempt to identify the relationship between anxiety and foreign language oral performance (as represented by OPI ratings). Results indicated that anxiety did not exert as much influence as ability on foreign language oral proficiency scores in an unofficial administration of the OPI. Since test anxiety research indicates that anxiety increases under an evaluative situation perceived as difficult and threatening, it is possible that anxiety will increase when the OPI is administered as an official test. Since important decisions about individual careers and available personnel may well be based on OPI results, close and continued monitoring of the effect of anxiety on OPI results is warranted.

Chapter Seven

Evaluating Student Attitudes Toward Second-Language Tests

Harold S. Madsen, Bruce L. Brown,   Brigham Young University
and Randall L. Jones

INTRODUCTION

While there has been extensive investigation into student attitudes in relation to second-language learning, for some reason, student attitudes toward test-taking—an experience that evokes the strongest expressions of feeling—has been largely ignored in ESL and FL literature. We began to recognize the need for measuring attitudes toward exams a few years ago when piloting an EFL test battery. A number of students, as well as some teachers, volunteered negative reactions to certain exams but rather positive comments on others. Evaluating these opinions, we found patterns of near consensus, which bore only an occasional relationship to exam difficulty.

Several reasons for evaluating student reactions to tests have become apparent: For one thing, using tests lacking face validity or exams causing high anxiety could create a negative attitude toward instruction, and this in turn could adversely affect progress in learning the language. Pimsleur (1970) argues that appropriate testing can help alleviate high dropout rate, underachievement, discipline problems, and negative student attitudes. Taylor (1971) holds that inappropriate testing systems are linked to high failure rate.

Another matter is the possibility of test bias and resulting student concern. Persons with certain cultural traits may be more susceptible to anxiety on a given language test than others are (Barabasz, 1970; Bronzaft, Murgatroyd, & McNeilly, 1974). Related to this is the possibility that strong negative reactions to a test may seriously weaken performance (though not consistently for all subjects) and thereby reduce the test's validity (Gaudry & Fitzgerald, 1971; Maurer, 1973; Osterhouse, 1975). And some tests may favor one group over another (Labov, 1972; Briere, 1973; Oller & Perkins, 1978; Farhady, 1979; Leach, 1979).

Still another reason for evaluating student reactions to tests is that this very process demonstrates teacher concern, while at the same time enabling students to participate in the evaluation process. Just as the regular monitoring of attitudes has been found appropriate in language teaching (Jorstad, 1974), similar monitoring of attitudes toward language tests holds the promise of improving language exams. And for those with a humanistic bent (cf. Disick & Barbanel, 1974), the study of test affect reflects an interest in the total person and not simply in the intellect or in skill mastery.

While the ESL/FL literature on test affect is quite limited and largely anecdotal, there is a helpful body of literature on test affect in other areas. An important area of test affect is that of test *anxiety*, more than 500 articles appearing in psychological journals in three decades.

Basic approaches to measuring anxiety include self-report, physiological techniques, and observation (Scovel, 1978, this volume). The latter, however, has not proved sensitive enough (Snyder & Ray, 1971). And while physiological approaches such as heart rate and galvanic skin response are occasionally employed (Morris & Liebert, 1970; Bronzaft & Stuart, 1971; Darley & Katz, 1973; Rosenzweig, 1974; Upshur et al., 1978), most studies use self-report because of its practicality and availability.

Over the years it had generally been assumed that anxiety was harmful or debilitating to test performance. But three decades ago, Alpert and Haber (1960) identified facilitating as well as debilitating anxiety. Later, additional theories on test anxiety were advanced, one of the most significant being Spielberger's construct of trait and state anxiety. The term "trait anxiety" was used to refer to a fairly stable personality characteristic, while "state anxiety" referred to the more transitory anxiety that tends to "fluctuate in response to different stimuli" (Wildemuth, 1977). Additional anxiety constructs in the psychological literature have contributed to our general understanding of the anxiety concept. For example, the "worry" versus "emotionality" dichotomy (mental concern as opposed to an automatic physical response) gives additional insight into various types and meanings of anxiety, as does the concept of "interference," which deals with anxiety as a factor that can result in biased or imprecise measurement in psychological testing. For an in-depth review of the test anxiety literature, see Hembree (1988).

In addition to the theoretical work, there is also a fairly extensive literature of empirical studies on test anxiety. Some studies have shown, for example, a relationship between gender and test anxiety (Manley & Rosemeir, 1972; Tryon et al., 1973; Morris et al., 1976). And on a wide variety of measures, persons with high test anxiety are outperformed by those with low test anxiety (Kestenbaum & Weiner, 1970; Holmes, 1972; Rosenzweig, 1974; Ohlenkamp, 1976). Anecdotal evidence confirms that anxiety can have a debilitating effect during a foreign language exam (Horwitz, Horwitz, & Cope, 1986, this volume). In this connection, Young (1986, this volume) looked at the relationship between anxiety and performance on the Oral Proficiency Interview. Initial results suggested that increased anxiety resulted in lower OPI performance, but when the effect of ability was taken into consideration, heightened anxiety no longer related to a decrease in performance. Nevertheless, as Young indicates (1986, this volume), this administration of the OPI was not an official test. The pressure of an OPI administration when it is used for actual grading or placement could increase anxiety significantly (as Stevenson [1979] found) and thus affect performance. Young's discovery, however, that examinee ability level is an important variable related to anxiety measurement is a useful insight. In fact, the relationship between student foreign language proficiency and exam anxiety is an important part of the results of the two studies presented later in this chapter.

The effect of various test conditions has also been investigated: unannounced exams (Warner & Kauffman, 1972; Gary, 1973), retesting (Cohen, 1971), use of humor (Smith et al., 1971), music (Stanton, 1973), feedback on test performance (Prestwood & Weiss, 1978), sufficiency of time (Ammann, 1970), as well as the effect of easy-to-difficult sequencing (Towle & Merrill, 1972; Stanton, 1973).

Initial ESL/FL information on test affect, as we have indicated, was anecdotal and peripheral to the central objective of the research. For example, Savignon (1972), in the course of developing a communicative competence test over a decade ago, noted the "overwhelming" positive reactions of students to that kind of testing. By the mid-1970s a European experiment comparing student performance on native-language versus foreign-language distractors disclosed that "most teachers discovered a (student) preference for offering the questions in the target language" (Groot, 1976, p. 48). Near the end of the decade, Mullen (1979, p. 188) provided a similar narrative summary of attitudes toward the cloze, indicating that examinees regarded it as "an inappropriate, even an unfair test."

About this time, studies commissioned at Brigham Young University began utilizing controlled experiments to investigate test affect. Maluf (1979), in evaluating differing distractor forms, looked briefly at student attitudes toward the tests they had taken. She found that advanced students strongly preferred FL distractors but that NL distractors tended to lessen the test anxiety of beginning students. Stevenson (1979) discovered significant differences in preference and anxiety among students who took three batteries of listening, reading, and grammar tests (nine exams in all) over a three-week period. The upper group of examinees rated all measures more positively than did the lower group. More recently Murray (1985) used a qualitative, introspective approach in a test anxiety study, which revealed that in addition to the impact of test type, differential test anxiety was aroused also by perceptions of item difficulty, time limitations, lack of familiarity with exam type, ambiguity in item stems, and low quality recordings for listening tests. The combined approaches of the earlier quantitative studies and the latter qualitative investigation constitute a form of investigative triangulation, which provides us with an improved perspective of the factors involved in test anxiety (Madsen & Murray, 1984).

Of the variables related to test anxiety, none is more interesting than the impact of exam form. One might assume, for example, that a face-to-face oral interview would normally be more anxiety producing than a paper-and-pencil test (as reported by Zeidner & Bensoussan, 1988). But Scott (1986) found no such effect in her assessment of student reactions to oral language tests; and observations of live oral testing by Jones indicates that oral tests are in fact less anxiety producing (Jones, 1985a, 1985b; see also Jones, 1976). Moreover, the nonthreatening nature of many oral interviews is corroborated by a variety of research studies. A controlled experiment by Shohamy (1980, 1982) revealed a strong preference for the oral interview over the cloze. Other studies have produced similar findings. For example, an affect study of a six-subtest ESL battery showed that the oral interview was the least anxiety-producing (Madsen, 1982). Murray (1985) found virtually the same results.

Naturally other variables must be considered as we attempt to interpret the anxiety experienced on language tests. For example, it has been shown that persons from various cultures tend to react differently to the same tests (Hansen, 1984; Scott & Madsen, 1983). And, as indicated above, unfamiliarity with an exam format can exacerbate test frustration (Scott, 1980; Scott & Madsen, 1983).

Psychological studies on test anxiety have produced considerable data on the traits of high- and low-anxiety subjects (Hembree, 1988). But far less information is available on state anxiety, particularly as this relates to varying test types. The initial study that follows investigates affective differences at varying ability levels. The second study examines differences in reactions to various test types across successive stages of the learning process.

STUDY ONE

Method

A major objective in both studies was to confirm that affective reactions differ significantly depending on the nature of the language test being assessed. In addition, Study One was designed to determine whether or not significant differences in affect would emerge between more proficient and less proficient students. Specifically, we compared those receiving A, B, C, D, or E as their final class grade. A secondary objective of Study One was to contrast the attitudes of beginning students with those who had received a year or more of instruction.

    Subjects. All 220 participants were enrolled in German courses at Brigham Young University. The majority were in beginning classes (German 101), some in second-semester classes (German 102), and the remainder in second-year coursework (German 201). The 101 group was composed of nine classes totalling 142 students. Of the 142 students, 38 received A's, 36 B's, 37 C's, 22 D's, and 9 E's. The German 102 group consisted of 47 students enrolled in three classes, and the German 201 group totalled 31 students in two classes. All of the respondents in Study One were given these tests and the affective rating instrument at the end of the semester.

    Tests and affective reaction measures. The battery of tests administered to German 101 students consisted of (1) dictation, (2) oral questions, (3) grammatical fill-in, (4) grammatical manipulation, (5) English to German translation, (6) German to English translation, and (7) true-false German culture. The dictation test presented spoken German sentences to students (such as, "Was gibt es heute zum Frühstück?"), which they were required to write down. Oral questions consisted of questions in German (such as, "Was machen Sie am Sonntag nachmittag?"), which were presented to students with the instruction that they then write a logical response. Grammatical fill-in required students to supply missing words in printed sentences (for example, "Add the correct indefinite article: Ist das _____ Taschenmesser?") Grammatical manipulation required students to modify in a specified way various German sentences (for instance, "Change to the conversational past tense: Sie studiert in Berlin"). English to German translation required students to translate English sentences such as "What time does the play begin?" into German. German to English translation reversed this procedure: Students were given German sentences, such as "Meine Eltern wohnen seit 15 Jahren in Offenburg," which they were to translate into English. And on the true-false German culture subtest, students read a sentence in English testing their knowledge of cultural information from the textbook, such as "Berlin is the capital city of the BRD," and then they indicated whether the statement was true or false.

    The battery for German 102 students differed from the 101 test in only two areas. It did not include the culture test, and a sentence completion task replaced the fill-in subtest. Sentence completion consisted of spoken sentences with the last word missing (such as "Ich muß für morgen einen Aufsatz _____.") The student wrote down a word that logically completed the sentence. The German 102 battery consisted, then, of (1) dictation, (2) oral questions, (3) sentence completion, (4) grammatical manipulation, (5) English to German translation, and (6) German to English translation. The second-year, German 201, test battery was identical in form to the 101 battery, except that dictation was not included.

The affective reaction questionnaire was tailored for this particular study. A Likert-type scale provided ratings from 1 to 10 on each of the following 10 questions:

1. How well do you think you did on this part of the test?
2. How pleasant was the experience of taking this part of the test?
3. How difficult did you find this part of the test?
4. How fair do you think this part of the test was?
5. How well did this part of the test correspond with what you have been doing in class?
6. How well do you think this part of the test reflects your knowledge of German?
7. How frustrating did you find this part of the test?
8. Some tests are very reliable, in that you would get the same score by taking it a number of times, whereas others are affected more by chance factors. How reliable do you think this part of the test is?
9. Some tests are better than others in differentiating between those who really have a skill or knowledge and those who don't. Others are affected by extraneous factors such as cleverness in taking tests or general ability or intelligence. To what extent do you think this part of the test discriminates well in this regard?
10. How well do you personally like this part?

Procedure. Immediately after each group of students had taken the test battery, they completed the affective reactions questionnaire described above for each of the individual subtests. Since statistical analysis of reactions by ability level was based on the final grade received in the course, subjects were not aware of their exact standing at the time they rated the tests.

Results. The major hypotheses of affect differences by test type, by student ability, and by longitudinal exposure to L2 will be assessed in three ways: first by inspection of tables of mean responses to affect questions by test type and by grade level, second by analysis of variance results indicating which differences are statistically significant, and finally the total pattern of the results will be displayed by a multivariate graphical method known as the Multigraf™ (Brown & Rencher, 1990).[1]

Inspection of the tables of mean affective reactions discloses general patterns related both to test type and to grade groups. Beginning with the results generated by German 101 students (Table 1), we can compare the mean affective rating of each grade group for every one of the seven subtests on all 10 questions of the affective reactions questionnaire. The maximum possible mean rating is 10.00, since responses were made on a 10-point scale. Note that the higher the numerical value the more positive the rating. Thus on question 1, "How well do you think you did on [this subtest]?" "A" students predictably rated themselves much higher on dictation, for example, (9.47) than "E" students rated themselves (7.89) on the same subtest.

From a cursory examination of Table 1 one can observe that on many of the questions, dictation receives the highest rating and German-English translation the lowest, thus indicating a preference for the dictation task. Grammar manipulation fares well on questions such as 2, 7, and 10, which refer to the emotional impact of the test. And on these same questions the

Table 1

TABLE OF MEANS FOR STUDY ONE, SHOWING THE TWO-WAY INTERACTION BETWEEN THE FIVE GRADE GROUPS ("A" THROUGH "E") OF GERMAN 101 STUDENTS AND THEIR RATINGS OF THE SEVEN LANGUAGE TESTS ON EACH OF THE TEN AFFECTIVE RATING QUESTIONS.

1. How well do you think you did on it?

	A	B	C	D	E
dictation	9.47	8.53	8.16	7.18	7.89
oral questions	8.29	7.42	6.68	6.27	5.56
grammatical fill-in	8.24	7.75	7.11	6.77	6.00
grammar manip.	8.82	8.31	7.41	7.55	7.00
culture true-false	7.68	7.61	8.14	7.05	6.22
English-German tr.	7.66	6.92	6.22	6.05	5.22
German-English tr.	7.58	6.72	5.70	5.59	4.22

2. How pleasant was the experience of taking it?

	A	B	C	D	E
dictation	8.47	7.39	7.68	6.73	7.33
oral questions	7.47	6.39	6.16	6.00	6.11
grammatical fill-in	7.61	6.83	6.86	6.73	6.00
grammar manip.	8.03	7.44	7.11	7.59	7.11
culture true-false	7.34	7.53	7.57	7.27	6.67
English-German tr.	6.82	6.22	5.16	6.27	4.89
German-English tr.	6.37	5.86	5.16	5.48	3.89

3. How difficult did you find it?

	A	B	C	D	E
dictation	8.84	8.06	7.65	6.9	7.67
oral questions	7.34	6.81	6.00	6.14	5.78
grammatical fill-in	7.39	7.28	6.59	6.95	6.00
grammar manip.	7.97	7.58	6.73	7.24	6.89
culture true-false	7.05	7.39	7.43	6.76	7.11
English-German tr.	6.32	5.69	4.84	5.55	5.11
German-English tr.	6.24	5.97	4.76	5.15	4.22

4. How fair do you think it was?

	A	B	C	D	E
dictation	9.26	8.83	8.92	8.36	8.44
oral questions	8.61	8.53	8.24	7.95	8.33
grammatical fill-in	9.00	8.53	8.51	8.09	8.89
grammar manip.	9.21	8.83	8.35	8.36	9.11
culture true-false	7.82	7.72	8.38	7.64	8.67
English-German tr.	8.37	8.11	7.46	8.09	7.78
German-English tr.	7.34	7.25	6.95	7.14	6.33

5. How well did it correspond to the class?

	A	B	C	D	E
dictation	8.79	8.67	8.24	8.27	8.89
oral questions	8.37	8.42	8.14	7.82	8.67
grammatical fill-in	8.61	8.03	8.27	8.18	9.22
grammar manip.	8.76	8.35	8.51	8.45	9.11
culture true-false	6.05	7.19	7.61	7.14	7.00
English-German tr.	8.05	7.64	7.46	7.55	7.56
German-English tr.	7.37	7.25	7.27	7.00	5.89

6. How well does it reflect your knowledge of German?

	A	B	C	D	E
dictation	8.77	7.86	8.22	7.27	8.33
oral questions	8.82	8.25	7.70	7.5	8.33
grammatical fill-in	8.39	7.86	7.95	6.86	8.11
grammar manip.	8.45	8.31	7.92	7.82	8.78
culture true-false	6.16	6.34	6.75	6.77	8.33
English-German tr.	8.42	7.89	8.05	7.18	7.67
German-English tr.	7.92	7.42	7.62	6.41	6.89

7. How frustrating did you find it?

	A	B	C	D	E
dictation	9.42	8.14	7.95	6.55	7.56
oral questions	7.61	6.61	6.05	5.55	6.22
grammatical fill-in	7.76	7.42	6.92	7.23	7.11
grammar manip.	8.39	8.14	7.16	7.82	7.78
culture true-false	7.45	7.47	8.03	6.68	8.00
English-German tr.	6.16	5.92	4.86	5.91	4.44
German-English tr.	5.61	5.50	4.19	4.64	4.00

8. How reliable do you think it is?

	A	B	C	D	E
dictation	9.21	8.50	7.69	8.09	7.33
oral questions	8.32	8.14	6.83	7.55	6.78
grammatical fill-in	8.45	7.56	7.28	7.73	7.44
grammar manip.	8.45	8.31	7.28	8.09	7.89
culture true-false	7.16	6.72	7.11	6.86	7.22
English-German tr.	8.42	7.72	7.08	7.82	6.78
German-English tr.	7.24	7.50	6.86	7.50	5.78

9. How well do you think it differentiates?

	A	B	C	D	E
dictation	7.86	7.47	6.86	6.91	7.00
oral questions	8.43	7.94	6.74	7.05	7.78
grammatical fill-in	8.16	7.81	6.94	6.77	6.67
grammar manip.	8.19	7.67	7.37	7.18	7.33
culture true-false	6.20	6.00	6.24	6.36	4.89
English-German tr.	8.49	8.44	7.23	7.00	6.67
German-English tr.	7.43	8.06	6.86	7.05	6.22

10. How well do you personally like it?

	A	B	C	D	E
dictation	8.95	8.31	8.32	7.5	7.22
oral questions	7.61	6.97	6.30	6.77	6.56
grammatical fill-in	7.89	7.36	7.05	7.27	6.56
grammar manip.	8.34	8.00	7.38	8.05	7.11
culture true-false	7.24	7.17	7.51	6.82	7.22
English-German tr.	6.92	6.25	5.57	6.45	5.89
German-English tr.	6.47	5.94	5.16	5.64	4.44

translation subtests are rated lowest, or in other words the most anxiety-producing. Moreover, questions such as number 9, which call for simply a cognitive or objective reaction to a test, likewise show differential ratings for certain test types. For example, the true-false culture test is consistently rated lowest or the least valid of all the exam types.

Even a casual look at Table 1 also reveals some differences in affective reactions by grade groups. Specifically, those who receive the highest grades at the end of the semester tend to rate the subtests higher than do those receiving lower grades. In short, the better students tend to have a more positive reaction to the tests than do the weaker students. At the same time, there also seems to be some interaction between the test being rated and the grade group of the persons doing the rating. Certain tests are viewed differently by students at various performance levels.

Since we are dealing with the ratings that respondents give to the various language tests on 10 different dependent variables, our data are multivariate. The traditional statistical procedure for dealing with multivariate data such as these is to use a multivariate analysis of variance (MANOVA) to test the overall multivariate effects for each of the factors ("language test type" and "grade groups" in our case) before using ordinary analysis of variance (ANOVA) to test the univariate effects for these two factors on each of the 10 dependent variables individually. Rencher and Pan (1990) have demonstrated with a simulation that this is in fact very good policy. They found that this is the only procedure, of those they evaluated, that is successful in keeping the alpha levels from being inflated. If one wishes the alpha level from the significance test to have meaning, one must not reject the null hypothesis on any of the univariate significance tests unless the overall MANOVA statistic for that particular effect is also statistically significant.

A two-way split-plot MANOVA was used for the analysis of the data in this study, with the first factor being the seven tests of language proficiency and the second factor being the five grade groups.[2] The multivariate Wilks' lambdas are significant for both of these factors, at the .0001 level for the language tests factor, and the .05 level for the grade groups factor. Also, the multivariate test for the interaction between these two factors is highly significant, at the .0001 level. Obviously the effects for the type of test being rated are much more pronounced than the effects of the grade group of those doing the rating, and the interaction between these two factors is also a strong effect.

Since all three multivariate effects are significant (language test, grade group, and their interaction) we are justified in examining the individual ANOVA results for each of these three. All 10 univariate F tests are significant (with an alpha level of $p < .0001$) for the language test factor. That means that the seven language tests differ significantly in the relative ratings they receive on all 10 of the questions listed in Table 1. For the grade groups factor, the univariate tests are significant on only 3 of the 10 questions: question number 1, how well they did ($p < .0001$); question number 3, how difficult the test was ($p < .05$), and question number 7, how frustrating the test was ($p < .05$). For the interaction between the two factors, the univariate tests were also significant for only three of the questions: question number 1, how well they did ($p < .05$); question number 6, validity ($p < .05$); and question number 7, how frustrating the test was ($p < .05$). The most obvious observation from these results is that the effect of *which* test is being rated is greater than the effect of which grade group is doing the rating and it is also greater than the effect of the two-way interaction.

The results of these statistical significance tests indicate that we can take the intertest differences that we see in mean affect ratings in Table 1 quite seriously. We can reject the null hypothesis, that these means do not differ in the population, at a very high level for each of the 10 affect questions. Another insight provided by the results so far (particularly the significant grade group effects and the significant two-way interaction between test type and grade group) is a caution in assuming that students are very similar to one another in their reactions toward the tests. In these results and those that follow, we see that high-performing students have a different pattern of affective ratings of the tests than do low-performing students, and also advanced students have a different pattern of affective ratings from beginning students. Furthermore, it is obviously the case that many factors in addition to the ones examined in this study may account for the reactions of particular students to particular tests.

Having inspected the mean affective reactions to the tests and the ANOVA results, we turn now to a visually descriptive summary of the results contained in Table 1. To display the total gestalt of the results of the multivariate analysis of variance, we have employed the simplest and the most basic of a number of recently developed multivariate graphical display techniques, the Principal Components Multigraf™ (Brown & Rencher, 1989). This is a method that can be used to display the information from all of the means in a multivariate analysis of variance in a single two-dimensional plotting.

Figure 1 is a Multigraf that displays some of the multivariate information from Table 1. In particular, it displays the multivariate information about the highly significant effects of language test type on the affective ratings. It shows the relative position for the means of each of the seven tests in the multivariate space of the 10 questions. Notice that each of the 10 questions appears in Figure 1 as an axis with two end points that are labeled as opposites on that question. For example, question 3 on test difficulty has an "easy" end point on the right side of the figure and a "difficult" end point on the left side of the figure.

When two or more axis end points are close together, this indicates that the variables (questions) are highly correlated with one another. Sometimes a number of axes will group together, indicating a cluster of variables that are highly interrelated. One such grouping that is reflected in the plottings focuses on the relative amount of anxiety generated by various subtests: Items such as "did well," "liked it," and "pleasant" (as opposed to "did poorly," "did not like it," "frustrating") we might refer to as emotive questions and they are oriented near the horizontal plane with low anxiety on the right of the figure and high anxiety on the left of the figure. A contrasting group of axes appears more cognitive, since the focus is not on the person but on characteristics of the tests such as validity: Items such as "differentiates well" and "accurately reflects" characterize this group, and they are oriented more toward the vertical plane, with the positive cognitive assessment at the top of the figure and the negative assessment at the bottom.

Seven locational points are plotted within the circle, one for each of the seven tests given to the German 101 students. If a test is located on the right side of the figure, whether high or low, this means it was rated positively on emotive variables, such as being relatively easy, pleasant, and not frustrating, etc. Similarly, if it is on the left side of the figure, regardless of its vertical position, it was rated as being difficult, unpleasant, frustrating, etc. Those that are high in the figure, regardless of horizontal position, were rated positively on cognitive variables such as validity and reliability. By contrast, the low position on the figure means that they were perceived as being deficient in such areas as validity and reliability.

When a test is plotted both high in the figure and to the right, this means that it was rated highly on both emotive and cognitive variables, such as ease and pleasantness, as well as validity and reliability. Emotive questions—those associated with the horizontal factor—are in general reflective of students' assessment of the test relative to themselves: How well they did, how much they liked it, etc. Cognitive questions—those most closely associated with the vertical factor—reflect students' assessment of the test relative to the group's actual knowledge of German and the intention and purpose of the class.

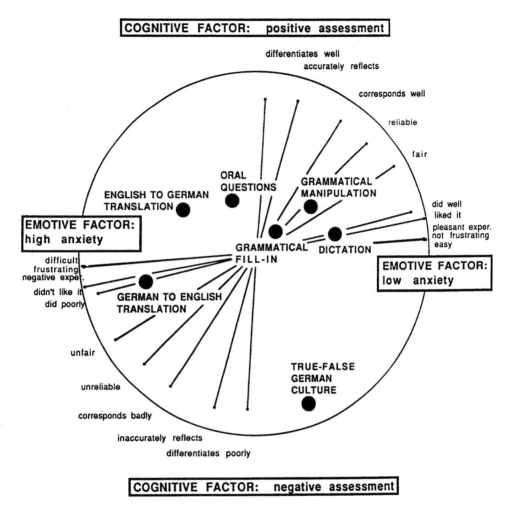

FIGURE 1 Principal Components Multigraf displaying the gestalt of the relative ratings given to each of the seven tests by German 101 students on the ten questions. This Multigraf is constructed from the seven by ten matrix of mean ratings for the seven tests on the ten questions, averaged over all 142 German 101 students in Study One.

Notice from Figure 1 that the test lowest in the figure, and therefore the one rated lowest on cognitive questions such as validity, is the culture true-false test. This is quite reasonable since knowledge of culture is not directly related to actual language skill. In referring back to Table 1, the table of means, one can verify that the culture true-false test does indeed have the lowest mean ratings on question 9—how well it differentiates between strong and weak students, and question 6, how well it reflects knowledge of German. It also has a relatively low mean rating on question 5 (its correspondence to class instruction) and on question 8 (test reliability).

The tests that are plotted toward the right, and therefore most positive on the horizontal emotive factor are dictation and grammar manipulation. Conversely, German to English and English to German translation items are ranked lowest in the emotive domain (on the left in Figure 1). This indicates that dictation and grammatical manipulation are rated by subjects as being relatively easy and pleasant, while the translation tests are rated as being relatively difficult and frustrating, particularly German to English translation. This can also be verified from Table 1.

It is interesting to note that these German 101 students not only rate German to English translation as the hardest and most unpleasant of the tests, but also less valid than any other language-skill test. And while culture true-false (which is not a language skill test) was ranked as much less valid than any other subtest, it was found to be one of the more pleasant to take.

We turn now from the visual plotting of overall ratings of tests to a visual plotting of how ratings relate to the grade group of the respondents. Figure 2 is similar to Figure 1, but this time the multivariate means that are displayed are those for each of the five grade groups, rather than the seven tests. We can see that the grade groups means do not vary nearly as much as the test means, and we remember that the grade groups factor was not nearly so significant statistically as the language tests factor.

Notice that the multivariate means for the higher grade groups (A and B) are both higher in the figure and more to the right, indicating that superior students tend to rate tests in general higher on both cognitive and emotive questions. In other words, superior students tended to see the exams they took as more valid and less threatening on the whole than less able students did. However, as we note in Figure 3, the emotive factor tends to differentiate grade groups more markedly than does the cognitive.[3]

Not only were the tests and the grade groups factors significant on the multivariate and some univariate tests, but the interaction between them was likewise significant. For most of the seven tests, the overall pattern of the more capable students' being in the upper right area of the figure tends to hold; but on the means for the culture true-false test, it does not. On the culture true-false test, it is the best students who are most negative toward it, specifically in the cognitive area—its adequacy as a reflection of German knowledge. A and B students, more than C, D, and E students, believe that it is not an adequate reflection of language knowledge. The significant interaction seems to be due principally to this reversal of the usual pattern of lower grade group students reacting more negatively toward tests.

The final issue in Study One is to examine whether the preferences found for German 101 students hold up at higher levels of German skill, as reflected in the German 102 and 201 classes. The means tables for the ratings by these more advanced students will not be given, but only the overall pattern of their results as displayed in two Multigrafs, Figure 4 and Figure 5.

Figure 4 is the Multigraf for the mean ratings given to six tests on the 10 questions by the 47 German 102 students. In this Multigraf, dictation is again favored as the easiest, least frustrating, most pleasant test. However, grammatical manipulation, which was rated by German 101 students as also very easy and pleasant, is rated by these 102 students as being the most difficult, unpleasant, and frustrating of all the six tests, sharing that lowest position on the horizontal emotive factor with German to English translation. It appears that the grammar dealt with by the end of the 102 class is much more challenging than that encountered near the end of a 101 class. But it is still surprising to note the dramatic drop in ratings for the grammatical manipulation test.

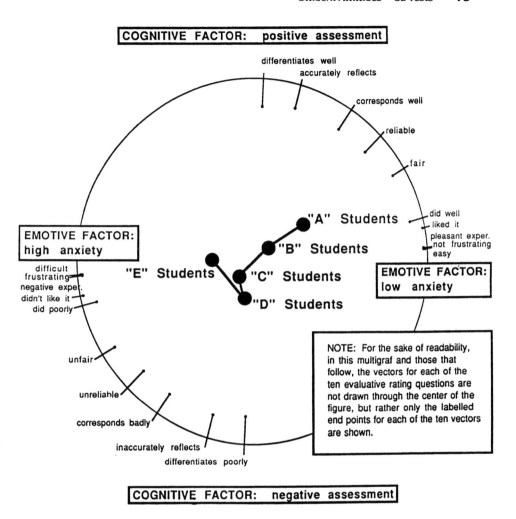

FIGURE 2 Principal Components Multigraf displaying the gestalt of the relative ratings given by each of the German 101 grade groups ("A" through "E"). This Multigraf is constructed from the five by ten matrix of mean ratings by the five grade groups on the ten questions, averaged over the respondents in each group and over the seven tests in Study One.

The culture true-false test was not administered to the German 102 students, but sentence completion, which was given in place of culture true-false in this battery for German 102 students, is found in the same topological location in the Multigraf that culture true-false was for German 101 students. This is the test that is lowest on the vertical (cognitive) factor, the factor associated with the perception of exam validity. In short, the sentence-completion subtest is simply not seen as a very valid measure of German.

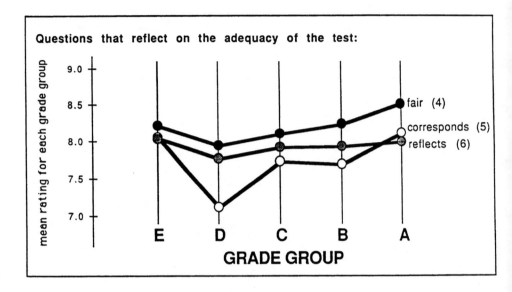

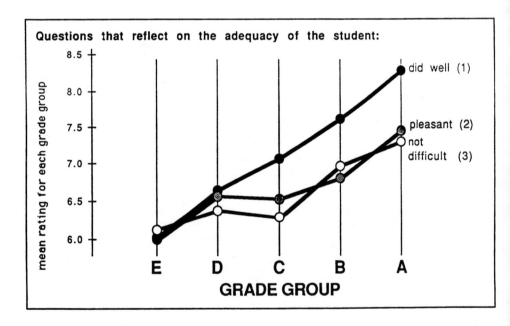

FIGURE 3 Univariate line graphs comparing the mean ratings given by each grade group ("A" through "E") of German 101 students on six of the ten questions, averaged over the respondents within each grade group and the seven tests being evaluated in Study One.

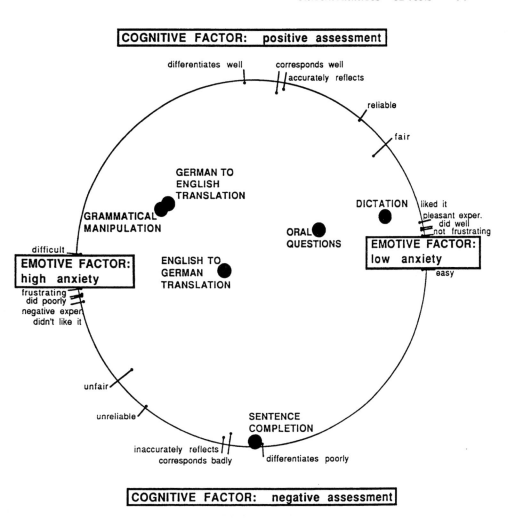

FIGURE 4 Principal Components Multigraf for the mean ratings given to each of the six tests on each of the ten questions by German 102 students in Study One.

The German 201 battery is identical to the 101 battery except that the 201 test does not include dictation. This permits a number of comparisons to be made. Figure 5 is the Multigraf for the mean ratings given to the six tests on the 10 questions by the 31 German 201 students.

Culture true-false is in virtually the same position in ratings by German 201 students as it was for German 101 students—easy and pleasant but not reflective of knowledge of German or class activities. However, we see some interesting shifts for the translation tests.

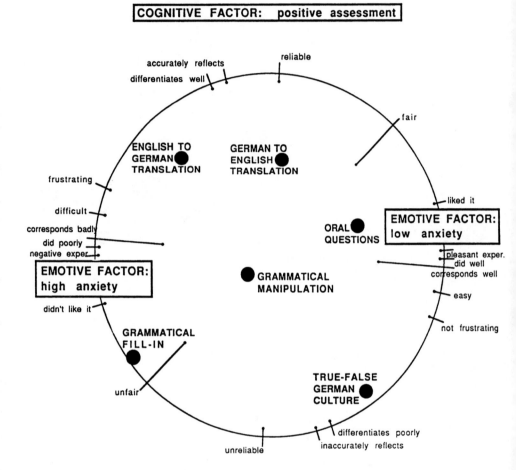

FIGURE 5 Principal Components Multigraf for the mean ratings given to each of the six tests on each of the ten questions by German 201 students in Study One.

Whereas for the German 101 and 102 students, English to German translation was rated as being easier than German to English; by the time students have completed German 201, the ratings are reversed. Now, German to English translation is rated as easier than English to German. Also, by the time a student is in 201, translation tests in general are rated well above the other tests in terms of validity and reliability. The sharpest contrast between the Multigraf for German 101 student ratings (Figure 1) and this Multigraf for German 201 student ratings involves the fill-in test. It was rated by the German 101 students as being quite high on all 10 of the questions (both emotive and cognitive). But in the Multigraf for these second-year (German 201) students, the fill-in test is in the lower left quadrant, indicating that it is now rated the very lowest on both dimensions. It appears that by the time one has developed a moderate amount of proficiency in German, the fill-in task is not seen as being very reflective of foreign-language skill, nor very reliable or fair.

STUDY TWO

In Study One, the reactions of German 101 students of differing ability levels to a variety of testing formats were investigated. In addition the affective reactions of German 102 and 201 students were briefly examined as an indication of how test reactions change as one gains more skill in the language. Since it is likely that many of the students who receive the lowest grades in German 101 do not continue into 102 and 201, our measure was probably slightly confounded. We were probably examining not only more advanced students but also more capable students. In this second study, the question of how affective reactions to the various tests shift as one gains more experience is further pursued, but this time with measures recorded at two times in the semester for both German 101 and 102 students, in order to trace more adequately the changes occurring across time.

Although the information sought is longitudinal, the design is cross-sectional. That is, rather than tracing one group of students through both German 101 and 102 and measuring the same group at different intervals, we have measured different groups at the four stages of progress (four weeks and seven weeks into the semester in German 101 and two weeks and then five weeks into German 102). Although there could be some advantages to measuring the same group over the four time periods, we feel these advantages would be more than off-set by the disadvantage of the carry-over effects and expectancy effects from having students repeatedly rating the same tests. Such repeated testing and rating could well alter the reactions that students would ordinarily have toward the tests.

Method

Subjects.   All 369 participants were enrolled in first-year German classes at Brigham Young University: 182 in German 101 (97 evaluated after four weeks of instruction, 85 other students evaluated after seven weeks of instruction); and 187 in German 102 (97 evaluated after two weeks of instruction, and 90 others evaluated after five weeks of instruction).

Tests and affective reaction measures.   The battery of tests was virtually the same for the two German 101 groups and the first group of German 102 students. All three groups were given (1) dictation, (2) oral questions, (3) sentence completion, (4) English to German translation, and (5) German to English translation. Only the sixth subtest differed, with the two German 101 groups having a true-false test on German culture, and the first group of German 102 students having a sentence formation test. Except for this sentence formation test, all of the subtests were described in Study One. In the sentence formation subtest, the basic components of sentences were given in their uninflected forms (such as

"Maria/wollen/mit/ihr/Eltern/fahren/nach Budapest"). From this, the students' task was to form grammatical sentences.

The second German 102 class also took six test types. Three were the same as those taken by the first 102 class, namely (1) oral questions, (2) German to English translation, and (3) sentence formation. Test number 4 was grammar fill-in, the same as described in Study One. The remaining two tests had not been administered previously in exactly the form used at this time: (5) listening comprehension, and (6) culture matching. The listening comprehension subtest consisted of tape-recorded connected discourse in segments approximately one minute long. Students were to select appropriate responses from multiple-choice options that were keyed by comprehension questions such as "Where does this conversation take place?" The Culture Matching subtest consisted of a list of geographical locations and significant sites, opposite a list of descriptions in English, such as "It is the largest gothic cathedral in the world." Students would match the site with the description.

Procedure.   The same 10-question affective reaction questionnaire was used, and the same testing procedure was followed as in Study One.

Results.   Table 2 displays the mean ratings for all of the tests that were measured across all groups, and Figure 6 is the Multigraf corresponding to it. Together they show the changes in affective reaction to the various tests as students progress through German 101 and 102. The small numbers next to each plotted point on Figure 6 indicate which group is doing the rating: These range from the four-week German 101 group (shown with "1" next to it) to the five-week German 102 group (with a "4" next to it).

The most obvious result is that students become progressively more negative toward the sentence completion test as they progress in the German 101–102 sequence. This is true of every question in the rating, but more pronounced for cognitive-factor questions dealing with validity and reliability.

Dictation again receives positive ratings from all three of the groups that were measured, particularly on emotive questions, that is, those related to pleasantness, test preference, and fairness. The culture true-false test is once again viewed as pleasant, but not a very good reflection of German skill.

German to English translation and oral questions are the only tests measured on all four groups. The general pattern is for German to English translation to be rated as even more difficult and frustrating at the two 102 levels than at the two 101 levels. Moreover, it is viewed by the somewhat more advanced second-year students as slightly less reflective of German knowledge and class instruction than it was by beginners. However, on the basis of what was found in Study One (Figure 5), it could be presumed that if similar measures were taken at the 201 level there would be a marked reversal of this trend as students reached a more advanced level. We would expect a sharp increase in ratings of German to English translation on the vertical (cognitive) dimension (since it was the highest test on this dimension for the German 201 students).

Table 3 and Figure 7 display the results of the ratings on all of those tests that were not repeated across the four groups. This includes the sentence formation test in the second-week German 102 group. And for the fifth-week German 102 group, it includes sentence formation, grammatical fill-in, listening comprehension, and culture matching. The main function of this final figure and its corresponding table is to give information about this potpourri of tests that were not included in any of the other Multigrafs (except for grammar fill-in, which was investigated in Study One).

Table 2

TABLE OF MEANS FOR STUDY TWO, SHOWING THE TWO-WAY INTERACTION BETWEEN STAGE OF PROGRESS IN LEARNING GERMAN AND THE RATINGS OF THE SIX LANGUAGE TESTS ON EACH OF THE TEN AFFECTIVE RATING QUESTIONS.

	1. How well do you think you did on it?				2. How pleasant was the experience of taking it?			
	101a	101b	102a	102b	101a	101b	102a	102b
dictation	8.88	8.52	8.71	—	7.85	7.54	7.56	—
oral questions	7.46	7.26	7.95	8.24	6.81	6.57	7.09	7.61
sentence completion	8.01	7.54	7.29	—	7.47	6.92	6.50	—
English-German tr.	7.54	7.37	7.30	—	7.07	6.99	6.44	—
German-English tr.	7.73	7.87	6.88	6.33	7.45	7.42	6.57	6.34
culture true-false	9.23	9.07	—	—	8.70	8.21	—	—

	3. How difficult did you find it?				How fair do you think it was?			
	101a	101b	102a	102b	101a	101b	102a	102b
dictation	6.22	7.19	6.63	—	9.23	9.11	8.89	—
oral questions	5.15	5.88	5.83	6.50	8.89	8.80	8.95	7.83
sentence completion	5.80	6.19	5.86	—	9.27	8.86	7.00	—
English-German tr.	5.04	5.81	4.92	—	8.87	8.91	8.60	—
German-English tr.	5.31	6.42	5.03	5.00	8.66	9.00	7.66	7.63
culture true-false	7.22	8.06	—	—	9.31	9.14	—	—

	5. How well did it correspond to the class?				6. How well does it reflect your knowledge of German?			
	101a	101b	102a	102b	101a	101b	102a	102b
dictation	8.97	8.78	8.82	—	8.24	7.99	8.39	—
oral questions	8.78	8.74	8.91	8.09	8.58	8.41	8.60	8.01
sentence completion	8.82	8.60	5.81	—	8.51	8.13	7.13	—
English-German tr.	8.36	8.28	8.31	—	8.76	8.46	8.45	—
German-English tr.	8.12	8.19	7.36	7.63	8.47	8.49	8.12	7.96
culture true-false	8.31	8.29	—	—	7.50	7.38	—	—

	7. How frustrating did you find it?				8. How reliable do you think it is?			
	101a	101b	102a	102b	101a	101b	102a	102b
dictation	8.00	7.98	3.33	—	8.68	8.84	7.40	—
oral questions	6.86	6.76	3.87	7.45	8.42	8.30	7.30	7.35
sentence completion	7.44	6.69	4.98	—	8.49	7.94	6.15	—
English-German tr.	6.93	6.94	4.88	—	8.49	8.20	7.02	—
German-English tr.	6.88	7.27	5.36	5.89	8.42	8.49	6.74	7.35
culture true-false	9.13	8.90	—	—	8.36	8.26	—	—

	9. How well do you think it differentiates?				10. How well do you personally like it?			
	101a	101b	102a	102b	101a	101b	102a	102b
dictation	8.32	7.99	7.57	—	8.24	7.61	8.50	—
oral questions	8.63	8.33	8.05	7.76	7.24	6.88	7.92	7.57
sentence completion	8.54	7.89	6.71	—	7.69	7.12	6.16	—
English-German tr.	8.85	8.37	8.42	—	7.51	7.00	7.26	—
German-English tr.	8.66	8.10	7.69	8.02	7.61	7.45	6.82	6.38
culture true-false	7.53	6.44	—	—	8.53	7.78	—	—

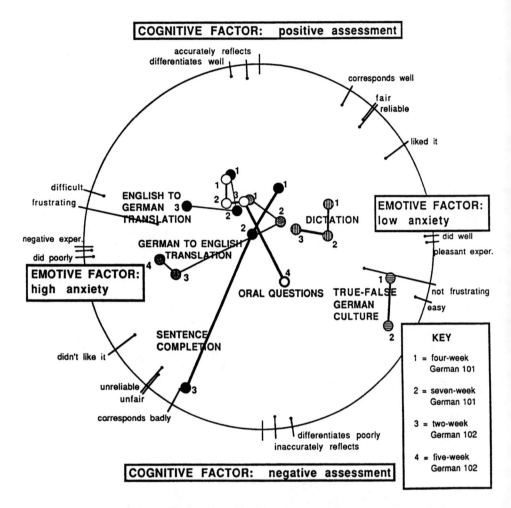

FIGURE 6   Principal Components Multigraf displaying developmental trend in the ratings given to tests in Study Two. This Multigraf displays the relative mean ratings given to six tests on the ten questions at four different stages of progress in learning German: four weeks into German 101, seven weeks into German 101, two weeks into German 102, and five weeks into German 102.

The grammatical fill-in test could be considered a kind of comparative anchor for these other tests, in that it was displayed in most of the figures of Study One. For German 101 students, the ratings of grammatical fill-in were near the center of the figure, but slightly positive on both emotive and cognitive factors (Figure 1). By contrast, it was the most negatively rated test by German 201 students (Figure 5). In Study Two (Figure 7), we see it again in a moderate position near the center for the five-week German 102 students. Two of the other three tests in this figure also receive quite moderate ratings. Sentence formation was ranked by both the second-week German 102 students and the fifth-week German 102 students. For both it was rated somewhat more positively on questions related to the vertical (cognitive) fac-

Table 3

ADDITIONAL TABLE OF MEANS FOR STUDY TWO, SHOWING THE MEAN RATINGS GIVEN BY THE TWO GERMAN 102 GROUPS TO FOUR LANGUAGE TESTS THAT WERE NOT ADMINISTERED TO THE GERMAN 101 GROUPS AND THUS WERE NOT INCLUDED IN THE DEVELOPMENTAL INFORMATION SHOWN IN TABLE 2.

	1. How well do you think you did?	2. How pleasant was the experience?	3. How difficult did you find it?	4. How fair do you think it was?
TWO-WEEK 102 GROUP:				
sentence formation	8.04	7.23	5.73	8.70
FIVE-WEEK 102 GROUP:				
sentence formation	7.87	7.52	6.20	8.36
listening comprehension	8.01	7.54	6.39	7.73
grammatical fill-in	7.88	7.49	6.47	8.01
culture matching	7.10	6.68	5.55	7.36

	5. How well did it correspond to class?	6. How well does it reflect your knowledge?	7. How frustrating did you find it?
TWO-WEEK 102 GROUP:			
sentence formation	8.40	8.44	3.87
FIVE-WEEK 102 GROUP:			
sentence formation	8.53	8.21	7.61
listening comprehension	7.97	7.93	9.43
grammatical fill-in	8.41	8.07	7.55
culture matching	7.14	5.78	6.45

	8. How reliable do you think it was?	9. How well do you think it differentiates?	10. How well do you personally like it?
TWO-WEEK 102 GROUP:			
sentence formation	7.51	8.26	8.23
FIVE-WEEK 102 GROUP:			
sentence formation	8.10	8.33	7.62
listening comprehension	7.19	7.70	6.82
grammatical fill-in	7.94	7.93	7.57
culture matching	6.41	6.02	6.30

tor than were other tests. The only major observation from this figure is that the five-week German 102 students are very negative toward culture matching, particularly on the cognitive factors of validity and reliability. This parallels somewhat the cognitive reactions to the Study One culture test. However, the matching culture test is viewed much more negatively on the emotive scale than was the true-false culture test in the first study. This new culture test is regarded not only as seriously lacking in validity but also as frustrating to take.

The positions of the tests from Figure 6 are plotted in the same multivariate space (the same orientation of the axes for the 10 questions) as those in Figure 7, and the relative positions of tests in these two figures can therefore be directly compared. From this comparison it can be seen that the five-week German 102 students are just as negative toward the culture-matching test as are the second-week German 102 students toward their sentence completion test.

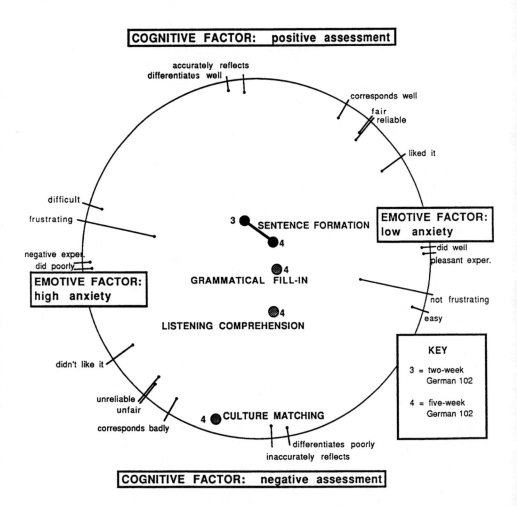

FIGURE 7 Principal Components Multigraf for the mean ratings given by the German 102 two-week group and the German 102 five-week group to five tests that were not administered to the other groups displayed in Figure 6.

SUMMARY AND CONCLUSIONS

Results of the two studies reported here lead us to the following conclusions: First, the initial hypothesis of differences in reactions to varied test types was confirmed. There are major differences in students' reactions to varying test types, and these differences are statistically significant. Moreover, it was found that these reactions tend to cluster into emotive and cognitive groupings. Looking at individual test types, we find that dictation and true-false culture tests were generally the least anxiety-producing, with translation producing the most anxiety and being the least favored, particularly in beginning classes.

Secondly, differences appear, too, among students grouped according to their final grade in the course. For example, "A" students in the German program placed a much lower value on the nonthreatening native language true-false culture questions than did weaker students. Also, the lower-performing students generally rated all of the tests lower than the higher performing students did, particularly on the more emotive questions. But differences between the ABCDE grade groups were less noticeable than the broad areas of agreement noted among the students in their ratings of tests.

Next, reactions to tests were found to vary depending upon one's stage of instruction. For example, it is not surprising that reactions to oral questions become more positive as one develops greater oral proficiency, and that German to English translation becomes less onerous at higher levels of instruction. But patterns of reactions to tests become quite stable at the intermediate level of instruction and beyond.

It is recommended that teachers consider the implications of these findings in conjunction with related language test anxiety research. It is now obvious from this study and others (Stevenson, 1979; Mullen, 1979; Shohamy, 1980) that there are major differences in anxiety generated by various forms of tests, and that this anxiety can actually result in a biasing effect against certain types of students (Madsen, 1982). In addition, this study and others (Scott, 1980; Murray, 1985) reveal that certain groups of students are more affected than others in experiencing test anxiety. Foreign language and ESL teachers would therefore be well advised to give careful consideration to the types of exams they use in evaluating students' language ability.

Studies have shown that certain accommodations can be made to lessen test anxiety (Hembree, 1988, pp. 67–72). Beginning students could benefit on occasion by having native language options (Maluf, 1979). Adjusting time constraints on language exams can help those who are anxiety prone (Madsen & Murray, 1984). Even the initiative of consulting with students about factors that produce test anxiety has been found to have a pronounced salutary affect (Murray, 1985; Zeidner & Bensoussan, 1988, p. 113). And besides this interview procedure there are additional techniques for assessing anxiety, with trait-anxiety measures such as the Alpert-Haber "Achievement Anxiety Test" (Alpert & Haber, 1960) and various state-anxiety measures such as the "Foreign Language Classroom Anxiety Scale" (the FLCAS by Horwitz, Horwitz, & Cope, 1986, this volume), the simple state-anxiety measure by Jones and Madsen (1980), as well as contemporary IRT (item response theory) "appropriateness measurement" procedures that investigate aberrant performance by individuals when taking tests (Weiss, 1983; Hulin, Drasgow, & Parsons, 1983; Madsen, 1987).

Finally, we conclude that assessing test affect is a significant area of psychometric investigation, one virtually as important as traditional concerns for assessing validity and reliability.

NOTES

1. DataMax™ and Multigraf™ are trademarks of ECHO Solutions, Inc. DataMax is a multivariate graphical general data analysis system, and the Multigraf is one of the procedures of DataMax. All of the graphical analyses in this paper were performed with a version of DataMax provided courtesy of ECHO Solutions, Inc., 1010 North State Street, Orem, Utah, 84057.

2. Since individual respondents are nested within grade groups but crossed with the tests being rated, the design was a two-way analysis with repeated measures over the language tests factor, but not

over the grade groups factor. The results were analyzed with the two-way split-plot model of multivariate analysis of variance using the RUMMAGE statistical analysis system (Scott, Carter, Bryce & Joiner, 1974; Bryce, 1982).

3. Figure 3, which is a set of simple univariate line graphs, shows in more detail the relative effects of grade group on emotive items as compared to cognitive items. Notice that the emotive items have a much stronger tendency to be linearly related to grade group than do the cognitive items, with those who receive higher grades having a much more positive emotional reaction to the tests overall (i.e., "pleasant, not difficult, did well") than those who received lower grades.

Chapter Eight

Oral Communication Apprehension and Hispanics: An Exploration of Oral Communication Apprehension Among Mexican American Students in Texas

Hugo Mejías   Pan American University
Ronald L. Applbaum   Westfield State College
Susan J. Applbaum   McAllen Independent School District
Robert T. Trotter II   University of Northern Arizona

INTRODUCTION

The U.S. Bureau of the Census classifies Hispanics as persons of Spanish origin or descent who designate themselves as Mexican American, Chicano, Puerto Rican, Cuban, and other/Spanish/Hispanic nationalities. Although tied together by a common cultural background-language and religion, these groups present distinct social-cultural and economic profiles (Ford Foundation, 1984, p. 6). The largest Hispanic group in the United States traces its origins to Mexico. Sixty percent of the 14.6 million Hispanics in the United States, excluding Puerto Ricans, are of Mexican origin (U.S. Bureau of the Census, 1981; Passel & Warren, 1983), with the majority of these individuals residing in the Southwestern United States.

In the United States, Hispanic enrollment and graduation from educational institutions is significantly lower than that of the general population and of other major ethnic and racial groups (U.S. Department of Education, 1982). One of the most significant factors affecting the educational attainment of Hispanics is their sometimes limited English-language background and proficiency (Fligstein & Fernández, 1982; Durán, 1983). This is not surprising since the proper use of English-language skills is a prerequisite to full and effective participation in public-school education in the United States (Astin, 1982). Such a requirement no doubt explains in part why studies have found that the communicative participation of Mexican American students is distinctly less than that of other students (Laosa, 1977; Ramirez, 1981).

Since most Mexican American students use two languages—English and Spanish—with varying levels of proficiency and competence in educational situations, they may experience communication apprehension or use their bilingualism to avoid educational situations in which they feel apprehensive (Krashen, 1981). The term *communication apprehension* (CA) refers to an individual's level of fear or anxiety associated with either real or anticipated communication with another person or persons. More than all other learning disabilities combined, CA is said to affect the behavior of students, with over 20% of all students experiencing high levels of CA (Hurt, Scott, & McCroskey, 1978; McCroskey, 1970, 1977a, 1982a). In light of these facts, it is reasonable to assume that CA may act as a general learning inhibitor for the bilingual and/or Mexican American student.

In discussing how important the use of language skills is in the schools, Hurt, Preiss, and Davis (1976) identify specifically the impact of oral communication on the learning environment:

> There is little doubt that the North American educational system places great reward on verbal behavior in the classroom. Pedagogical devices such as testing, group discussions, story-telling, experimental learning, and the like, all demand frequent verbal output on the part of students. Out-of-class activities such as counseling sessions, and even recess, also demand verbal interaction.

For the high CA student, normal educational situations such as those described by Hurt, Preiss, and Davis will be perceived as threatening. Such students are apt to feel anxious in social situations in which they have little control (McCroskey & Richmond, 1980) because their participation is not voluntary but rather is required by someone in authority. Typically, students are required to participate in class meetings, group discussions, oral reports to classmates, and conferences with counselor and teachers. Because students have little control over communication in these contexts, their required participation may result in heightened anxiety, withdrawal, less persistence in a second language, and negative academic consequences (Krashen, 1981).

The level of communication apprehension manifested by the student is potentially critical in the learning process because students who experience a high degree of CA are unlikely to participate fully in the learning situation. If a student is apprehensive about communicating in a particular language—whether English or Spanish—he or she will have negative affective feelings toward oral communication and will likely avoid it. In light of the fact that even native English-language speakers who are highly apprehensive are more passive in the classroom, the student who is not highly proficient in English would be expected to exhibit high CA levels and passive classroom behavior.

When students use two languages, they may avoid situations in which they must function in a language with which they feel apprehensive. Non-native English speakers who are apprehensive in English, then, tend to avoid situations in which they are called upon to function in English (Allen, O'Mara, & Andriate, 1984a). This apprehension in the second language, moreover, is usually somehow related to apprehensiveness in the primary language (Fayer, McCroskey, & Richmond, 1984; McCroskey, Fayer, & Richmond, 1983).

PURPOSE OF THE STUDY

Until now, no data have been reported on CA among Mexican Americans. This study was therefore undertaken to generate normative data on the CA of Mexican Americans at both the high school and college levels. Data collected by the study were then compared with previous research data drawn from high school and college-level students, primarily from the United States, Puerto Rico, and other non-native bilingual populations. In making this comparison, the following research questions were examined:

1. Are CA norms for Mexican American high school and college students speaking English similar to those of other Hispanics speaking English?
2. Are CA norms for Mexican American college students speaking either English or Spanish similar to those of other Hispanics speaking English or Spanish?
3. Are the CA scores of Mexican American high school students speaking Spanish different from their CA scores when speaking English?

Because it has been suggested that within the Mexican American culture, attitudinal differences exist between genders (Cuéllar, Harris, & Jasso, 1980), the following additional questions were also examined:

4. Are there gender-related differences between CA levels of male and female Mexican Americans speaking English in various contexts?
5. Are there gender-related differences between CA levels of male and female Mexican Americans speaking Spanish in various contexts?

In order to answer these questions, two separate studies were conducted. The first of these involved the testing of college students at Pan American University, and the second involved the testing of high school students in south Texas.

Measures

College. The CA of college students was measured by the Personal Report of Communication Apprehension (PRCA-24) instrument, which focuses on apprehension concerning oral communication (McCroskey, 1970, 1982a). This instrument was chosen largely because of its high reliability and predictive validity.

Two versions of the 24-item PRCA developed by McCroskey and Beatty (1984) were administered to all subjects (see Figure 1). The first version was directed toward measurement of CA associated with speaking in English, while the second version was intended to assess feelings of apprehension associated with speaking in Spanish. Both versions of the PRCA-24 were administered in English.

High school. The CA of high school students was measured by the Personal Report of Communication Apprehension (PRCA-10) displayed in Figure 2 (McCroskey, 1970, 1982a). The short form of the PRCA was used with high school students because time constraints did not permit employing the longer form and because the researchers sought to reduce potential student fatigue (Hurt & Preiss, 1978; McCroskey, 1978). Two versions of the

Directions: This instrument is composed of 24 statements concerning your feelings about communication with other people. Please indicate in the space provided the degree to which each statement applies to you by marking whether you (1) Strongly Agree, (2) Agree, (3) Are Undecided, (4) Disagree, or (5) Strongly Disagree with each statement. There are no right or wrong answers. Many of the statements are similar to other statements. Do not be concerned about this. Work quickly, and just record your first impression.

_____ 1. I dislike participating in group discussions.

_____ 2. Generally, I am comfortable while participating in group discussions.

_____ 3. I am tense and nervous while participating in group discussions.

_____ 4. I like to get involved in group discussions.

_____ 5. Engaging in a group discussion with new people makes me tense and nervous.

_____ 6. I am calm and relaxed while participating in group discussions.

_____ 7. Generally, I am nervous when I have to participate in a meeting.

_____ 8. Usually I am calm and relaxed while participating in meetings.

_____ 9. I am very calm and relaxed when I am called upon to express an opinion at a meeting.

_____ 10. I am afraid to express myself at meetings.

_____ 11. Communicating at meetings usually makes me uncomfortable.

_____ 12. I am very relaxed when answering questions at a meeting.

_____ 13. While participating in a conversation with a new acquaintance, I feel very nervous.

_____ 14. I have no fear of speaking up in conversations.

_____ 15. Ordinarily I am very tense and nervous in conversations.

_____ 16. Ordinarily I am very calm and relaxed in conversations.

_____ 17. While conversing with a new acquaintance, I feel very relaxed.

_____ 18. I'm afraid to speak up in conversations.

_____ 19. I have no fear of giving a speech.

_____ 20. Certain parts of my body feel very tense and rigid while giving a speech.

_____ 21. I feel relaxed while giving a speech.

_____ 22. My thoughts become confused and jumbled when I am giving a speech.

_____ 23. I face the prospect of giving a speech with confidence.

_____ 24. While giving a speech I get so nervous, I forget facts I really know.

Scoring:
Group $= 18 - (1) + (2) - (3) + (4) - (5) + (6)$
Meeting $= 18 - (7) + (8) + (9) - (10) - (11) + (12)$
Dyadic $= 18 - (13) + (14) - (15) + (16) + (17) - (18)$
Public $= 18 + (19) - (20) + (21) - (22) + (23) - (24)$
Overall CA $=$ Group $+$ Meeting $+$ Dyadic $+$ Public.

FIGURE 1 PRCA-24. (Personal Report of Communication Apprehension)

Directions: This instrument is composed of 10 statements concerning your communication with other people. Please indicate the degree to which each statement applies to you by marking whether you (1) Strongly Agree, (2) Agree, (3) Are Undecided, (4) Disagree, or (5) Strongly Disagree with each statement. There are no right or wrong answers. Work quickly, and just record your first impression.

_____ 1. I look forward to expressing myself at meetings.

_____ 2. I am afraid to express myself in a group.

_____ 3. I look forward to an opportunity to speak in public.

_____ 4. Although I talk fluently with friends, I am at a loss for words on the platform.

_____ 5. I always avoid speaking in public if possible.

_____ 6. I feel that I am more fluent when talking to people than most other people are.

_____ 7. I like to get involved in group discussion.

_____ 8. I dislike to use my body and voice expressively.

_____ 9. I'm afraid to speak up in conversations.

_____ 10. I would enjoy presenting a speech on a local television show.

To compute the PRCA score, follow these 3 steps:

1. Add the scores for items 2, 4, 5, 8, 9.
2. Add the scores for items 1, 3, 6, 7, 10.
3. Complete the following formula:
   PRCA = 3 − (total from step 1) + (total from step 2).

FIGURE 2　PRCA-10. (Personal Report of Communication Apprehension—short form)

10-item PRCA were administered to all students (see Figure 2). The first version was intended to measure CA associated with speaking in English. The second version was directed toward assessing feelings of apprehension associated with speaking in Spanish. Both versions of the PRCA-10 were administered in English.

Subjects

College.　The study sample was composed of 429 undergraduate students enrolled in basic psychology and basic studies courses at Pan American University, Edinburg, Texas. Ninety percent (388) of the subjects were of Mexican American ancestry. Among the Mexican American students, 254 (65.5%) were female and 134 (34.5%) were male.

Participation in the study was voluntary, although the psychology students did receive course credit for participating in the research project. All subjects were debriefed immediately following administration of the PRCA-24 measures.

High school.　The second study sample was composed of 284 secondary-level students drawn from a large south Texas public high school, which incorporates grades 9

Table 1

MEAN CA IN ENGLISH-SPEAKING AND SPANISH-SPEAKING COLLEGE STUDENTS

Context	English			Spanish		
	M	F	M/F	M	F	M/F
Dyad	14.836	15.780	15.371	16.142	16.949	16.811
Group	15.224	16.209	15.779	16.507	17.268	17.114
Meeting	16.410	17.996	17.296	17.582	18.602	18.231
Public	18.388	20.358	19.664	19.007	20.173	19.618
Overall	64.858	70.343	68.110	69.239	72.992	71.774
Overall s.d.	15.011	15.598	15.727	16.878	16.371	15.840

Table 2

HIGH CA BY SEX/CONTEXT/LANGUAGE COLLEGE STUDENTS

	Language/Sex			
	English		Spanish	
Context	M	F	M	F
Dyad	3.0	9.4	9.7	11.4
Group	4.5	8.7	9.0	13.4
Meeting	7.5	13.0	14.2	18.1
Public	15.7	30.3	19.4	28.0
Overall	16.4	28.0	23.1	33.1

through 12. The students were drawn from 10th and 11th grade regular English classes. Eighty-eight percent (252) of the students were of Mexican ancestry. Among the Mexican American students, 136 (53.9%) were female and 116 (46.1%) were male. Participation in the study was voluntary, and students received no course credit or reward for their participation in the research project. Subjects were debriefed following administration of the PRCA-10 measures.

RESULTS

Table 1 shows the overall CA and context CA subscore means for college students speaking English and Spanish. The data presented show an increase in the means of context subscores as we move from *dyad* to *group* to *meeting* to *public* contexts. The data indicate that the mean CA scores in Spanish are higher than mean English CA scores on both the overall CA measures and the subscore measures. Moreover, female students show higher mean CA scores than do male students on overall CA and subscore measures across both languages.

Table 2 presents the percentage of college students with high CA by sex and language on all CA measures. The data indicate that (1) female students have a greater percentage of high CAs than do male students on overall CA; (2) female students have a greater percentage of high CAs than do male students when speaking either English or Spanish; and (3) female

Table 3

LEVEL OF COMMUNICATION APPREHENSION BY SEX: COLLEGE STUDENTS

Context	Spoken Language	Female Mean	Male Mean	S.D.	F. Ratio	(p)
Dyad	English	15.7795	14.8358	4.4251	4.021	.0456*
	Spanish	16.9488	16.1418	4.7847	2.505	.1143
Group	English	16.0287	15.2239	4.6523	3.961	.0473*
	Spanish	17.2677	16.5075	4.7162	2.287	.1313
Meeting	English	17.9961	16.4104	4.660	10.403	.0014*
	Spanish	18.6024	17.5821	4.7584	4.065	.0455*
Public	English	20.3583	18.3841	4.8557	14.963	.0001*
	Spanish	20.1732	19.0075	4.7104	5.435	.0203*
Overall	English	70.3425	64.8582	15.5985	11.128	.0009*
	Spanish	72.9921	69.2388	16.6224	4.513	.0343*

* Significant differences between male and female measures.

Table 4

CA IN ENGLISH-SPEAKING AND SPANISH-SPEAKING HIGH SCHOOL STUDENTS

Sex	Language					
	Spanish			English		
	Mean	Mdn.	S.D.	Mean	Mdn.	S.D.
FEMALE	35.64	36.15	7.15	34.16	43.04	6.35
MALE	35.68	35.71	6.35	34.10	34.36	6.59

students have a higher percentage of high CAs than do male students in all four communication contexts. Table 2 also shows that as the number of participants in the communicative context increases, the percentage of high CAs in all but two group contexts also increases.

Table 3 shows an analysis of the level of CA by sex and communicative context for college students. One-way analysis of variance procedures was used to examine differences between male and female students on the overall CA and subscore context measures. Female students produced CA measures that were significantly different from those of male student CA measures on overall CA, meeting CA, and public CA measures when speaking Spanish.

Table 4 shows the CA scores of Mexican American high school students speaking English and Spanish. The data indicate that the mean CA scoi.s for both male and female Mexican American students when speaking either English or Spanish are higher than those found in other studies of comparable age groups. In addition, the Spanish CA scores were higher than the English CA scores for both sexes. The Anglo students in this study, however, showed CA scores similar to those found in previous studies. Anglo male and female CA scores in English were 30.77 and 32.22, respectively, and in Spanish, 35.6 and 36.0, respectively. These data indicate no significant differences between the CA of Anglo male and female students.

Table 5 presents the percentage of high school students with high CA by gender and language. The data analyses of Table 5 indicate that Mexican American students have a

Table 5

HIGH CA BY SEX AND LANGUAGE: HIGH SCHOOL STUDENTS

	English		Spanish	
	Male	*Female*	*Male*	*Female*
Mexican-American	49.1	45.6	59.5	59.6
Anglo	22.2	28.8	100.0	92.3

higher than normal percentage of high CAs when speaking either English or Spanish. Anglo students' scores, on the other hand, indicated that these students experienced a high level of CA only when speaking Spanish.

DISCUSSION

The Mexican American CA results in this study are different from those reported by researchers examining other Hispanic groups. The CA studies of Puerto Rican university students by Allen, O'Mara, and Andriate (1984a, 1984b) and by McCroskey, Fayer, and Richmond (1983) found much lower levels of CA in Spanish and higher CA levels in English than were found for the Mexican American population in this study. These differences, however, can be explained by the fact that the two populations had different *native* languages, even though in both cases Spanish was the dominant language. Since Spanish is the Puerto Rican students' dominant as well as native language, one would expect these students' CA level in Spanish to be lower than their CA level in English. Research has repeatedly shown that bilingual, non-native students in the United States similarly experience less CA in their native language than in English when the native languages were the dominant language for those subjects. For the Mexican American subjects in our study, however, English was the dominant, although not necessarily the native, language; thus, relative CA levels found in this study were in fact consistent with data from previously studied bilingual populations.

It should also be noted that the CA levels for the Mexican American students in this study were not as extreme as those previously found for Puerto Rican students. Puerto Rican students showed less CA in their native language and more CA in their second language than did the Mexican American students in our study. A comparison of the Mexican American sample with the Latin American sample examined by Allen, O'Mara, and Andriate (1984a) shows similar patterns. One significant difference between these two populations, however, is that the Latin American women's CA scores were significantly lower across all contexts than were those of the Mexican American women.

Our study, then, appears to support previous studies' findings that the level of communication apprehension is a function either of the individual's native language or of his or her dominant language. Bilinguals experience less CA in their native or dominant language than in their second language, and this occurs across communication contexts. Additionally, the CA scores increase as we move from the more informal, personal contexts to the more formal, less personal contexts.

Previous research has indicated that approximately 20 percent of the United States mainland population experiences high levels of CA (McCroskey & Richmond, 1980). In keeping with this finding, the Mexican American college women in our study showed high

CA frequencies in Spanish as well as an extremely high percentage of CA in the public communication context. The Mexican American college males, however, were in the high CA range on overall CA only in Spanish. Moreover, relatively few Mexican American college students revealed a high CA in dyad, group, and meeting situations in both English and Spanish.

Although CA values differ significantly across cultures and in a variety of contexts, the communication norms of a specific culture will dictate whether the CA level is a problem. If an individual were to have a CA level exceeding the norm, it might hinder the individual's ability to interact with others of the same culture. For example, if a Mexican American experiences high CA in dyadic classroom situations, CA might create a barrier to normal classroom interaction, and the individual's failure to behave as expected might be perceived negatively by other communicators, including teachers and school administrators.

While it has been suggested that CA is an affective response and, thus, may be unrelated to the performance skills (proficiency) of an individual, it is possible also that one factor underlying students' proficiency evaluations is their perception of their oral performance in specific contexts. This perception, moreover, may be shaped in part by the students' CA levels. Since behavior change can lead to affective change under certain circumstances, it may be possible in such cases to reduce CA by improving the students' performance skills and, thus, modifying the students' perception of their performance skills.

This study, like previous studies of bilingual college students, found significant positive correlations between subjects' CA in the two languages. Previous research has suggested that CA is a trait that can be generalized across both languages for bilinguals, in the sense that CA in a second language is best predicted by CA in a dominant or native language. If we assume that CA in a second language is thus related to CA in the dominant language, the findings of this study may suggest that reducing CA in the dominant language may also reduce CA in the second language.

It has been suggested in this study that as the CA level in the dominant or native language increases, students will experience greater difficulty in learning a second language. Furthermore, it is known that individuals with high CA levels in certain learning situations may avoid those contexts. Accordingly, if CA is manifest in the learning situation required for increasing the students' second linguistic competence, students will very likely experience difficulty learning the second language. While the underlying assumptions for this conclusion are supported by this study, neither this study nor any of those reported here has actually tested or established any relationship between CA and language learning at either the college or high school level.

An area of significant difference between our study and other research on CA among bilingual speakers is that of gender-related CA. While previous research has not indicated any consistent CA patterns between male and female college students, Allen (1984) reported that Latin American women are less apprehensive than Latin American men. Fayer, McCroskey, and Richmond, on the other hand (1984), examining Hispanic college students in Puerto Rico, concluded that CA was not a function of gender. These authors did note, however, that Hispanic males reported higher overall CA and higher CA measures in each context, except group, than did females. The findings of both studies conflict with our own. In our study the CA measures of Mexican American male and female college students were significantly different from those of Anglos and Hispanics examined in previous studies. Mexican American females in our study consistently produced higher CA scores than did Mexican American males both overall and across all communication contexts when speaking either English or Spanish. The gender differences revealed, by our study, however, may in fact be the result of cultural bias relative to sex roles.

Yet another finding of this research is that CA increases with the increasing formality and social complexity of communicative situations. In our study, both male and female Mexican American college students showed a pattern of increasing CA scores across communicative contexts, moving from dyad to group to meeting to public context. Although this CA pattern had not been reported in most previous research, it does appear in the data reported by Fayer, McCroskey, and Richmond (1984) on United States Hispanic pharmacy students. In addition, the CA scores of Latin American subjects in the Allen, O'Mara, and Andriate (1984b) study exhibited this pattern when the subjects were speaking English. Such a pattern seems to conform to general teacher observations and student comments that CA is experienced more intensely in more formal situations involving greater numbers of participants, such as in classroom interactions or when speaking before an audience; accordingly, less CA is experienced in more personal communication situations, such as in dyadic interactions and small-group encounters.

In a number of ways our study of high school students produced results similar to those of our college student study. The Mexican American high school males and females both showed high CA scores significantly above the overall CA norm in both English and Spanish, whereas the Anglos indicated a normal range of high CAs in English, but an exceedingly high percent of high CAs in Spanish. Moreover, CA levels of the Mexican American high school students in this study were exceedingly high and consistent with the high levels of CA found among other studies using Hispanic adults and college students. In contrast with the results of our study of college students, however, no significant differences in CA emerged between genders in the sample of high school students.

Finally, our study has implications for classroom instruction. The normal high school classroom requires students to communicate orally, frequently in a question-and-answer or dialogue mode. We would therefore expect that students who are not proficient orally would not receive as much reinforcement and support from their teachers and would not participate in as many classroom activities as students who are proficient orally. More specifically, students with high CA in the classroom context are likely to restrict their oral communication. Such a response may be detrimental to academic performance in a particularly subtle way. Since silence is rewarded by certain teachers and actually demanded in certain learning activities, the student with high CA is apt to perceive silence as a desirable response to classroom activities, and in this way the behavior is reinforced. As a result, rather than coping with the problem of communication apprehension, students would avoid confronting their fear of communicating in the classroom situation.

Some students may actually lack the skills necessary to be highly proficient in the classroom, while others may possess the appropriate behaviors but may be unable to perform adequately due to high CA. This research project dealt with the identification of the latter problem. Based on the results of our study, one may conclude that a significant number of Mexican American students in high school may be unable to perform adequately because of their excessively high levels of CA. Such avoidance in the learning environment could of course involve a complex interaction with other factors. For instance, a lack of proficiency or understanding of the course content by the student—e.g., solving quadratic equations in algebra—could interact with an aversion to ask questions, resulting from high CA. Such a student might be unwilling or unable to request the necessary clarification of content or to acquire the skills needed for learning the course concept. The failure to attain clarification might ultimately be reflected in the student's inability to respond correctly on an examination. And, in turn, improper examination responses are likely to lead to lower achievement measures and a lower course grade. In this sense the CA of Mexican American students may be a critical factor in determining classroom success and retention at both the high school and college levels.

APPLICATION

Because of the negative impact CA may have on students' educational performance, treatment of this complex oral communication dysfunction is critical. Three general treatment methods are recommended: (1) systematic desensitization, (2) cognitive modification, and (3) skills training.

Systematic desensitization (SD) focuses on reducing the CA associated with the act of oral communication. The student is taught how to relax in the presence of the anxiety stimuli and, thus, the anxiety is reduced in subsequent oral communication situations. SD treatment appears to be situation-specific, that is, treatment may reduce anxiety in public communication contexts, but not dyadic contexts. Reduction of the apprehension or anxiety does not appear to generalize across contexts.

Cognitive modification (CM) focuses on changing the student's own cognitive appraisals. CA is viewed as resulting from a negative self-evaluation of one's performance in an oral communication situation and the expectation of adverse consequences. Students are taught to manage their self-evaluation and to develop more facilitating self-talk. Students learn to evaluate more realistically the consequences of their behavior (Kanter & Goldfried, 1979). Like SD, this treatment has found to be effective when dealing with anxiety in public contexts, but it does not generalize to interpersonal situations (Fremouw & Zitter, 1978). SD appears to be more effective than CM with individuals showing only high anxiety in public contexts, whereas CM appears to be more effective for individuals reporting a more generalized, cross-situational CA. One element of this treatment appears to be particularly effective in reducing anxiety and that is to provide individuals with insight into the unproductive thinking that induces their anxiety (Thorpe, Amatu, Blakey, & Burns, 1976).

Skills training (ST) focuses on developing the communicator's behavioral repertoire in oral communication situations. It is assumed that students perform poorly in communication situations because they lack the requisite skills, and successful performance will lead to a decrease in anxiety. The student is taught the behavioral skills required for success in the particular oral communication context. Like some CM treatments, it would appear that skills training learning in one communication situation may not transfer to other contexts.

Glaser (1981, p. 337) has recommended the following:

These programs which seek to reduce anxiety toward communication most effectively would emphasize SD or CM. On the other hand, to reduce avoidance of communication situations and to produce actual behavior change, ST is the treatment of choice. A reduction in anxiety does not imply a decrease in avoidance behavior nor the learning of more effective response.

Part Four

Students' Perspectives on Language Anxiety

While Part Three of the text helps teachers recognize the effects of anxiety on their students' language performance, Part Four explores the language learner's own perceptions of anxiety. What are students' experiences with language anxiety? What do students identify as sources of language anxiety? Which classroom practices and instructor characteristics are associated with lower—or higher—levels of anxiety? By offering students' self-reports of anxiety, the papers in this section can help teachers recognize anxiety reactions in their own students and organize instruction in more satisfying ways.

In the first article, Price interviews anxious foreign language students and offers their compelling accounts of disturbing learning experiences. Even years later, several individuals find it painful to recall a particular language class. As uncomfortable as language teachers may be with such criticism, we cannot hope to banish debilitating anxiety from the language classroom without acknowledging the fear, frustration, and sometimes anger of our students.

Ironically, students may still be anxious even when instruction has been purposefully designed to reduce stress. Koch and Terrell find that students experience considerable anxiety in response to a number of activities, particularly oral activities, used in the authors' Natural Approach classes. It seems likely that regardless of the language teaching method, speaking the language in front of an entire class is difficult for a large number of students. On the other hand, both articles point to ways in which students can be more comfortable participating in oral activities. Teachers might consider using some of the investigative approaches described here, such as interviews or questionnaires, to learn which aspects of language learning are difficult for their students and to stimulate a dialogue about language anxiety.

Chapter Nine

The Subjective Experience of Foreign Language Anxiety: Interviews with Highly Anxious Students

Mary Lou Price   Texas Education Agency

INTRODUCTION

My interest in studying foreign language anxiety grew out of my experiences in the classroom. As a college instructor of French, I became increasingly aware of students' reluctance to speak French, of their self-deprecatory remarks regarding their language skills, of their obvious relief when they finally completed their language requirements. I began to consider the possibility that a number of students were experiencing a great deal of anxiety about their foreign language classes, and I began to conduct my classes in such a way as to reduce anxiety. The more attuned I became to the issue of anxiety, the more my students seemed to be willing to discuss their feelings about foreign language learning. I eventually became interested in studying foreign language anxiety through interviews with students.

Although anxiety has long been recognized by educators as a potential problem in the foreign language classroom, relatively little research has been conducted in this area. Investigations of foreign language anxiety have been for the most part quantitive studies, primarily correlational research. In the 1960s and 1970s, a number of studies on the relationship between foreign language proficiency and learner variables examined anxiety among other variables (Chastain, 1975; Pimsleur, Sundland, & McIntyre, 1964; Tucker et al., 1976; Gardner et al., 1976; Swain & Burnaby, 1976; Backman, 1976). Results of these studies were not conclusive, perhaps because of the difficulty in measuring anxiety, as well as the fact that a number of different anxiety measures were used in the studies.

In the last decade, foreign language anxiety research has taken several directions. One direction has been to reexamine the anxiety-proficiency relationship using measures designed to assess the specific construct of foreign language anxiety (Young, 1986, this volume).

Other studies have focused on the relationship between anxiety and learner variables (West-cott, 1973; Horwitz, 1986, this volume; Price, 1988). A third direction in recent research has been the examination of the effects of anxiety on the foreign language learner (Kleinmann, 1977; Steinberg, 1982; Young, 1986, this volume; Madsen, 1982; Ely, 1986.)

An alternative approach to investigation of these relationships is qualitative research, which allows the researcher to obtain descriptive information on variables not easily assessed through empirical research. It can also provide a way to view phenomena from the point of view of the subject. A small number of researchers have attempted to use qualitative methods to investigate foreign language anxiety. In McCoy's (1979) study, language students identi-fied 11 sources of anxiety about foreign language classes. Bailey (1983) studied language learners' diaries and found a relationship between anxiety and competitiveness among for-eign language learners. Horwitz, Horwitz, and Cope (1986, this volume) used information obtained during a support group for anxious language students to develop a theory of foreign language anxiety.

THE PRESENT STUDY

The interview is one qualitative technique that has been successfully used in many fields, but not in the study of foreign language anxiety. Interviews can be used both to obtain a subjec-tive description of the interviewee's own experiences and to investigate specific questions of interest to the researcher. The present study uses student interviews to examine the question of foreign language anxiety from the perspective of the anxious language learner. The goals of this study are twofold:

1. to obtain a detailed description of what it is like to be an anxious student in a foreign lan-guage class, and
2. to use student insights as a source of information on questions of potential interest to the foreign language educator.

The following questions are addressed in the study:

1. What is it like to be an anxious foreign language student?
2. What aspects of foreign language classes cause the greatest anxiety?
3. What causes certain students to experience high levels of foreign language anxiety?
4. What role does the instructor play in the anxiety level experienced by language stu-dents?
5. What do anxious learners believe would make language learning less stressful for them?

METHODOLOGY

The first step in conducting the interviews was to obtain a pool of students who considered themselves to be anxious about foreign language classes and were willing to be interviewed. Subjects were recruited in several ways. An informal questionnaire was developed and admin-istered to several lower-level language classes. This questionnaire contained a number of questions about students' reactions to foreign language classes, including several questions concerning anxiety. Those students whose responses suggested high levels of anxiety were contacted and invited to participate. Former students and acquaintances who had at some time indicated to me that they were very anxious about language classes were also contacted. Finally, other language instructors were asked for referrals of students who appeared to be highly anxious in their classes. Obtaining subjects proved to be quite easy. Most of the individuals contacted were willing to participate, and some appeared quite eager to discuss their experiences.[1]

During the initial contact with students, I explained the nature of the study, that it was voluntary, and that all interviews would be conducted in English. Those who indicated a willingness to participate were scheduled for an interview.

Fifteen subjects were interviewed. Of the original 15, five were subsequently eliminated from the study either because their interviews did not indicate that they experienced high foreign language anxiety or because they were unable or unwilling to answer the interviewer's questions. Of the 10 remaining subjects, eight were females and two were males. All were current or former students of the University of Texas at Austin.

Each interview lasted approximately one hour and was recorded with the subject's permission. The first part of each interview was open-ended. The subjects were asked to describe present and past foreign language courses. The goals of this portion of the interview were to establish a rapport with the subject and to obtain a detailed description of each subject's experiences. The second half of the interview was more structured, focusing specifically on anxiety. During this portion of the interview, the following questions were asked:

1. Can you tell me something about how you have felt during your language classes?
2. What bothered (bothers) you the most about foreign language classes?
3. Are there other things about foreign language classes that bother you?
4. Do you have any idea as to why you feel so anxious in your language classes?
5. Do you have any ideas as to how language classes might be made less stressful?
6. What role have your instructors played in how you have felt during foreign language classes?

Analysis of the interviews was conducted by listening to and transcribing the taped interviews, then writing descriptions of each subject's experiences and identifying common threads in the interviews.

THE INTERVIEWS

The Experience of Foreign Language Anxiety

As they shared their experiences, it was clear that just thinking about their language classes evoked a great deal of emotion for the subjects. As they spoke, they sighed, fidgeted, laughed nervously, and told the interviewer repeatedly how "horrible" it had been, how "awful" they had felt, how much they had "hated" this or that class. The following case studies illustrate some of the emotions and reactions to language classes experienced by these students.[2]

Anne.   Anne was a very talented graduate student in music who had recently taken a required class titled "French for Graduate Students." This course was designed to help graduate students develop reading proficiency in the target language. As such, it did not require students to speak or write French at any time. Furthermore, it was offered on a pass-fail basis. One might expect that it would produce minimal anxiety. However, Anne was terrified at taking the course and remained terrified throughout the term. She took her French books everywhere during the course and couldn't stop thinking about the course. She had recurrent nightmares about the class, including one in which she arrived late to class and discovered that the instructor was handing back tests and refused to hand her test back because it was "so bad." The worst part of the experience for Anne was waking up early every morning and being too keyed up to get back to sleep. She described one particularly stressful day, the day before the first exam. "I cancelled everything I was supposed to do because I couldn't sit through anything, knowing I had to study French. I sat in Jerry's office [a classmate] and we tried to study. We were hysterical! I finally decided to go in to work, but I was worthless. I was so nervous that after about an hour, my boss suggested that I go on home. I headed back to Jerry's office. I remember thinking on the way, 'I just can't do this. I'm going to have to drop this course.' Jerry and I decided to go out to dinner. At dinner, we started laughing—it was that laughter—you laugh because you're afraid that you'll cry. We still talk about that dinner."

Anne passed that exam and the course as well, but she didn't feel that she had become any less anxious about language courses and didn't understand why she experiences such high anxiety.

Beth.   Beth had graduated from college eight years earlier. She had warned me that she had a bad case of "language phobia" and that it was going to be difficult for her even to discuss her experiences. She began the interview by explaining that she had taken French in high school and in college and had always done well, but she had dreaded every class. In her words, "French classes were very, very stressful for me, because I didn't speak well. . . . Everything came out in a Texas accent, which was horrible, because the professors would stop me and make me go over and over it and I still couldn't get it right! The more they made me do it, the more frightened I became!"

Her personal horror story was the day that Beth had to give an oral report at the end of her third semester of college French: "It was an absolute nightmare—the worst thing I ever had to do in my life. At the end of my talk, the teacher stopped dead in his tracks. The room was dead quiet. He said, 'That is the absolute worst thing I have ever heard.'"

Beth claims that, eight years later, she can't think about that day without getting upset. "I don't laugh about it now. It was the most traumatic experience I've ever had." She claimed that she hasn't tried to speak or read French since that time and concluded her interview with this observation: "I'd rather be in a prison camp than speak a foreign language."

Joan.   Joan was enrolled in a second-semester French course. She described her numerous attempts at fulfilling her college language requirement. She remembered that she had been excited about the idea of learning French before her first language class began. But, on the first day of the semester, the instructor came in "speaking French a mile a minute." According to Joan, it was all downhill after that moment. She failed the first few tests miserably and finally dropped the course. The next semester, she enrolled again, began to have conflicts with the instructor, changed sections, hired a tutor, studied two to three hours a day, and passed. That summer, she went to France, built up her confidence, and came back to try the second semester in summer school. Within a few weeks she was failing and dropped. She signed up for a correspondence course but says that she couldn't make herself even begin to do the work. She dropped that class and enrolled again for the fall semester. At the time of her interview, she was failing and wasn't sure what to try next. Joan was angry as well as anxious—at her instructors, at the university for putting her through this, and at herself for failing.

Classroom Sources of Anxiety

Subjects were asked to indicate what aspects of foreign language classes bothered them the most. Answers to this question were surprisingly consistent. They all responded that the greatest source of anxiety was having to speak the target language in front of their peers. They all spoke of their fears of being laughed at by the others, of making a fool of themselves in public. Several had painful memories of being ridiculed by other students, particularly in secondary school language classes.

The subjects were also concerned about making errors in pronunciation. Several were particularly ashamed of their Texas accents. They knew that they were not pronouncing words like a native French speaker and expressed great embarrassment at their "terrible" pronunciation. "It's embarrassing to mispronounce at our age," said one. From another, "You think, 'She says it every day for five times.' Why can't I say it?" An older subject recalled that she had barely spoken in her college French classes because she was too intimidated about pronunciation. "I would go back to my room and practice for hours," she claimed. She added, "You knew that you were never, never going to be able to say it like he did. . .you were going to fail at pronouncing those words."

A third source of stress for these students was the frustration of not being able to communicate effectively. Several mentioned that they knew they were intelligent adults but couldn't communicate that way in French. Said one subject, "You feel frustrated because you're an interesting adult and you sound like a babbling baby." Another offered, "My French is not good. It's not really fluent enough to carry on anything meaningful. I feel extremely uncomfortable speaking. I feel like I'm stupid." From a third, "You're sitting there thinking, 'I'm a smart parson. I should be able to do this and I can't do it.' It's frustrating. I want to speak. I want to tell her things and I know that I don't have the words. Try as I might, I cannot get a coherent sentence out of my mouth. I wouldn't be surprised if my teacher thinks I'm a total dingbat. I wouldn't blame her."

An additional source of anxiety for many of these students was the difficulty of their language classes. A recurrent complaint was that they worked harder in their language classes than in their other classes, but they didn't do as well. One subject mentioned that she had studied French three hours a day in college, but had still made a *C*—the only *C* of her college career. The discrepancy between effort and results seemed to be most disturbing to students who were used to making high grades. These students seemed to feel less in control in language classes than in other courses.

Causes of Anxiety

While we can only speculate about why students might experience such high levels of anxiety, the interviews do suggest several possibilities. One is the level of difficulty of foreign language classes and the relatively poor results some students achieve compared to their results in other classes. Foreign language courses may be more demanding and more difficult than other courses, thus eliciting higher anxiety than other courses.

Another factor that may play a role is the speaker's beliefs. Many of these subjects had beliefs that were potential sources of anxiety. The majority of the subjects believed that their language skills were weaker than those of the other students. They believed that they weren't doing a good job and that everyone else looked down on them. All of the subjects brought up the notion that learning a language requires a special aptitude, an aptitude which they didn't possess. Paradoxically, several also believed that they should have done much better than they did, that if they had only worked a little harder they could have been successful at this task.

Quantitative research has investigated the relationship between foreign language anxiety and certain personality variables. The present interviews suggest two personality variables that may be related to foreign language anxiety—perfectionism and fear of public speaking. Several subjects mentioned that they were very anxious about public speaking and several believed that they were overly perfectionistic.

Another possibility is stressful classroom experiences. The role played by experience is difficult to evaluate from these interviews, as the backgrounds and classroom experiences of the interviewees were quite varied. Some students had been anxious from the very first moment they entered a language class. Others had started out with a positive attitude and had only become anxious after having had a particularly painful experience. Some students had obtained low grades throughout their language classes, while others had been quite successful. Interestingly, the one stressful experience related by almost all of these subjects was that of going from a relatively easy high school language class to a fast-paced and much more demanding college class.

The Role of the Instructor

From these interviews it was clear that instructors had played a significant role in the amount of anxiety each student had experienced in particular classes. Each had vivid memories of past teachers and how these teachers had treated them in class. In some cases, instructors had alleviated their anxiety. One student mentioned that she became much more calm after being in a class where the teacher encouraged mistakes and periodically discussed the importance of making mistakes in order to learn. Another student relaxed on the first day of an intermediate French class in which the instructor walked around the room and asked everyone to describe his and her language learning background. The student realized then that the other students were not any more advanced than she.

Conversely, some teachers had increased students' anxiety, such as those who criticized students' accents or the high school instructor who walked around the room with a big yardstick and flung it on the desk of anyone who wasn't listening, yelling, "Pay attention!" The most common complaint about instructors was that many of them had made classroom time a performance rather than learning time. As Anne, the student mentioned earlier, put it, "It was never a learning experience. You either did it right or you didn't."

How Can Language Learning Be Made Less Stressful?

The last question in each interview was, "Do you have any ideas as to how language classes might be made less stressful?"

Interestingly, all of the subjects seemed to have already given some thought to this question and had immediate answers. In many cases, their responses appeared to be addressing the question of what would have made languages *easier* for them to learn. Several believed that they would need to live in the country of the target language in order to learn it. Others believed that they should have begun at a different age. Several subjects thought they should have started earlier, while some of the older subjects thought they would have done better if they had started later, when they were more mature and confident and had fewer personal issues to deal with.

Some very concrete suggestions for alleviating anxiety were offered. There was a general feeling that smaller classes would help a great deal. Several mentioned that getting to know the other students helped them to feel more relaxed by reducing the fear of being ridiculed and taking away the feeling that the others are all smarter and more confident. The subjects suggested a number of measures that instructors could take to reduce anxiety, such as giving students more positive reinforcement, encouraging them to make mistakes, and helping them to develop more realistic expectations of themselves by letting them know that they weren't supposed to be fluent or have a perfect accent after two semesters. The most frequent observation made by these subjects was that they would feel more comfortable if the instructor were more like a friend helping them to learn and less like an authority figure making them perform.

CONCLUSION

On the basis of these interviews, a number of suggestions can be made regarding ways to reduce anxiety in the language classroom. Most strikingly, students' fears of public embarrassment must be taken seriously when planning activities. One recommendation would be to include a number of small-group or one-on-one activities in each day's lessons. This would allow the anxious student to practice the target language without the entire class as an audience. When the student is speaking in a large group situation, corrections should be made as tactfully as possible. Naturally, the student should never be ridiculed.

For the students to feel comfortable about using the target language in the classroom, it is important that they view the classroom as a place for learning and communication rather than as a place where they perform for the instructor. While a certain amount of evaluation is necessary and useful, students should not feel that they are performing each time they use the target language. Time could be allotted for communicative activities in which the student is corrected either not at all or only when absolutely necessary for comprehension. During such activities, the instructor would focus on the message the student is trying to communicate rather than on the accuracy of the student's grammar and pronunciation.

A number of specific suggestions can be made on the basis of these subjects' own ideas as to how language classes could be made less stressful. Students need to be encouraged to make mistakes and should be reminded periodically of the instructional value of mistakes. They should also be given realistic expectations—that is, they should be told what they can reasonably expect to accomplish in the amount of time they will be studying the target language. It should be made clear to them that they are not expected to achieve native-speaker pronunciation and fluency. Finally, if we want students to use the target language actively, they need to be given a great deal of encouragement and positive reinforcement.

The experiences of these students provide a great deal of information about the role of anxiety in foreign language classes. They tell us that there are students for whom language classes are a source of fear, shame, and humiliation. They also offer insights on what it feels like to take a foreign language class when one is anxious, as well as what makes students anxious and what teachers can do to alleviate that anxiety. One important conclusion to be drawn from these interviews is that students can provide valuable information to the language instructor, not only about anxiety but also about other aspects of the language classroom. As we design courses and plan classroom activities, it is important that we keep our students in mind and use their insights and impressions to help us in the decision-making process.

NOTES

1. In fact, long after the interviews were completed, if I casually mentioned my research to friends and acquaintances, I often received a response along the line of, "Interview me. I have language anxiety."

2. The names of the three subjects have been changed to protect their confidentiality.

Chapter Ten

Affective Reactions of Foreign Language Students to Natural Approach Activities and Teaching Techniques

April S. Koch   The Pennsylvania State University
Tracy David Terrell University of California, San Diego

INTRODUCTION

Perhaps even more frustrated than the language instructors who fail to teach their students a foreign language are the students who are too nervous, insecure, unmotivated, or indifferent to both the instructor and culture of the target language to be open to language instruction. Research has confirmed that attitudinal factors relate to success and failure in second language acquisition and would imply that language instruction must take these factors into account. The teaching techniques associated with the grammar-translation approach, such as tedious grammar exercises and translations, and those associated with audio-lingualism, such as pattern drills and memorization and recitations of dialogues, can foster negative attitudes toward the target language and language learning in general.

One approach to foreign language instruction that claims to be affectively oriented is the Natural Approach (henceforth, NA).[1] Developed in the late 1970s and early 1980s, the NA is a communicative approach that attempts to provide comprehensible input in the target language and opportunities for the students to develop communicative competence by using the target language in meaningful classroom activities.[2] NA is an approach that emphasizes the acquisition of target language skills in "stages." Students first are allowed a Comprehension stage in which they are asked to attend carefully to oral input and respond indicating comprehension, but are not forced to produce the target language. In the second stage, Early Production, students are encouraged to produce target language words or short phrases in response to input. In the third stage, Speech Emergence, students begin to put words together to produce longer utterances. In all stages, the development of good listening skills is seen as the basis for the acquisition process and consequently the foundation for the speaking skills. The input and interactional activities of the class focus on using the target language to express ideas and feelings about topics the students are interested in. The study of the target language grammar is seen as an aid to the acquisition process but it is not the primary focus of the NA class. Since it is thought that acquisition cannot take place in a high anxiety context, efforts are made to lower the anxiety levels of the students by providing a nonthreatening cooperative atmosphere during the class hour. In the following sections, we will describe NA activities and techniques designed to work within these general guidelines.

Although the fundamental principles of the NA as well as the methods and techniques are designed to promote affectively positive attitudes, these claims had never been tested empirically. Only a data-based investigation of the students' actual responses can reveal the precise effect of NA's class activities and instructional techniques on attitude and motivation. Consequently, a study (Koch, 1984) was conducted to determine which facets of NA result in positive attitudes and which, if any, actually increase anxiety in the classroom. This paper focuses on the results of that previous study on one specific attitudinal variable: anxiety.

BACKGROUND OF THE STUDY

Dictionaries offer "fear" as a synonym for anxiety. Spielberger and Diaz-Guerrero (1976, p. 6) maintain that although both fear and anxiety are unpleasant emotional reactions to a stimulus perceived as threatening, the "threatening" stimulus of the former is known, while that of the latter is not. Anxiety, fear, and even anger, however, produce similar physiological responses; they activate the adrenal medulla, which can secrete the heart- and hair-raising hormones of adrenaline and noradrenaline. It is believed that the secretion of adrenaline is related to anxiety and the secretion of noradrenaline to anger (Levitt, 1981, pp. 78–79).

Language studies have revealed a consistent relationship between anxiety and foreign language proficiency. Gardner, Smythe, Clément, and Gliksman (1976, pp. 198–213) reported that classroom anxiety correlated with speech skills in French as a foreign language in grades 7–11 in Canada. Naimon, Fröhlich, Stern, and Todesco (1978) claimed that classroom anxiety and fear related to failure for a group of French students in grades 8–12. These studies all indicate that the activities in the foreign language class that create an atmosphere of panic, fear, anger, and other unpleasant feelings, which are psychologically and physiologically associated with anxiety, can impede language acquisition. As the NA specifically aims to create a relaxed atmosphere, an investigation of its specific effects is especially warranted.

METHODOLOGY

Students in the first two years of NA Spanish classes at the University of California, Irvine, received a questionnaire in the eighth week of the trimester.[3] At that time students are presumably familiar with the NA class activities and instructional techniques. One hundred and nineteen students (76 females and 43 males) completed the questionnaire.[4] From the first-year Spanish classes there were 89 subjects consisting of 34 students from three 1A (first quarter) classes, 27 from three 1B (second quarter) classes, and 28 from three 1C (third quarter) classes. From second-year Spanish classes there were 30 subjects comprised of 8 students from one 2A (fourth quarter) class, 17 from two 2B (fifth quarter) classes, and 5 from one 2C (sixth quarter) class.

The age of the students ranged from 17 to 44 years old; the average age was 20. All except 6% of the students were native speakers of English. Only 2% were majoring or planning on majoring in Spanish. Four-fifths of the students had previously studied a foreign language and over half had previously studied Spanish. Students who had previously studied a foreign language were asked to name the approach that was used: Thus, 69% claimed grammar-translation, 46% audio-lingualism, and 17% direct method.[5] Native speakers taught all of the classes involved in this study, although this is not a requirement of NA. Since the number of students in the second-year group is small, the following discussion will concentrate on the results from the first-year students, especially in more detailed breakdowns.

In general, the responses to the questionnaire indicated that the majority of the students perceive themselves to be very calm, self-confident, and motivated. There were, however, nine students who claimed to be "very" or "extremely" nervous persons. These students comprise a special opportunity to study anxiety. Therefore, these "nervous" students' reactions to the questions pertaining to anxiety will be compared to those of the "regular" students to determine if "anxious" students will have a higher anxiety level in the NA class.

One could argue that there are more effective ways than a questionnaire to assess student attitudes in the NA class. The questionnaire could, in fact, invite one serious concern. Schumann (1976a, p. 493) maintains that in order to please the experimenter, participants in a survey might not be completely honest with their answers. Realizing that the subject of study is the method used in their classes by their instructors, students might refrain from criticism. It is also possible that students will not accurately assess themselves psychologically, culturally, and academically to avoid recognizing any negative traits in their personalities. Consequently, direct observation of the students' behavior in class might yield more objective and conclusive data. Such an investigation, however, would exclude student behavior not directly visible to the observer. On the other hand it is important that a study concerned with students' feelings about an approach include the opinions of the subjects of study.

It is possible that a longitudinal study, owing to the longer period of investigation and intense analysis of the responses of a few students rather than a superficial analysis of the responses of many students, could be more conclusive. Yet, since a variety of students with diverse attitudes and feelings will be in an NA class, it is necessary to understand the effect of the approach on a cross section of all kinds of students. In addition, a longitudinal study of such a large number of students would have been impractical. Thus, the present cross-sectional study emerges as a compromise.

STUDENT PERCEPTION OF ANXIETY IN AN NA CLASS

Table 1 examines the responses indicating the anxiety of the 92 regular students and the 9 nervous students [6] in an NA class (RESP = responses; EXTR = extremely nervous; VERY = very nervous; MODR = moderately nervous; NOT = not nervous at all).[7] The data indicate that about one-third of the students surveyed report that they are not at all anxious in an NA class and that almost 90% of the regular group believe that they are moderately to "not at all anxious" in their classes. In contrast, about one-fifth of the nervous students are very or extremely nervous in an NA class.

Table 2 reports the anxiety level of students when asked to perform in front of their classmates. The responses suggest that the overwhelming majority of all students are not overly anxious when they perform in front of their classmates, but a sizable number of the nervous students (about one-fifth) report extreme anxiety in this common class situation.

Table 3 reports students' comparison of anxiety levels in an NA class compared to previous language classes[8] (−NER = less nervous; = NER = about the same as in other methods; + NER = more nervous than in previous methods). From the data we can only

Table 1

**STUDENT PERCEPTION OF ANXIETY
IN NA CLASSES**

RESP	REG (92)	NERV (9)
EXTR	3%	11%
VERY	10%	11%
MODR	54%	56%
NOT	33%	22%

Table 2

**STUDENT PERCEPTION OF ANXIETY
IN THE PRESENCE OF CLASSMATES**

RESP	REG (92)	NERV (9)
EXTR	2%	22%
VERY	10%	0%
MODR	44%	44%
NOT	44%	34%

Table 3

**ANXIETY LEVEL IN NA COMPARED
TO CLASSES TAUGHT WITH OTHER
METHODS**

RESP	REG (92)	NERV (9)
−NER	40%	39%
=NER	26%	31%
+NER	34%	30%

conclude that students have varied reactions to their NA class: About one-third claim that they feel less nervous than in other approaches, another one-third feel that it makes them more nervous, and the remaining third claim that there is no difference in their anxiety levels. Interestingly enough, the nervous students offer the same responses on this question as do the regular students.

The data from Tables 1, 2, and 3 show that although more students are less anxious in an NA class, students have different reactions to NA and the approach is not successful in reaching low levels of anxiety for all students. In order to explore this issue further we will attempt in the rest of this paper to ascertain the effects of specific NA class activities and teaching techniques on the students.

STUDENT RESPONSE TO NA ACTIVITIES

Activities Judged to Produce Anxiety

In Table 4 we list (in descending order) all activities that one-fifth or more of the students indicated as anxiety-producing[9] (ORAL = oral presentations; SKIT = skits and role playing; WORD = defining a word in Spanish; SITU = saying how you would react in a given situa-

Table 4

NA ACTIVITIES THAT PRODUCE ANXIETY

ACT	REG (92)	ACT	NERV (9)
ORAL	75%	ORAL	100%
SKIT	53%	SKIT	50%
WORD	34%	SITU	50%
—	—	WORD	44%
SITU	28%	CHAR	33%
CHAR	25%	—	—
OPIN	23%	MAPS	22%
NUMB	20%	NUMB	22%
		LIST	22%
		QZGM	20%

tion; CHAR = charades; OPIN = giving an opinion about an issue; NUMB = working with numbers; MAPS = working with maps and other similar realia; LIST = figuring out what does not belong in a list of items; QZGM = quiz games). The data indicate that only three of the 23 activities rated by the students make more than a third of the regular students anxious: oral presentations (ORAL), oral skits and role playing (SKITS), and defining words in Spanish (WORD). As ORAL and SKIT are performance activities, it seems logical that they would produce some anxiety in any teaching approach. But ORAL and SKIT are activities that are important not only because they give students the opportunity to speak for an extended period of time, but also because they require the speaker's audience to listen to someone other than the teacher. Though many students find them stressful, it is doubtful that we would want to discontinue their use. There is no immediate explanation for the low rating of the other activities, but we will come back to this issue as the examination of the data and the discussion proceeds.

The self-described nervous students identified five of the 23 activities as anxiety-provoking. For example, ORAL makes all nine of these students nervous. In addition, several activities show up here but do not make more than one-fifth of the regular students significantly anxious (e.g., working with maps and advertisements (MAPS), working with numbers (NUMB), figuring out what does not belong in a list of items or a picture (LIST), and quiz games (QZGM).

In Table 5[10] we examine these data longitudinally for first-year students in order to examine changes in anxiety levels for these activities changes as the year progresses. (See above for most abbreviations; new abbreviations are: STEP = describing the steps of an activity; IMAG = imagining situations.) The data reveal that ORAL and SKIT are the top anxiety producers in all three first-year levels. Interestingly, the data also suggest that there is a significant decrease in anxiety in general from first quarter to third quarter. In the first quarter, nine of the 23 activity types surveyed were judged to produce anxiety. By the third quarter only five of the 23 activities are still rated by the students as making them nervous. Making oral class presentations (ORAL) is clearly the activity that produces the most anxiety (in 92% of the students in the first quarter), but in the third quarter even ORAL makes only a little over one-half of the students nervous. Skits (SKIT), on the other hand, continue to produce anxiety in about one-half of the students throughout the academic year. Defining words in Spanish (WORD) is also not rated as easier by the end of the course.

In the following section we turn to the other side of anxiety by looking at activities that students judge to produce comfort.

Table 5

ACTIVITIES THAT PRODUCE ANXIETY: FIRST-YEAR BREAKDOWN

ACT	1A (34)	ACT	1B (27)	ACT	1C (28)
ORAL	92%	ORAL	86%	ORAL	57%
SKIT	51%	SKIT	50%	SKIT	43%
SITU	34%	OPIN	31%	WORD	31%
NUMB	34%	—	—	—	—
IMAG	33%	NUMB	27%	SITU	28%
—	—	WORD	25%	CHAR	27%
WORD	28%	IMAG	22%		
CHAR	27%	CHAR	21%		
QZGM	27%				
STEP	26%				

Activities Judged to Produce Comfort

In Table 6 we list the activities judged by at least one-fifth of the students to be "comfortable." Activities marked with an asterisk are those considered to produce anxiety by more than 20% of the students. (New abbreviations: INTV = interviews in pairs; RANK = preference ranking; TPR = total physical response commands; MING = obtaining information by mingling with other students; SCHD = creating charts and schedules; STRY = inventing a story for a picture; STPR = Simon says with TPR; MUSC = music; READ = reading short stories; HIST = historical and political lectures.)

The most popular activity, INTV, may make students feel comfortable because it gives them the opportunity to get to know their classmates. RANK and IMAG are affective-humanistic activities that permit students to express their own ideas. RANK is an activity that enables students to voice their opinions without the necessity of complex language. IMAG might make students comfortable because it permits them to be creative. A comparison of Tables 4 and 6 is instructive. Of the seven activity types ranked as anxiety-producing by more than 20% of the students, only one (ORAL) was not also rated as comfort-producing by more than 20% of the students. The most interesting example is WORD (defining words in Spanish). It is ranked as the third most anxiety-producing activity by 34% of the students, yet it is the third-ranked comfort-producing activity by 44% of the students. Other activity types also show this disagreement. CHAR (charades) produces anxiety for 25% and comfort for 22%. As these results were replicated repeatedly in this study, we must conclude that students vary greatly in their individual reactions to NA activities. In other words, an activity that produced anxiety for one may provide comfort for another and vice versa.

Table 6 also indicates that although nervous students may be comfortable with many NA activities, they are far less comfortable than the regular students. Only five of the 23 activities make one-third or more of the nervous students comfortable compared to 11 for regular students. IMAG and LIST, activities that comfort the regular students, also comfort the nervous ones; but otherwise even the types of activities are different for the two groups. For example, preference ranking (RANK) is judged to produce comfort by more than one-half of the regular students, but only about one-fifth of the nervous students share this opinion.

In Table 7 we examine these same data longitudinally to determine if comfort levels for these specific activities change significantly over the course of the first year. The data sug-

Table 6

NA ACTIVITIES JUDGED TO PRODUCE COMFORT

ACT	REG (92)	ACT	NERV (9)
INTV	56%	IMAG	71%
RANK	54%	NUMB	55%
WORD*	44%	LIST	44%
IMAG	42%	MING	43%
LIST	40%	MUSC	33%
TPR	39%	—	—
MAPS	38%	SKIT	25%
MING	35%	SITU	25%
SCHD	35%	RANK	25%
OPIN*	34%	TPR	22%
STRY	33%	INTV	22%
—	—	WORD	22%
STPR	31%	OPIN	22%
MUSC	26%	HIST	20%
SITU*	25%		
QZGM	24%		
NUMB*	23%		
STEP	23%		
CHAR*	22%		
SKIT*	22%		
READ	21%		

gest that first-quarter students find the most comfort in TPR, interviews (INTV), using their imagination (IMAG), working with maps and charts (MAPS), and Simon says with TPR (STPR). We speculate that this is because all of these are simple activities that do not require complex responses in the target language.

Second-quarter students respond positively to interviews (INTV), preference ranking (RANK), using maps and charts (MAPS), defining words in Spanish (WORD), and using the imagination (IMAG). INTV, IMAG, and MAPS continue to be comforting but the drop in high ratings given to TPR/STPR may result from these being judged as a "beginners" activity. The new additions to this top list are defining words in Spanish (WORD) and preference ranking (RANK). These are "intermediate"-level activities requiring responses in the target language that are more complex than first-quarter students can easily manage. It is also interesting that second-quarter students rate fewer activities as producing comfort than either first- or third-quarter students. This may be due to midyear fatigue: First-quarter students are normally very excited about NA and the whole array of new activities. However, by the second quarter they have participated in most of the activity types and the newness has worn off. In addition, the language of the activities is now quite a bit more complex and the entire language learning task seems more difficult than in the first quarter.

Interviews (INTV), preference ranking (RANK), obtaining information by mingling with other students (MING), creating charts and schedules (SCHD), and inventing a story for a picture (STRY) are the most comfortable activities for third-quarter students. These are clearly activities that require somewhat more complex target language production. In general, third-quarter students are more comfortable with NA since 20 of the 23 activities are rated by at least 20% of the students as comfort-producing. These data support the notion

Table 7

ACTIVITIES THAT PRODUCE COMFORT: FIRST-YEAR BREAKDOWN

ACT	1A (34)	ACT	1B (27)	ACT	1C (28)
TPR	54%	INTV	70%	INTV	54%
INTV	53%	RANK	52%	RANK	50%
IMAG	46%	MAPS	41%	MING	48%
MAPS	46%	WORD	38%	SCHD	47%
STPR	43%	IMAG	37%	STRY	46%
MING	41%	MUSC	37%	LIST	45%
READ	38%	TPR	36%	IMAG	44%
SCHD	36%	STPR	35%	OPIN	39%
—	—	—	—	WORD	38%
STRY	31%	LIST	30%	TPR	36%
OPIN	31%	MING	30%	CHAR	33%
NUMB	31%	READ	27%	QZGM	33%
SKIT	30%	STRY	25%	—	—
RANK	27%	OPIN	23%	SKIT	32%
QZGM	27%	SCHD	23%	ORAL	29%
SITU	26%	STEP	20%	MUSC	29%
STEP	26%			MAPS	28%
MUSC	24%			STPR	28%
CHAR	23%			STEP	24%
				NUMB	23%

that even beginning students have different needs and preferences as they pass through the stages of language acquisition in a first-year course.

One example from the above data is especially interesting, namely the large number of second-quarter students who rate interviews (INTV) as producing comfort. Although the first-quarter students have the skills to handle very simple questions such as "What is your name?" and "Where do you live?," they are not advanced enough to ask and answer more complex questions. Third-quarter students rank INTV high, but because they have more advanced language skills, many prefer more complex topics of conversation. Second-quarter students, however, too advanced for the simplicity of first-quarter activities and not advanced enough for the socio-cultural orientation of the third quarter, are at the perfect stage to interview their classmates effectively.

Ratio of Comfort to Anxiety

In order to arrive at any conclusions concerning the use of NA activities and anxiety, we must now consider the interaction between comfort and anxiety. To construct Table 8, we subtracted the number of students who claimed that an activity produced anxiety from the number who claimed that the same activity produced comfort. For example, the highest-ranking activity was preference ranking (RANK), rated by 54% as producing comfort and 10% as producing anxiety. The resulting comparison is 54% − 10%, or 44% as a sort of absolute comfort index. When the difference between the percentages is 3% or less, the anxiety/comfort levels were arbitrarily considered to be equal. The resulting ranking is based on magnitude of difference.

Table 8

COMFORT/ANXIETY FOR ACTIVITIES

ACT	COMF	>	NERV
RANK	54%		10%
INTV	56%		13%
LIST	40%		2%
MAPS	38%		1%
SCHD	35%		1%
TPR	39%		9%
MUSC	26%		0%
IMAG	42%		18%
MING	35%		12%
STPR	31%		9%
STRY	33%		11%
READ	21%		0%
ART	14%		0%
QZGM	24%		10%
HIST	13%		0%
OPIN	34%		23%
WORD	44%		34%
STEP	23%		15%

ACT	COMF	≅	NERV
CHAR	22%		25%
SITU	25%		28%
NUMB	23%		20%

ACT	COMF	<	NERV
ORAL	14%		75%
SKIT	22%		53%

The data presented in Table 8 reveal the ratio of comfort to anxiety for each of the 23 activities. There are only two activities that produce more anxiety than comfort—oral presentations (ORAL) and skits (SKIT). Interestingly, as we have seen, these are also the two most anxiety-producing activities. The other three activities that make some students anxious, defining a word in Spanish (WORD), dealing with a given situation (SITU), and charades (CHAR), produce at least as much comfort in other students as anxiety. Other activities that produce high levels of both comfort and anxiety are giving an opinion (OPIN) and working with numbers (NUMB).

The comparison of comfort and anxiety ratings demonstrates that NA activities can produce diverse responses in students. Table 8 also indicates that there are several activities which, although they are not found among the top comforting activities, have significantly favorable ratios of comfort to anxiety. Highlighted are such content activities as historical and political lectures (HIST), music (MUSC), art (ART), and reading short stories (READ). Although these activities do not make a great percentage of the students comfortable, they also do not produce any anxiety. Thus, these would seem to be "safe" activities.

Let us now turn to an examination of the reactions of students to specific teaching techniques used in NA.

STUDENT RESPONSE TO NA INSTRUCTIONAL TECHNIQUES

Instructional Techniques Judged to Produce Anxiety

In Table 9 we list the instructional techniques used in NA that were judged by at least one-fifth of the students to be anxiety-producing. (QUIZ = oral quizzes; CALL = being called on in class to speak; LGRP = working in groups of 7–15; ERRO = speech errors not corrected during oral activities; GRAM = limited grammar instruction during class; ENGL = discussion of grammar NOT given in English; SPAN = class taught completely in Spanish; STUD = working with different students; PAIR = working in pairs; SGRP = working in small groups of 3–6; STOP = small-group topical conversation.) The data presented indicate that only three of the 16 NA techniques studied make one-third or more of the normal students anxious.

Not surprisingly, oral quizzes (QUIZ) were on the list. QUIZ is a technique employed in the early stages of language instruction to evaluate student comprehension. The instructor makes a statement, usually about a picture or a situation in the classroom, and asks students to indicate whether the statement is true or false. It is possible that the anxiety stems from the fact that American students are accustomed to written examinations and that any oral exam will produce anxiety in a large number of them. Being called on individually (CALL) will make any student anxious who is not ready to speak. In early stages, NA employs the technique of "random volunteered responses," which permits one or more students to answer or respond to a question or remark at the same time without being called on. However, as the course progresses, NA instructors do call on individual students as they perceive that the student is "affectively ready" to respond in the target language. It appears that even in NA, which stresses individual responses less than other approaches, nonvolunteered responses provoke anxiety among many students. Perhaps instructors should attempt as early as possible to identify students who are particularly sensitive to being called on individually.

The anxiety produced by LGRP is of interest since group work is an integral part of the NA class. Students perform many activities in groups. The idea is that students interacting in small groups relax and speak the target language more freely. The results of this study seem to indicate, however, that whereas being paired with a classmate for interviews (INTV) or put into groups of 3 to 6 (SGRP) does not make students anxious, it appears that being put into larger groups does. Possibly students perceive that there is no appreciable difference between large groups (7 to 15 students) and the entire class.

While QUIZ, CALL, and LGRP are a source of anxiety for most students, ERRO and GRAM are anxiety-producing to about one-forth to one-third of the students. Speech errors are not directly corrected during NA communication activities, for it is believed that such corrections will make students anxious. Terrell (1981, p. 123), however, notes that many adults find it difficult to endure a perceived high degree of inaccuracy in their speech. Most students want to know if their output is accurate, and many students believe that speech correction is necessary in order to learn to speak a language well. Since not having speech errors corrected makes some students anxious, it appears that this technique meant to lower anxiety levels actually has the opposite effect on a significant minority of students.

Related to error correction is the issue of explicit grammar instruction. In NA foreign language classes, instructors normally assign grammar explanations and self-correcting verification exercises. And, although some NA instructors do regularly follow up in class on gram-

Table 9

NA TECHNIQUES RATED AS PRODUCING ANXIETY

TECH	REG (92)	TECH	NERV (9)
QUIZ	59%	CALL	75%
CALL	57%	LGRP	62%
LGRP	33%	ERRO	44%
—	—	GRAM	44%
ERRO	32%	QUIZ	37%
GRAM	26%	SPAN	33%
ENGL	20%	—	
		STUD	25%
		ENGL	22%
		PAIR	22%
		SGRP	22%
		STOP	22%

mar assignments, grammar is never the single focus of the oral activities during the class period. Rather than using class time to drill grammatical forms and patterns, NA instructors attempt to include new forms and structures in the input relating grammar to the students' personal lives, interests, etc. Personalized exercises emphasize meaning over form. The de-emphasis on grammar in the NA class (GRAM) also makes about one-fourth of the students anxious. These results make it clear that some students wish to spend more class time on form. For these students, NA's decreased emphasis on formal grammar instruction designed to lower levels of anxiety actually had the opposite effect.

Table 10 displays the data of Table 9 longitudinally. The data suggest that all of the techniques become less threatening as students become more proficient in the target language; however, calling on students individually (CALL) continues to provoke anxiety throughout the year as do oral quizzes (QUIZ). Indeed, these are the only two NA techniques out of 16 that continue to bother large numbers of students at the end of the first-year course. Even working in large groups (LGRP) is no longer judged to be a problem by third-quarter students.

The responses to the de-emphasis of formal grammar instruction (GRAM) displayed in Table 10 raise interesting questions. The de-emphasis on grammar produces anxiety among only one-forth of the first-quarter students, but this number rises to almost one-half in the second quarter. By the middle of the academic year, on the other hand, many second-quarter students, who are now more experienced in the language, appear to want more explicit grammar teaching. Then by the third quarter there is a large decrease in anxiety, since the de-emphasis on grammar (GRAM) is not even among the top five anxiety-producing techniques and only one student in 10 is bothered by the de-emphasis of grammar.

One interpretation of these data is that the much-debated question of whether or not to emphasize grammar is poorly formed. The question is not whether to emphasize grammar, but when it is appropriate to do so. It is possible that beginners in the comprehension stage (novice mid) and beginning the "early speech" stage (novice high) can only utilize very small amounts of grammar instruction—mostly as an advance organizer for the input and to give them more confidence in the acquisition process.[11] Therefore, most first-quarter students are delighted to have a language class that does not emphasize grammar since frequently their past experiences with grammar instruction have been negative. Students at the end of the

Table 10

TECHNIQUES: DECREASE IN ANXIETY FROM 1A TO 1C.

TECH	1A	1B	1C
QUIZ	68%	67%	41%
CALL	48%	52%	43%
LGRP	46%	55%	17%
ERRO	40%	46%	26%
GRAM	26%	40%	11%

"early speech" stage and beginning the "speech emergence stage" (intermediate low) have begun to produce large amounts in the target language and often want to confirm the correctness of their output. Thus, toward the end of the first year of instruction, NA students are more confident using what they have learned and become more interested in what they express than how well they have expressed it. It may be that they have gained a certain level of accuracy they are happy with and wish to concentrate on expanding their range of vocabulary and ability to talk about a wider range of topics.

In contrast to the de-emphasis of grammar (GRAM), the policy of no direct correction of student speech errors (ERRO) continues to be a problem throughout the year for some students. Almost one-half of the students in the first and second quarter are bothered by the fact that the instructor does not directly correct errors during oral activities. On the other hand, only one-quarter of the students continue to be bothered by the absence of error correction by the third quarter. We continue to believe that direct interruptive error correction serves no purpose whatsoever. However, it would seem that the entire area of "negative feedback" needs to be reexamined. We had assumed that students would be able to use the "expansions" of the instructor—the "corrected" responses by the instructor to correct their own speech. But apparently many students do not utilize these expansions and continue to want direct correction.

NA Techniques Judged to Produce Comfort

In Table 11 are listed the techniques that at least one-fifth of the students judged to produce comfort. (New abbreviations: PICT = use of pictures to present new vocabulary; PERS = personalization of vocabulary; ASSO = acquisition of vocabulary through association; CTOP = classroom topical discussion; NCAL = not being called on individually.) These data indicate that 13 of the 16 techniques make at least one-third of the students feel comfortable, and all of them produce comfort for at least one-fifth of the students. Importantly, the data suggest that it is the personalized aspect of the NA that makes students feel the most comfortable. Using pictures to present vocabulary (PICT), pairing students with their classmates (PAIR), personalizing grammar (PERS), having students work with different students (STUD), associating vocabulary with students and objects in the class (ASSO), and putting students into groups of 3 to 6 (SGRP) produce comfort for more than one-half of the students. (That personalizing grammar [PERS] makes so many students comfortable suggests that it is only the perceived grammatical de-emphasis and not the technique employed to

Table 11

NA TECHNIQUES RATED AS PRODUCING COMFORT

TECH	REG (92)	TECH	NERV (9)
PICT	64%	NCAL	89%
PAIR	62%	SGRP	67%
PERS	62%	PERS	55%
STUD	54%	CTOP	55%
ASSO	52%	STUD	50%
SGRP	52%	SPAN	44%
SPAN	48%	PAIR	44%
CTOP	47%	ASSO	37%
NCAL	43%	PICT	33%
STOP	40%	ENGL	33%
CALL	40%	GRAM	33%
ENGL	35%	ERRO	33%
GRAM	35%	STOP	33%
—	—	—	—
ERRO	30%	CALL	25%
LGRP	25%		
QUIZ	20%		

Table 12

TECHNIQUES THAT PRODUCE COMFORT: FIRST-YEAR BREAKDOWN

TECH	1A (34)	TECH	1B (27)	TECH	1C
PERS	69%	PAIR	74%	PERS	63%
PICT	68%	PICT	73%	SGRP	61%
CTOP	60%	ASSO	66%	PICT	57%
PAIR	59%	CTOP	65%	ASSO	54%
STUD	56%	STUD	65%	PAIR	53%
SPAN	50%	CTOP	60%	NCAL	52%
ASSO	50%	SPAN	59%	CTOP	48%
SGRP	50%	ENGL	44%	SPAN	46%
NCAL	46%	PERS	44%	STOP	46%
ENGL	42%	CALL	44%	STUD	46%
STOP	41%	STOP	42%	GRAM	44%
GRAM	39%	NCAL	41%	QUIZ	41%
CALL	36%	GRAM	36%	CALL	39%
—	—	—	—	LGRP	37%
ERRO	30%	QUIZ	22%	—	—
		LGRP	20%	ENGL	31%
				ERRO	26%

teach grammar that bothers students.) The data presented in Table 11 reveal that nervous students are as comfortable with NA techniques as are regular students.

In Table 12 we present the same data longitudinally. The data indicate that the comfort ratings for most of the techniques do not vary greatly during the three-quarter sequence. Personalization of grammar (PERS), use of pictures to present vocabulary (PICT), acquisition of vocabulary through association (ASSO), working in pairs (PAIR), and classroom topical discussion (CTOP) were popular at all levels of instruction.

Table 13

TECHNIQUES: RATIO OF COMFORT TO ANXIETY

TECH	COMF	>	NERV
PICT	64%		1%
PERS	62%		5%
ASSO	52%		0%
PAIR	62%		11%
CTOP	47%		2%
STUD	54%		11%
SGRP	52%		10%
NCAL	43%		5%
STOP	40%		4%
SPAN	48%		19%
ENGL	35%		20%
GRAM	35%		26%

TECH	COMF	≅	NERV
ERRO	30%		32%

TECH	COMF	<	NERV
QUIZ	20%		59%
CALL	40%		57%
LGRP	25%		33%

Techniques: Ratio of Comfort to Anxiety

In order to estimate the real levels of anxiety in an NA class due to specific techniques, in Table 13 we display the ratio of comfort to anxiety for the various NA techniques rated. An examination of the data reveals that four of the techniques that are perceived as the most comfortable retain their top status even after subtracting anxiety ratings: using pictures to present vocabulary (PICT), personalization of grammar presentations (PERS), acquisition of vocabulary through association (ASSO), and working in pairs (PAIR). Techniques like classroom topical discussion (CTOP) and not calling on individuals (NCALL), and small-group topical discussion (STOP) are not rated by as many as producing comfort as the four top techniques, but the data suggest that they are "safe" techniques since very few subjects find them anxiety-producing. Finally, although oral quizzes (QUIZ), calling on students individually (CALL), and large-group discussions (LGRP) are the most anxiety-producing techniques, it is worth noting that a number of students judge these techniques to be comfortable. For example, although 57% identify being called on individually (CALL) as anxiety-producing, a full 40% find that this same technique makes them secure, probably because they see it as beneficial in the acquisition process.

Two techniques, limited grammar instruction in class (GRAM) and the avoidance of direct error correction (ERRO), deserve additional attention. In the preceding section we noted that these two techniques produced anxiety in relatively large numbers of students. The data in Table 13, however, present the other side of the picture. Although 26% of the students find the de-emphasis of grammar in NA anxiety-producing, a greater number of students (35%) found this technique comforting. In addition, although 32% claim that avoidance of error correction makes them anxious, 30% offer the opposite opinion. It seems that students are divided in their judgments of the value of grammar instruction and error correction. Perhaps this should not be such a great surprise as the language-teaching profession itself is so divided on these important issues.

CONCLUSIONS

The purpose of this paper was to identify the particular activities and techniques of NA that contribute to lower levels of anxiety in students. However, we have found that there are no simple answers to this question. It is true that many activities and techniques were found to produce low levels of anxiety for most students. For example, activities such as preference ranking (RANK), interviews (INTV), figuring out what does not belong on a list of items (LIST), working with maps and other realia (MAPS), creating charts and schedules (SCHD), and total physical response (TPR) produce comfort for large numbers of students and at the same time are judged by almost no one to produce anxiety. In other cases, however, even when the activity is identified as comfort-producing by many students, a sizable minority considers the activity to produce anxiety. For example, almost one-half of the students claim that imagining situations (IMAG) produces comfort, while almost one-fifth believe that it leads to anxiety. In addition, several activities elicit a split opinion: Playing charades (CHAR) and dealing with a specific situation (SITU) are considered by almost equal numbers of students as making them comfortable or anxious. Even performing in skits (SKIT), which is considered by a full 53% of the students as anxiety-producing, is taken to be comforting by 22%. Of all of the NA activities in the survey, only presenting oral reports (ORAL) is considered by a large majority to be anxiety-producing with only 12% considering it to be comfortable.

Students rated most NA techniques as producing comfort rather than anxiety. Of the 16 techniques examined, only three were rated by more students as resulting in anxiety rather than comfort. However, as in the case of NA activities, there were diverse responses. Some techniques are "safe," with most students rating them as comfortable: Using pictures to present vocabulary (PICT), personalization of grammar (PERS), acquisition of vocabulary through association (ASSO), pair work (PAIR), and classroom topical discussion (CTOP) are rated high by large numbers of students with almost none considering them to be anxiety-producing. However, while more students rate teaching completely in Spanish (SPAN), using no English (ENGL), and a de-emphasis of grammar in the class (GRAM) as comforting, a large minority find these same techniques to be anxiety-producing. The reverse also holds: Techniques such as oral quizzes (QUIZ), calling on individuals (CALL), and large-group discussion (LGRP), which are anxiety-producing for large numbers of students, are still rated highly by from one-fifth (QUIZ) to two-fifths (CALL) of the students.

In general, student responses indicate that the activities and techniques that relate to the students on a personal level result in the most comfort. The students' responses also indicate that increased exposure over time to many NA activities and techniques results in a decrease in anxiety. On the other hand, several activities and techniques meet with mixed reactions even after the students have had considerable experience with them, and student reactions vary at different stages of proficiency. First-quarter students like activities and techniques that do not require complex responses in the target language. Third-quarter students seem more tolerant and like to take chances; hence they prefer more complex activities and are pleased with the de-emphasis on grammar and the chance to produce the target language free from error correction.

This paper has offered a glimpse into the reactions of typical NA students. The hope of NA is that, should students begin language study feeling anxious about studying a foreign language, the approach will help assuage their fears. The affective-humanistic activities that enable students to express their feelings are particularly aimed at making them feel comfortable. Working in small groups, discussing relevant topics, and relating grammar and vocabulary to their personal interests make most students feel comfortable. Although certain performance activities such as oral presentations and role-playing and difficult problem-solving activities make some students anxious, we would not want to give up these activities; rather, we would hope to find ways to make these activities less threatening.

Conversely, the most important finding, we believe, is that although some activities and techniques appear to please a majority of students, others elicit varied reactions. This variation of response appears to be due to individual learning styles and to changes that take place in the individual students during the first year of instruction. Consequently, activities and instructional techniques should not be thought of as intrinsically "good" or "bad" but rather "useful" or "not recommended" for certain students at particular levels of language acquisition. Thus, there would seem to be no simple remedy for student anxiety. Instructors cannot choose activities, techniques, or even a language-teaching method or approach without taking into consideration the students' individual learning styles, interests, and affective reactions.

NOTES

1. See Terrell, 1977, 1981, 1982, 1986; Krashen & Terrell, 1983; Terrell, Andrade, Egasse, & Muñoz, 1986.

2. Other approaches that also make affective claims are TPR (Asher, 1977), Community Language Learning (Curran, 1976), and Suggestopedia (Lozanov, 1979). See also Moskowitz, 1978.

3. The questionnaire is not included in this paper because of length restrictions; however, it is found in Koch, 1984.

4. Because of this relatively small number of students, we did not apply standard statistical procedures to the data.

5. Percentages do not add up to 100 because of multiple experiences with different approaches.

6. Students with no previous foreign language experience were not included in this section.

7. The Appendix also contains the decoding of all abbreviations.

8. The 18 students who have not previously studied a foreign language cannot compare the NA to any other approach and were excluded from this section.

9. In this and following tables of data we omit any item that was mentioned by less than 20% of the students. In addition, we have visually separated all items mentioned by more than 30% of students.

10. Percentages do not add up to 100% in this and subsequent tables because of the expression of multiple answers.

11. Comprehension stage consists of interaction with input, but no demands for target language output are made on the students (1–10 instructional hours). Early speech stage includes interaction that requires students to produce words or short phrases in the target language (10–50 instructional hours). Speech emergence stage consists of activities that require the student to produce sentences and more complex discourse.

APPENDIX

NA Activities

ART	Art
CHAR	Charades
HIST	Historical and political lectures
IMAG	Imagining situations
INTV	Interviews with other students
LIST	Figuring out what does not belong in a list of items
MAPS	Working with maps and advertisements
MING	Obtaining information by mingling with other students
MUSC	Music
NUMB	Working with numbers
OPIN	Giving an opinion about an issue
ORAL	Oral presentations
QZGM	Quiz games
RANK	Preference ranking
READ	Reading short stories
SCHD	Creating charts and schedules
SITU	Dealing with a given situation
SKIT	Skits and role-playing
STEP	Describing the steps of an activity
STPR	"Simon Says" with Total Physical Response
STRY	Inventing a story for a picture
TPR	Total Physical Response
WORD	Defining a word in Spanish

NA Techniques

ASSO	Acquisition of vocabulary through association
CALL	Being called on to speak
CTOP	Classroom topical conversation
ENGL	Discussion of grammar not given in English
ERRO	Speech errors are not directly corrected in oral activities
GRAM	Limited grammar instruction in class
LGRP	Working in groups of 7 to 15
NCAL	Not being called on individually
PAIR	Working in pairs
PERS	Personalization of grammar

PICT	Pictures to present vocabulary
QUIZ	Quizzes given orally
SGRP	Working in groups of 3 to 6
SPAN	Class taught in Spanish
STOP	Small-group topical conversation
STUD	Working with different students

Teaching Strategies: Helping Learners Cope with Language Anxiety

Parts Three and Four of this text offered suggestions for reducing language anxiety, including classroom activities, instructor behavior, and evaluative formats. Part Five, on the other hand, focuses on ways that instructors can help language learners themselves deal with language anxiety. It explores such issues as: How can language anxiety be addressed directly in the language classroom? How can teachers facilitate the identification of students' individual sources of language anxiety? How can teachers help dispel students' anxiety-provoking beliefs about language learning?

An important theme of this section is that increasing students' knowledge about the language-learning process will help them become more effective and self-confident language learners. Foss and Reitzel describe an anxiety-management model from the field of speech communication. Specifically, they maintain that language anxiety emanates from students' perceptions of their performance rather than the actual performance. Thus, the individual learner must be actively involved in any effort to decrease anxiety.

Crookall and Oxford suggest a related approach to anxiety reduction called *learner training*. In learner training, students are encouraged to think about the language-learning process in order to become better—and less anxious—language learners. Their article also includes teacher-training activities to help instructors become sensitive to language anxiety in students and themselves. Until this point, we have considered language anxiety primarily as a concern for students. Crookall and Oxford remind us that language teachers are also language learners and users who may be susceptible to language anxiety. As we work to banish anxiety from the language classroom, we must consider teacher anxiety and how it affects instructional practice.

Chapter Eleven

A Relational Model for Managing Second Language Anxiety

Karen A. Foss and Armeda C. Reitzel   Humboldt State University

> Why can't I speak what to think a lot in English? I'm so bitter, trying hard. I'd like to speak a lot, however, I can't. Finally, I think My basis abilities of English ran short. I'm disgusted with myself.

This comment, taken from a student's journal in an ESL class,[1] captures the anxieties experienced by many second language learners in their efforts to master a new language. The relationship between communication competence and communication anxiety has concerned theorists in speech communication and in second language acquisition. Members of both disciplines are concerned with the teaching and enhancement of communication capabilities and recognize that anxiety about communication often functions as an impediment to that goal.

Although *communication competence* and *communication anxiety* have been defined in various ways, there is general agreement about the meanings of the terms. Communication *competence* is the knowledge of and ability to use appropriate communication patterns effectively in an interaction (Bostrom, 1984, p. 25). Communication *anxiety* is the abnormally high and debilitating level of fear associated with real or anticipated communication with one or more persons (McCroskey, 1977C). It can manifest itself as a trait—a general reluctance on the part of an individual to communicate regardless of context—or it may occur only in specific situations, such as when giving a speech or conversing in a foreign language.

Although anxiety reactions of various kinds have been recognized and studied extensively by psychologists and educators, foreign language classroom anxiety only recently has been isolated and distinguished from other forms of anxiety (Horwitz, Horwitz, & Cope, 1986, this volume). Foreign language anxiety seems to share certain characteristics with communication anxiety, for example, high feelings of self-consciousness, fear of making mistakes, and a desire to be perfect when speaking (Friedman, 1980; Horwitz et al., 1986).

However, the anxiety associated with foreign language learning also differs from general communication anxiety. It seems to be a "distinct complex of self-perceptions, beliefs, feelings, and behaviors . . . arising from the uniqueness of the language learning process" (Horwitz et al., 1986, p. 128). Language learners have the dual task not only of learning a second language but of performing in it, whereas anxious speakers in a communication classroom generally have only performance concerns. In addition, second language learners may have difficulty understanding others, a problem that usually is not common for native speakers.[2] Furthermore, foreign language anxiety entails a risk to self beyond that experienced by a native speaker because the speaker knows he or she cannot present the self fully in the new language. Horwitz et al. (1986) summarize:

> Adult language learners' self-perceptions of genuineness in presenting themselves to others may be threatened by the limited range of meaning and affect that can be deliberately communicated. . . . Probably no other field of study implicates self-concept and self-expression to the degree that language study does. (p. 128)

Various methods for treating communication apprehension in general communication and in language classrooms appear in the literature. Foss (1982) describes the range of treatment techniques that have been used in speech communication classes, including *learning theory* approaches, such as biofeedback, cognitive restructuring, and systematic desensitization; approaches based on *skills training*, such as oral interpretation, assertiveness, and conversational skills training; and treatment via the *basic communication skills course*. Several methods of treatment also are outlined in a volume edited by Daly and McCroskey (1984). McCoy (1979) describes how three of the most common treatment methods—systematic desensitization, cognitive restructuring, and modeling—can be applied to second language classrooms. Finally, Lucas (1984) offers a series of exercises based on the assumption that skills practice will eliminate much language-learning anxiety.

In much of the previous work on language-learning anxiety, however, the methods presented have not been adapted to the specific characteristics of the second language classroom. Many of the methods suggested, such as systematic desensitization, hypnosis, or biofeedback, demand levels of training and expertise beyond those of ESL teachers. In addition, language teachers often have neither the time to devote to handling extreme cases of anxiety nor the funds for the special equipment involved (Horwitz et al., 1986, this volume).

Even skills approaches—which can be handled within the constraints of the language classroom—have been less effective than expected because of the special difficulties of second language learners. By *skills approach* we mean any method based on the assumption that correct performance of a behavior results in competence. The speaker, however, must simultaneously recognize and consider his or her behavior as competent if skills approaches are to be rewarding. No matter how competent a performance is, some students will not judge their communication positively and thus are not reinforced for their skill levels. For these students, skills approaches may increase anxiety because such approaches place them in a situation that they continually evaluate negatively. What is needed, then, is an approach to language-learning anxiety that takes into account the significance of self-perception throughout all phases of language learning and performance and that can be handled within the time and funding constraints of the classroom.

We see self-perception as a critical factor in both language-learning anxiety and communication anxiety. In fact, its role has been widely recognized by researchers in both fields (Friedman, 1980; Horwitz et al., 1986, this volume). Communication apprehensives—

whether those speaking their native language or those learning a new one—typically have low self-esteem, perceive themselves as less worthy than others, perceive their communication as less effective than that of their peers, and expect continued failure no matter what feedback they actually receive (McCroskey, Daly, Richmond, & Falcione, 1977). With second language learners, there are the additional feelings of incompetence about grasping the language in the first place and about the inability to present oneself in a way consistent with one's self-image. In both forms of anxiety, negative self-perceptions set in motion a perpetuating cycle of negative evaluations that may persist in spite of evaluations from others to the contrary.

Perception of self plays a key role in how students approach the acquisition and use of a second language. Learning to reflect upon experiences and going through some introspection can help students become more in tune with their impressions of their second language competence and provide them with a means for modifying their approaches to language learning. Sometimes student perceptions of self may correspond to the instructor's evaluations of students' strengths and weaknesses. For example, the following excerpt from a student's journal shows his concern with listening comprehension, an area in which one of us, as his ESL instructor, also felt work was needed:

> Today I was in a trouble. Because I'm not good at hearing. The I. E. L. I. consists of three levels. Now I'm in the best class. . . . But it is a miracale. I guess I'm the lowest in the highest class. And it is very difficult to me. . . . But I must do my best. So after today I'll make sure every assignment every day.

In other situations, however, the instructor's perception of a student's ability and the student's own perception of ability may differ. One of the best students in a high-level class wrote the following: "But basically I think I'm in low level of the class. That could be a good chance to try to study as hard as I could. Then if I catch up other students, it shows that I can make progress." This admission came as a surprise, since she was perceived by the instructor to be one of the top students in the class. Thus, students' perceptions of their competencies may differ from those of their instructors, and it is those self-perceptions that students must learn to analyze and work with in order to overcome communication apprehension in second language situations.

What is needed, then, to deal with communication anxiety in the second language classroom is a model of competence that incorporates the steps involved in language acquisition and performance as well as the role of self-perception as it operates across communication interactions. We propose that the model of relational competence developed by Spitzberg and Cupach (1984) for use in the field of speech communication provides such a framework and deserves the attention of ESL scholars and teachers.

THE RELATIONAL COMPETENCE MODEL

Spitzberg and Cupach (1984) call their model *relational* because they argue that competence can be determined only in the context of a particular relationship:

> We choose to view relationship as a confluence of behavior and perception. To us, it is at least as important to know how people view the behavior of self and other in terms of relational definitions as it is to know what behavior is actually performed. (p. 151)

In this model, then, competence is not an objective performance but a matter of perception that varies across interactions: "Competence is not something intrinsic to a person's nature or behavior; it is an impression that a person has of self or other" (p. 115).

Although Spitzberg and Cupach (1984) do not ignore the fact that actual behaviors play a role in perceptions of competence, they simply emphasize "the importance of discovering these norms anew in each contextual episode" (p. 107). The relativity of competence is emphasized in a recent elaboration of the model: "The relational competence model does not argue against the importance of objective behavior. . . . The question changes from 'what behaviors *are* competent?' to 'what behaviors *are most likely to be viewed* as competent?' " (Spitzberg & Hurt, 1987, p. 30). Competence, then, is a matter of degree, and perceptions of competence can vary from situation to situation and even within a particular episode. For example, a behavior that someone perceives to be a terrible faux pas on one occasion might pass unnoticed by that individual and others on another.

Spitzberg and Cupach (1984) make perception crucial to all stages of their model of competence. If competence is assumed to be an interpersonal impression that depends on the individuals involved, their relationship, and the nature of the particular encounter, the perceptions of those involved must take priority. They suggest that a communicator is competent if perceived so by self and/or others. The process of perception becomes the link between cognitive aspects of learning and performance aspects. In terms of language learning, then, Spitzberg and Cupach's model suggests that distinctions between the stages of acquisition/learning and performance are less important than the recognition that perception will determine how a student handles each phase.

This relational model makes a distinctive contribution to the notion of competence as it has developed in the discipline of communication. Whereas most conceptualizations have treated competence as an individual trait, determined by judging an individual's behavior in isolation, Spitzberg and Cupach (1984) insist that self-perceptions and interactional contexts be taken into account before making assessments about competence. The notion that competence can be determined only by looking holistically at the interactional situation makes this model truly communication oriented. This focus seems to us a useful framework for conceptualizing how anxiety interferes with the attainment of competence in second language classrooms and for developing ways to reduce that anxiety. The focus is placed not on the individual performances of students but on self-perceptions of behaviors as they occur in specific episodes and contexts.

Spitzberg and Cupach's (1984) relational model of competence includes five fundamental components or processes: motivation, knowledge, skills, criteria outcomes, and context. Each of these is discussed in turn, with an elaboration of the special factors involved in the application to the second language classroom. Taken together, these components provide a comprehensive starting point for developing exercises to help students recognize and handle their anxieties as they interact in a variety of settings.

Motivation

Motivation is the foundation of the model, since it means the difference between communicating and not communicating. By *motivation,* Spitzberg and Cupach (1984, p. 119) mean the affective approach or avoidance response to a particular communication situation. Obviously, if a person avoids a particular situation, the opportunity to communicate simply is not available. Some second language learners may choose not to communicate in a situation because they judge their capabilities in the new language to be so poor that not communicating is perceived as more rewarding than doing so. For some, symptoms of anxiety—excessive perspiration, shakiness, and the like—may be what keeps them from communicating. Avoidance at the motivational level reinforces the perception of incompetence because the individual never puts himself or herself in a position to increase skill levels and to be evaluated positively by others. Indeed, many students may resort to skipping classes or dropping out of language programs completely. Scovel (1978) summarizes: "debilitating anxiety . . . motivates the learner to 'flee' the new learning task; it stimulates the individual emotionally to adopt avoidance behavior" (p. 139).

At times, students may rebel against the second culture/language because of culture shock. Dodd (1982) suggests that foreigners sometimes may fight or flee the second culture during the transitional stage of culture shock. For instance, students may choose not to associate with native speakers or use the second language as a way of "fighting" against the second culture. They are not motivated to use the language because they do not view the second culture in a positive light. Others may cope with culture shock by withdrawing ("fleeing") from contact with the second culture. The motivation to learn and use the second language, then, depends on students' perceptions of their abilities in the second language and their feelings toward the second culture. Again, it is the students' perceptions of the context of communication, including the culture within which the communication is to take place, that plays a big role in students' responses to communication activities.

Knowledge

Once a person decides to approach a situation, a certain amount of knowledge about how to communicate in that context is necessary. Knowledge, then, is the second step in the model. It consists of a repertoire of behavioral patterns and strategies upon which a person draws in order to decide how to communicate in a given situation (Spitzberg & Cupach, 1984, p. 123). This stage, for the second language learner, is the process of intuitively acquiring and consciously learning the language. For many, this stage of the process may be especially anxiety producing because the task of tackling a second language appears overwhelming. Again, the symptoms of tension, fear, or panic that accompany some students' efforts to study the new language may render their efforts at learning ineffective. The efforts of students who perceive themselves as incompetent only reinforce rather than dispel this perception.

Skills

Closely related to knowledge are skills, the third component of the relational competence model. This refers to the fact that although a person may be motivated to interact competently and may understand, theoretically, how to manage the fundamentals of a language, he or she needs certain skills to converse successfully in the new language. Again, Spitzberg and Cupach (1984, p. 129) do not negate the importance of skills training but argue that it must be viewed as part of an integrated process, heavily dependent on self-perception. Students' perceptions may or may not be consistent with their actual skill levels: Their actual performances may be adequate or even extremely fluent according to the perceptions of others, but they themselves may not evaluate them positively.

Outcomes

The fourth component of the model is outcomes. Spitzberg and Cupach (1984) identify several outcomes likely to be taken as evidence of communication competence, including communication satisfaction (how satisfied one is with the interaction), relational trust (the extent to which all parties involved feel positively toward the other in the interaction), and interpersonal attraction (an individual who is more satisfying and confirming to talk to frequently is seen as more likable).

In the second language classroom, the instructor typically is seen as responsible for establishing and evaluating appropriate outcomes. Students also need to become evaluators of outcomes and levels of competence in order for them to develop realistic perceptions of their performances. In addition, fluctuating expectations for competence should be emphasized over absolute determinants of behavior. Students need to become used to the idea that "a 'negative' outcome involving some dissatisfaction may still reflect competence if that outcome is *relatively* better than its alternatives" (Spitzberg & Cupach, 1984, p. 110).

Context

Context is the final component of the relational model. It demands that attention be given to the subjective dimensions of environment as well as to its objective features. Each person, via his or her perceptions, creates an environment that facilitates or hinders language learning. For Spitzberg and Cupach (1984), the self-perceptions of the context often are more important than the context itself and can fluctuate greatly across time and situation. Perceptions of the general context—that is, the second language culture—may vary in an individual as knowledge and feelings toward the culture develop. In addition, an individual's views toward specific situations—dating, for example—may differ due to factors such as past experiences, present mood, and locale.

STRATEGIES FOR MANAGING ANXIETY

The balance of this article discusses treatment strategies for handling language-learning anxiety at each step of the relational model. In each case, these sample exercises are designed to highlight the role of perception as a critical but often overlooked factor in language learning and to concentrate on developing competence in various interactional settings. Although the exercises we describe are appropriate for particular ESL levels, they can be easily adapted to other levels as well.

Motivation

Anxiety during the motivational phase of competence development has consequences for each subsequent stage of the relational model—knowledge, skills, outcomes, and context—and must be addressed by the second language teacher if satisfactory progress at the following stages is to occur. The two approaches described for dealing with high motivational anxiety address individual perceptions that may block the initiation of communication activity. One approach is based on rational emotive therapy, whereas the other is an exercise designed to help students determine precisely what part of the process of speaking the new language produces the most anxiety for them personally.

Rational emotive therapy.

Rational emotive therapy. Rational emotive therapy is based on the assumption that irrational beliefs are the source of much anxiety when anticipating a communication situation such as conversing in a second language (Grieger & Boyd, 1980; Straatmeyer & Watkins, 1974). If these beliefs can be recognized, students can learn to interpret such situations in more realistic ways and thus may choose to approach rather than avoid situations demanding conversation.

The language teacher can begin by presenting the idea that we all operate, to some extent, from individual irrational belief systems. Some of these are given to us by our culture, some by our families, and others simply are picked up unconsciously from life experiences. Much of the time these beliefs are harmless—or at least do not interfere with our abilities to live effective lives. Such beliefs, however, can be detrimental to second language students if they interfere with language learning.

Following this discussion, the instructor asks students to generate a list of their fears about speaking the new language. Simply putting these on the board and allowing students to realize that they are not alone in their fears can, in and of itself, encourage students to relax in their efforts to speak the second language. Each of these beliefs—from "I'll make mistakes and people will laugh" to "My accent is awful"—can be shown to be grounded in irrational and unproductive assumptions.

For instance, the fear of making mistakes may come from a basic belief that one is not worthy unless one is thoroughly competent and adequate in all aspects of life. The fear of being laughed at may come from an unconscious yet entrenched belief that one must be approved of by every person one encounters. Similar irrational ideas that cause and sustain anxiety for language learners are the following: (a) "It is catastrophic when things are not the way I would like them to be—that is, I cannot speak this language fluently and that is horrible"; (b) "It is easier to avoid than to face certain of life's difficulties and responsibilities"; and (c) "There is one correct way to handle a particular situation, and if I don't do it correctly, the outcome will be disastrous."

Each student selects two or three beliefs from the list that seem to be contributing most to his or her anxiety. For each belief, students work through a series of questions designed to convince them of the lack of logic behind this belief. These questions, with a sample set of responses, are listed below.

1. *What irrational belief do I want to dispute?* That I must speak the language perfectly in order to be liked by those with whom I converse.
2. *What evidence exists of the falseness of this belief?*
   a. No proof exists that people will not like me if I cannot speak their language perfectly. Who knows—they may appreciate my efforts to try to speak the language and will end up liking me just as much as if I spoke fluently.
   b. If someone I like rejects me for not speaking the language perfectly, that will be unfortunate, but I will not die.
   c. No law of the universe says I must be liked by everyone.
   d. If I am not liked by one person, I can still be liked by others.
   e. In the past, I have done things imperfectly—and people have still liked me.
   f. I might speak the language perfectly, and people could still not like me.

3. *Does evidence exist of the truth of this belief?* No, not really. I can't think of a situation in which I knew for a fact that a person didn't like me because I couldn't speak the language perfectly. Even if my greatest fears are realized, and no one in my host country likes me because I cannot speak their language well. I can still cope. I know there *are* people in the world who like me, who appreciate my efforts to learn a second language, and with whom I can have meaningful relationships.

Students can refer to and rethink these worksheets throughout the course to remind them that much of their anxiety is a matter of beliefs that really do not make much sense when examined seriously. If worksheets are shared in small groups, students gain considerable support from their peers and develop more realistic expectations about their own performance.

Anxiety graph. A second activity especially useful for helping students confront anxiety when contemplating a communication situation is the anxiety graph. The technique was devised by Brownell and Katula (1984) for managing anxiety in public-speaking situations, but we have adapted it for use in the second language classroom. Although the literature on communication anxiety implicitly acknowledges that anxiety is not a constant phenomenon throughout a communication interaction, instructors often fail to point out that not every phase of an interaction is equally anxiety producing for every student. Thus, students typically contemplate an event in its totality, evaluate it negatively, and end up with an inaccurate perception of the amount of anxiety actually experienced.

The anxiety graph is designed to help students to gain an accurate understanding of the nature of their anxiety, to pinpoint when anxiety is highest in a given interaction, and to approach the situation more realistically, given this information. On the graph, a completed example of which is shown in Figure 1, students chart their anxiety about a conversational encounter immediately after it occurs. This can be repeated throughout the course to graph an individual's anxiety over time. An instructor can also use the graph in individual conferences, discussing with each how best to cope with the anxiety experienced most frequently. We prefer for students to share their graphs in groups, a process that enables them to see how similar their responses are to those of other students.

Again, the point of the exercise is for students to perceive a situation realistically and to be rewarded by others for the appropriate and effective aspects of their communications. The anxiety graph can help students internalize the fact that speaking a new language is not a uniform process that is consistently difficult and anxiety provoking.

Knowledge and Skills

Although we recognize that the cognitive process of knowing a language is distinct from the ability to put that knowledge into practice, the following exercise addresses the anxiety associated with these two phases in an integrated fashion. Thus, we have chosen to treat the knowledge and skills components of the competence model together here.

Three activities commonly used in communication classrooms to help students gain knowledge of and skills in the language and culture are role playing, drama, and oral interpretation. Since many second language teachers already employ role playing and drama in their classrooms, the use of oral interpretation is discussed here as another possible vehicle for lowering anxiety at the knowledge and skill levels.

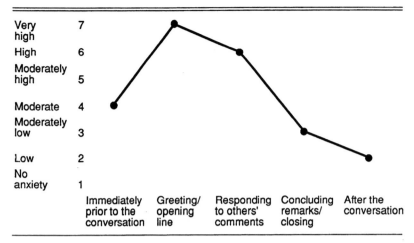

From "The Communication Anxiety Graph: A Classroom Tool for Managing Speech Anxiety" by W. W. Brownell and R. A. Katula, 1984. *Communication Quarterly, 32,* p. 245. Copyright 1984 by the Speech Communication Association. Adapted by permission.

FIGURE 1   An anxiety graph

Oral interpretation, an integral component of most speech communication programs, involves the practiced oral reading of a script before an audience. Performances may be done solo or in groups. Oral interpretation requires the careful selection and practice of material before the actual performance. A set of scripts (poems, portions of poems, or portions of stories) is selected by the instructor, who may or may not choose to involve students in this process. The scripts typically reflect a central theme, such as "the challenge of being an immigrant in the United States" or "the changing roles of women and men."

The scripts are practiced for correct pronunciation, intonation, volume, and timing. Emphasis is placed on interpreting the texts in terms of the meaning in and behind the words on the paper. Nonverbal communication—facial expression, hand movements, eye contact, and so on—is planned and practiced. After the groups and/or individuals have practiced, they perform their interpretations in front of an audience. The scripts are not memorized, but they are practiced well enough that students do not have to read every word from the scripts they are holding. The group preparation, evaluation, and performance lessen communication anxiety for many students, as does the fact that they are performing the works of others (Hopf, 1970; Mier, 1983; Pelias, 1984; Schmitt, 1975; Washington, 1983).

As an introduction to oral interpretation, we have had beginning ESL classes perform quality children's literature—stories that have become classics for American children and can be thought of as modern folktales. Such stories can lead into discussions about cultural beliefs, values, and behaviors in addition to serving as material for performance. Among the literature available for use is *Charlotte's Web, The Velveteen Rabbit, The Phantom Tollbooth,* and all of Dr. Seuss's writings. We have arranged for students to perform a selected piece for several audiences, including other ESL classes and local elementary school classes.

We had special success recently with Dr. Seuss's *Green Eggs and Ham.* Students thoroughly enjoyed all aspects of the exercise, from discussing the vocabulary and the cultural values suggested by the poem to practicing pronunciation, delivery, and appropriate facial expressions. Many students really "hammed it up" while performing the piece to the various audiences. One student, who did a wonderful job of playing the character who did not want to eat green eggs and ham, wrote about the experience in her personal journal: "Oral Skills class yesterday was so fun to me. We read the topic continued from the day before yesterday loudly." This student normally complained about not understanding and not being able to speak in English, but she did an excellent job of interpreting her part. More important, she also felt that she did a good job with her performance. Such positive responses on the part of both students and teachers suggest that oral interpretation can be an upbeat way to help students overcome some of their performance anxieties.

Outcomes

The outcome component of the relational model involves the individual's impressions of the communication event. What is important is how he or she views and feels about the communication that has occurred. The opportunity to reflect upon the outcomes of communication is necessary for developing specific objectives for continuing competence. At the same time, it allows students to realize, once again, the importance of their perceptions in determining the outcome of a particular communication episode.

Journals have become a common practice in many English, language, and communication classes (Popkin, 1985). In addition to dialogue journals, which encourage "personal communication and mutual understanding between each individual student and the teacher" (Staton, 1983, p. 2), journals may be used to examine personal value systems (Highnam & Geist, 1981), to explore intercultural issues encountered in the new culture (Mansell, 1981), and to assess current competencies (Hunt, 1979).

We have used journals as a vehicle for intrapersonal reflection on the language-learning process. Daily journals can help students track their feelings of apprehension in the second language situation. In addition to talking/thinking through anxieties, students also can write through their feelings of inadequacy to arrive at a more realistic, positive sense of their progress. The following excerpt is a representative sample of the evolution in perceptions— from negative to increasingly optimistic—that we observed among our students:

> Oh, my god, at Reading class and writing class I couldn't understand what they said. I could understand a little. I don't know whether what is correct or not. I understand what they said roughly in some parts though I couldn't speak a word. What should I do? I remembered what Kumi's saying, "The student of University may teach you English as a tutor." Before returning on my way, I told Tom my troubles. Tom said to me it passed two weeks. Don't worry, but try to look for someone who be able to speak in English. I'm relieved. There is no hurry. Remember "Slow and steady won the race."

Journals also can be used to help students develop realistic communication goals. The student begins by recording all instances of interpersonal communication during a 3-day period. The recording should include with whom, about what, when, where, and why conversation occurred. Subjective impressions should be noted whenever possible, since these reveal the perceptual set from which the student is operating. Instructors can use this information to help students sort out the typical perceptions of situations that consistently produce high anxiety.

With this information, each student then develops a hierarchy of specific goals to work toward in the remainder of the class. Instructors should help students develop realistic goals so that they experience success as they progress up their chosen hierarchies. The journals continue during this phase as well, with students keeping track of their perceptions about their interactions as they attempt to accomplish their goals.

Toward the end of the course, another 3-day sample of interpersonal communication is recorded and evaluated by the student. The second sample is compared with the first to determine whether changes have occurred and whether the student's level of confidence has increased.

Context

Context, the fifth and final component of the Spitzberg and Cupach (1984) model, involves identifying the objective environment and the subjective perceptions that influence how students interact in that environment. The use of case studies is discussed as a way of encouraging students to examine contextual differences and to understand the role perceptions play in understanding context. A cultural artifact exercise that facilitates students' understanding of the culture they are studying is also described.

Case studies. Case studies involving an ethical issue are excellent for helping students become aware of their perceptions of situations and how important context is to those situations. One case study we have used asks students to consider what they would do if they discover that cheating is going on in a class in which they are doing poorly. Students need to deal with two levels of analysis: (a) What is the situation/problem? and (b) What should be done about the situation/problem? Not only are there many different perceptions about what should be done, but there are as many different ways of describing exactly what the situation or problem is.

Students become aware of the different ways of looking at a specific situation from a variety of individual and cultural viewpoints. More important, students can get in touch with their own ways of perceiving and discussing events. Such objective awareness of their own subjective reactions to situations and people can increase students' understanding and interpretation of their communication competence in various contexts.

Cultural artifact exercise. This exercise requires students to bring to class one or two physical objects that signify some aspect of their culture. Students share their objects and ideas about the objects with other students in small groups or with the entire class. For example, in order to introduce the assignment to students, we have brought in such items as McDonald's Big Mac containers or microwavable TV dinners to illustrate the "fast food" syndrome of many Americans who are constantly on the run and prefer to eat quickly rather than enjoy leisurely meals.

This activity allows students and teachers to compare and contrast their cultural "artifacts" and what those artifacts symbolize to them in a nonthreatening manner. By bringing in physical objects, students focus on tangible entities; these serve as concrete visual aids to assist in the explanation of a bit of their culture. The concrete object, then, helps students present more subjective, abstract concepts in the second language and to understand the variations possible within and across cultures.

CONCLUSIONS

In this article, we have used a relational model of communication competence as a starting point for discussing ways of handling communication anxiety in second language classrooms. Although the communication anxiety a native speaker suffers is not identical to that experienced by ESL students, self-perceptions of competence are crucial in the management of anxiety for both groups of students. Thus, the exercises we have suggested for each stage of the competence model acknowledge and work with students' perceptions.

We hope that this article will serve as a catalyst for future work—theoretical and pragmatic—about the relationship among perception, anxiety, and competence. Ultimately, we hope the ideas we have offered here will directly benefit students by helping them to feel increasingly positive about their communication experience. Rather than having students say "I can't," we hope to have students who can deal with their anxieties by working through their feelings, as the student who wrote the following excerpt did:

> We had a awful discussion today. Before the discussion, I was afraid that most of students speak too fast. That was a fact. In the discussion they speak too fast. But I could understand. Because if I could not understand, they speak slowly again. I could understand. I concentrated and tried to understand. So it was hard, but very interesting. And I found out that [my teacher's] voice was the fastest one. I've never hear such fast voice like a machine-gun-fire. But now I know that I'm getting used to American's voice slowly.

NOTES

1. All examples from student journals are taken from two ESL classes—Oral Skills, Level A, and Writing, Level 3, sponsored by the International English Language Institute, Humboldt State University, Arcata, CA, summer 1987.

2. For reasons unrelated to their knowledge of the second language, nonnative speakers may experience—just as some native speakers do—a phenomenon called receiver apprehension, which refers to "the degree to which students are fearful about misinterpreting, adequately processing and/or being unable to psychologically adjust to messages" (Cooper, 1984, p. 254). Very little is known about the causes and treatment of this type of apprehension.

Chapter Twelve

Dealing with Anxiety: Some Practical Activities for Language Learners and Teacher Trainees

David Crookall and Rebecca Oxford   The University of Alabama

INTRODUCTION

This chapter does not attempt to take an academic look at language-learning anxiety. Rather, it proposes a few activities that can be used with learners to help them recognize and deal with that anxiety, as well as some other activities that can be used with teachers in training to encourage them to think for themselves (instead of just reading) about anxiety. A preamble will provide a useful backdrop to the activities presented in the latter part of the article, reminding readers of the importance of attending to learner anxiety, but warning them that anxiety cannot be eliminated completely.

The well-known notion of the language learner's "affective filter" (Krashen, 1982) seems rather too abstract to convey the real sense of anxiety that may arise in some foreign and second language learning situations. The phrase serves, nevertheless, to remind teachers that *negative affect*—commonly manifested as anxiety—is something they should be concerned about. For many learners a mild degree of anxiety can be helpful and stimulating; however, a high level of language-learning anxiety can become debilitating (Brown, 1987). It is a form of serious personal discomfort, and most people simply fail to perform at their best under such constraints.

Severe language-learning anxiety causes other interlocking problems. For example, it lowers students' situational (classroom-related) self-esteem, reduces their confidence in themselves as language learners, strengthens inhibition, lessens willingness to take risks (an essential for learning to communicate in a new language), and decreases the probability of achieving a high degree of language proficiency (Oxford, 1990).

For those of us who have been out of school for a long while and who might have forgotten, here is a forceful reminder of the multiple roots of foreign language-learning anxiety.

In the typical language classroom, learners are often asked to perform in a state of ignorance and dependence which may engender feelings of helplessness. They have to produce unfamiliar sounds in front of an audience. When they do not perform adequately, they may be subjected to comment and correction, sometimes for reasons that are not clear to them. Most of them do not possess the linguistic tools to express their own individuality. In any case, there is usually little opportunity for this, since the interaction is dominated by the teacher. (Littlewood, 1984) .

The second language situation (where someone is trying to learn a language in the community where that language is the main mode of daily communication) generally offers more authentic practice opportunities than does the foreign language environment and might therefore be considered less anxiety-provoking. However, the second language classroom can often engender anxiety that is just as potent as that generated by the foreign language classroom. And outside of the classroom, learners of a second language can face even greater emotional hurdles.

With their limited communicative competence, they [second language learners] may have difficulties in relating to others and presenting their own selves adequately. For example, making casual conversation or expressing spontaneous reactions may be difficult, and attempts to do so may result in misunderstandings and laborious efforts to explain. Unless they have firm confidence in themselves, they may come to feel that they project a silly, boring image, and become withdrawn. Their sense of alienation may be increased by the fact that they are having to re-learn the conventions which surround simple daily events, such as eating in a restaurant or approaching an acquaintance. To use two terms commonly applied to this kind of experience: they may develop a sense of "reduced personality" and experience various degrees of "culture shock." (Littlewood, 1984)

CHANGING CLASSROOM PATTERNS

Although teachers cannot whisk away every atom of learners' anxiety, particularly outside the language classroom, they can do a great deal to help lessen the anxiety of the classroom—usually by making the classroom as friendly and relaxed as possible. Teachers can make a point of being warm and personable, and of rewarding effort, risk-taking, and successful communication.

They can also improve the classroom climate through the use of pair work, small-group work, games, simulations, and structured exercises that alter the communication pattern of the classroom.[1] Instead of the all-too-typical format in which communication occurs mainly with the teacher, who highlights and corrects the embarrassed student's errors in front of onlookers, the pattern becomes one of student-to-student communication, with the emphasis on conveying meaning rather than underscoring mistakes. As the classroom structure and communication patterns change, we can expect debilitating anxiety to lower and students to begin to relax. Learners then usually become more concerned with trying to communicate their viewpoint than with avoiding public humiliation, saving face, or impressing the teacher with the ability to parrot "correct" answers. Encouraged by teachers, students too can make a contribution, such as having realistic expectations and being less competitive. Finally, language departments are able to contribute by altering their priorities and constraints.

If the recommendations above are followed carefully and consistently, then anxiety in the classroom is likely to be minimized, and language-learning efficiency strengthened. However, we do not live in a perfect world. We may have to work under constraints imposed by institutional policies or situations that are difficult to change in a short space of time. For example, the classroom may have chairs bolted to the floor, making group work and moving about difficult.

Parts of an institutional syllabus may require that certain skills be "taught" (and, it is hoped, learned), such as making presentations—a particularly anxiety-producing situation. For example, in many ESL classrooms in the United States, students preparing to enter universities have to learn how to make presentations and cannot get out of it, however much they or the teacher would like to do so. Tests and exams that are little related to classwork can also generate particularly high levels of anxiety.

We may start a new class by pairing up students and being noncritical but even so quickly find that some students' anxiety remains fairly high. Indeed, classroom procedures, such as group work, which we advocate and consider as anxiety-reducing, may actually be quite the contrary for some students, whose only experience has been near-silent listening to frontal teaching and speaking only when spoken to. Changing the classroom structure and communication patterns may sometimes actually increase anxiety in some students.

Students who have been brought up in very formal or authoritarian educational systems may not feel instantly comfortable in classrooms in which they are encouraged to communicate informally with their peers and in which the teacher takes on a facilitating rather than directing role. For example, games and simulations—which often call for being a bit daring or for "hamming it up"—may cause a degree of embarrassment to certain introverts who prefer to hide themselves behind academic rule-learning. Communicative activities, which reveal that there are often many equally correct and divergent answers, may create discomfort for strictly convergent thinkers who believe they can handle only a single right answer.[2] Many students are also used to competing (against their peers or the system, to earn grades), and some may balk at large doses of cooperation and sharing. There are a few who may be confused or thrown off balance by any kind of change or novelty, no matter how benign or even positive.

Students like these, who feel temporarily more anxious because of these changes, are likely to relax with time as they get used to the new routine and atmosphere. Generally speaking, when teachers make the classroom a nonthreatening place where students are not required to do repeated solo performances in front of everyone else, students often respond by relaxing and becoming less anxious.

But what about those learners whose anxiety is not just a temporary response to institutional demands or to changes in classroom procedures and roles? Some people are naturally more anxious than others in any learning situation, or they may need quite a bit of time to settle down to a new class. Moreover, some students are anxious about almost *any* kind of learning situation, or have a generally anxious personality or exhibit various self-esteem problems. Also, teachers may be under pressure or "naturally nervous" and thereby inadvertently stimulate latent anxiety in their students.

Some students may thus, for a variety of reasons, and despite our best efforts, be filled with various kinds of anxiety. No teacher can therefore guarantee that a class will be anxiety-free. There are times when, and circumstances where, we may become aware that anxiety has reached a point when it should be dealt with, perhaps more explicitly than by some of the above-mentioned suggestions.

ADDRESSING ANXIETY DIRECTLY

Whatever the reason for anxiety, it is possible to address the problem in a fairly direct way. Instead of limiting our efforts to creating situations in which we hope anxiety will not rise (e.g., using group work), or to behaving so as to minimize anxiety (e.g., being friendly), we can deal with anxiety directly and explicitly.

This, however, requires that we accept that anxiety does exist, that in some situations and for some students, strong anxiety persists. If we are able to admit to ourselves and to our students that anxiety levels do occasionally rise above a beneficial level, we can then take a stance that, rather than limiting ourselves to trying to avoid dealing with anxiety head-on (implicit, for example, in the "be friendly" stance), actually goes beyond this and deals with anxiety explicitly and openly as a normal human feeling. This is an attitude which considers that both students and teacher can share the problem, and both can deal with it together.

All too often the teacher is cast in some way as an opponent of the student, in some kind of battle to get the student to learn, despite anxiety—or by avoiding situations that may tend to create anxiety. If, instead, teacher and student were to consider themselves in partnership and view themselves as trying together to overcome the problem of anxiety, then neither would see the other as a source of difficulty, and both could work together to deal with the common problem. After all, it is in the interests of both students and teacher that anxiety be kept at relatively benign levels. Thus, instead of the teacher saying, "I should do this, otherwise my students will get anxious," the teacher could say, "If the students and I feel anxiety is a little too high, perhaps we could stop for a while and together see what its causes are and how we may reduce it."

This kind of practice properly falls within the realm of learner training—a concept that has been gaining ground fairly recently. Thus far not a great deal has been written on the topic, but we believe that it has much to offer our students. Basically, the philosophy behind learner training can be summed up as follows. We teachers are expected to follow various courses in order to train as teachers. Learners, on the other hand, are somehow expected, willy-nilly, to learn without receiving any training in that pursuit. If training teachers to teach is important, how much more important is it to train learners to learn—after all, it is precisely the act of learning that we teachers wish our student to accomplish.

> Learner training aims to help learners consider the factors that affect their learning. . . . It focuses their attention on the process of learning so that the emphasis is on *how* to learn rather than on *what* to learn. (Ellis & Sinclair, 1989; emphasis in the original)

In more concrete terms

> We could very profitably spend time on sensitizing students to (some of) the methodological, linguistic and learning aspects of their course, on sharing with them some of our problems as teachers, and inviting them to express freely their problems as learners, on making them aware that, although we cannot learn the language for them, their learning problems are also our problems. . . . [N]ine hours of language learning proper and one hour of learner training may be better than a ten-hour diet of "pure" language learning. (Crookall, 1983)

One of the aims of learner training is to help learners "discover the learning strategies that suit them best so that they may become more effective learners [and] take on more responsibility for their own learning" (Ellis & Sinclair, 1989). Strategy training is thus an important part of learner training.³ And a broad conception of learner training should also include dealing with anxiety.

Dealing with anxiety in an explicit and purposeful way is part of true learner training. If we spend some of our class time not on actually teaching the language directly but rather on dealing directly with the anxiety that students may be feeling, then the time spent on language learning will be more effective. By helping students to deal with anxiety, we are training them to be better learners. It is important for teachers to provide learners—especially language learners—with the opportunity for active involvement in both the learning of the language and in the learning process—something that years of formal schooling may have dampened or even crushed.

ACTIVITIES

The activities described below are all designed to be used to help students and teacher to deal with anxiety. A word of warning, however, is in order. The activities are not a form of (professional) psychotherapy or psychodrama. They are classroom vehicles for ordinary human beings to talk about ordinary everyday anxiety problems that naturally arise in a variety of language-learning situations. The following quote, from Maley and Duff (1982), in reference to their drama techniques, is fully applicable to our activities presented below.

> . . . dramatic activities are not a substitute for the psychoanalyst's couch. They are not sessions of self-liberation (complexes and hang-ups cannot be cured through them). (p. 6)

In the same way, the anxiety-reducing activities outlined below cannot solve any sort of deep-seated or generalized personality problem. They will, however, be useful to teachers and students who simply want to understand and reduce the usual sort of overanxious feelings that sometimes tend to arise in language-learning situations.

The activities have been divided into those that can be used with language learners themselves, and those that can be used by supervisors with teachers in training (or, for that matter, by fully trained teachers who want to look at their own anxieties). Some learner activities can be adapted for teacher training (as seen below)—and vice versa, depending on your kind of student group. In mono-lingual classes, especially the lower levels (which may be those where anxiety is greatest), the activities can be carried out in the students' native language.

Many of the activities are in the form of games and simulations, whose value and power have been explored elsewhere (Crookall & Saunders, 1989; Crookall & Oxford, 1990). We have kept the notes on each activity to a strict minimum, for reasons of space, but they should enable you, as supervisors or teachers, to create your own full-blown materials.

Activities for Learner Training

Agony column. Tell students that they are going to do a small editorial simulation, in which they will take on three roles, one in each stage of the simulation: (1) themselves as language learners, (2) an "Agony Aunt" (such as Abby, Ann Landers, or Heloise)⁴ in a magazine or newspaper, and (3) advisors/counselors.

For stage 1 (expressing anxiety), ask students individually to write a letter to the Agony

Aunt of an imaginary language-learning magazine for students. The letter should not be too long (say, 200 words), but each student should explain a particularly difficult thing they find in language learning. It can be anything, from the problem of making mistakes to not liking the teacher. (The letter should end by asking for advice.) You might give students the option of your not looking at their agony letters except if they want you to do so, and that only their fellow students will see the letters. Students should put their names on the letter so that they can get the reply back at the end of stage 2. Alternatively, each student can be given a number, and the letters referred to by that number.

For stage 2 (advising on others' anxieties), ask students to group together in threes or fours. Collect the letters written in stage 1, and then distribute them so that each group gets letters written by people from outside the group. Students now discuss each of the three or four letters carefully. Students consider what sort of reply they will make, and then write out their response. At this point students should begin to realize that they are not alone in experiencing anxiety, and this will be reassuring. An additional step in this stage might be for the letter to be sent on (without the first replies) to a second group to receive a second reply.

In stage 3 (discussing one's own anxiety), the letters are handed back to their original authors, accompanied by the replies. At this point there may be a variety of reactions to the replies. Some students will find them helpful, while others may feel they are unsatisfactory. In either case, discussions should now center on students' own anxieties, their reactions to the replies received and the suitability and soundness of the advice given. Students who find the replies helpful should be encouraged to build on this and suggest additional ideas of self-advice. Unsatisfied students should be asked how they would have responded to such a letter (i.e., what advice they would give for their own anxiety). In these discussions, students should also be encouraged to seek advice from their colleagues in the group.

Stage 4 would consist of (1) a debriefing session, in which one representative from each of the small groups meets in a larger group, and (2) a whole-class feedback session chaired by the teacher.

Variation.   The teacher can become Agony Aunt during the course. Here students write short letters to the teacher about learning problems in general, or about anxiety in particular. The teacher spends a little time individually with the student talking about the problem or writing back.[5]

Ghost avengers.   In this activity students are told something like the following: *Imagine that some years ago you passed away from this world and that you have now become a member of the Association for Worldly Experience (AWE), which has a Special Language Learners' User Group (SLLUG). One of the main aims of AWE is to encourage and help its members to go back to earth regularly to haunt acquaintances who have caused anxiety to its members while they were earth dwellers.*

The SLLUG, of which you are an active member, has decided to have a brainstorming session to decide what members can do to get revenge on their earth-bound colleagues when you make your next trip there at the next solstice. The brainstorming session is in three stages. Each stage will be explained as we come to it.

In the first stage, you work on your own and write brief notes, as fast as you can, on all the things you would like to do to your past earthly language teachers. For example, insist that they speak with a funny accent to their colleagues, lose their pay if they don't get a good grade on a professional exam, or a variety of more dire events than these.

For the next stage, you work in small groups of three or four. Here you take turns—each person reading out just one of his or her avenging actions. After each person reads out the proposed action, you can add variations of your own, or you may think of new things. Make a note of these.

For the third stage, you should go back to some of the more interesting proposed actions and ask the person to explain why he or she wanted to take that action. When you have heard the explanation, and perhaps asked for clarification, you may wish to provide feedback and comment on how you interpret things.

In your discussions, think about how the proposed action reflects your own experience. Remember, this should be a fun game, but questions about the moral suitability of a particular proposed action can also be discussed, especially if it reflects your real experience in learning a language.

Mistakes panel. The object of this game is to encourage students to take an amusing look at errors and to realize that they are not taboo—and that they can contribute to learning. Students work in groups of three or four. Ask them to collect mistakes over a few classes, or else to think up some mistakes with examples. These are written on cards—one set of cards (each containing the same series of mistakes) needs to be made for each group. Each mistake carries a unique identification number (from one to the total number of mistakes).

Then each group becomes a competition panel, assessing the mistakes of the other groups. Here the panel is asked to rate each mistake on a number of criteria, awarding one to three points for each criterion. The criteria might be: amusement (how funny they are), creativity (how original they are, especially if students make up mistakes), logic (how reasonable is the mistake in terms of the language, e.g., saying "comed" instead of "came"), communicative intelligibility (how well can one still understand the message, despite the error—often a context will be needed for this), and learning contribution (how much can be learned from this error). A table can be drawn up, such as Table 1, and points totalled.

The points from each panel for each mistake are then added together, to make a grand total. For example, ratings of 10, 8, 12, 7, (for mistake 14, given by groups 2 to 5) produce a total of 39. The winning mistake can then be calculated.

If you wanted to have group winners, the total of all the totals for each of the mistakes offered by a group can be calculated, and the group with the highest score wins. For example, Group 4 gets totals of 39, 41, and 35 for its three mistakes, making a grand group total of 115. If this is done, the fun element should probably be emphasized and the competition played down.

Discussions among students and between students and teacher during the panel evaluations can help students learn to be at ease with errors. In this game the best mistakes are rewarded!

Table 1
MISTAKE RATINGS

Mistake No.	Amusement	Creativity	Logical	Intelligibility	Learning	Total
1	2	3	1	1	3	10
2	1	1	2	3	1	8
3	2	2	2	2	1	9
etc.						

Anxious photos.   Give students a series of photos or pictograms depicting a wide range of situations in which they use or learn the language, e.g., at a railway station; with a host family; in class all students facing the teacher; small groups in class. Each student groups the photos into sets (criteria to be chosen by learners) reflecting his or her feelings about the anxieties that arise in those situations. Each student then invites one or two colleagues to his or her table to explain why they have put the photos in those combinations. The visiting student(s) should help by asking questions about the anxiety and why it arises. They then move to the next colleague's photo groupings, and do the same.

After this, each student returns to his or her grouping and silently brainstorms the different ways in which the student has dealt with his or her own anxiety, and the ways in which the student thinks his or her colleague(s) might deal with anxiety. They then meet again. Finally, they construct a table, with the situations down the side and the anxiety reducing strategies across the top. They then put a cross in the intersecting columns and rows that are valid for them.

You may have to help students formulate (and provide short names for) some of the anxiety-reducing strategies. They should also distinguish between situations over which they have some control, and those over which they have little.

Reversed accents.   In a monolingual class, students can be asked to speak to each other in their mother tongue, but imitating the accent of someone from the target language speaking their mother tongue. This can be amusing and effective and requires only minutes if done at the start of several classes.

Other activities.   Keeping a diary of feelings about language learning often helps learners to discover sources of anxiety and to find ways of coming to grips with it. In class, students (if they agree freely to do so) might share their thoughts, and thus get some peer support and ideas from others. An emotional checklist is also useful, as is positive self-talk to counter anxiety.[6]

Activities for Teacher Training

Trigger pictures.   Photos or short video clips showing various types of anxiety are needed. Trainees work in pairs or threes. Their first task is to identify the type and source of anxiety depicted in the picture or video clip. They pool their thoughts and discuss their ideas. The second task is to propose two or three possible "remedies" for each of the situations. The entire class then discusses.

Agony column.   For details of this activity, see the previous learners' section. Used in teacher training, Agony Column can be used to look either at learner anxiety or at teacher anxiety (i.e., the anxieties teachers themselves have, and which may affect learner anxieties).

If Agony Column is run for the purpose of examining learner anxiety, you will need a series of letters written to a language-learning Agony Aunt. These may be made up, but better still they can be obtained by asking students to write such a letter as part of their writing course or their learner training (as in the learners' section above). Trainees work singly, and write their several replies to the authors of each of the letters. In pairs or threes, trainees discuss each others' answers. If you wish to use the exercise for getting teachers to examine their own teacher/teaching anxieties, then the game can be run in much the same way as described above for students.

Ghost avengers. This can be done in exactly the same way as described under the learners' section. In addition, as a follow-up activity, some real notes (on proposed actions) from a previous learner session can be used for a discussion. If learners are willing to be videotaped while playing Ghost Avengers, then this will also provide food for thought for the teacher-training session.

Linguethics. Trainees are told the following. You are members of a new Board of Ethics in Language Teaching (BELT) for your area (class, school, locality, country, world—you choose). You have been asked to draw up a new code of ethics, to be called the User Priorities (UP). The part you are working on just now is designed to curb actions and behaviors on the part of teachers, students, and administrators that seriously increase anxiety for language learners. Again, working individually, then in small groups, followed by whole-class feedback, is a good way of organizing this activity. In addition, if you wanted to concentrate on more specific elements, settings, or attitudes, role profiles may be written.

Correction decisions. In this activity, trainees are asked to discuss specific errors and mistakes made by learners. After a short discussion on the differences between error and mistake, the trainees are provided with a dozen or so typical examples of student errors/mistakes. The types of errors/mistakes should range all the way from slips of the tongue, through mistakes due to inattention as well as grammar errors, to serious breakdowns in communication. The mistakes/errors can be written on paper and/or provided on audiotape or videotape. Make a copy of Table 2 on a large sheet of paper, remembering that columns should be much longer and columns D to F should be the widest. Trainees fill in their individual tables, then in groups discuss issues in order to come to a consensus on filling in a group table. In a teacher-led plenary feedback session, groups then compare their tables.

Table 2
MISTAKE/ERROR EVALUATION

A Mistake or error	B Type of mistake or error	C Importance of error (e.g., for communication)	D Would you do anything about it? (Yes/No)	E Why do you think something needs to be done?	F What options exist for making amends (i.e., correcting)?	G What are the anxiety consequences of those options

CONCLUSIONS

We hope that you will use some of the above activities in your classroom, that you will adapt them and that they will inspire you to think of and develop others. Once you have tried some of the activities, you might be able to think of ways to get students to develop new activities. This would not only be an enjoyable and worthwhile exercise, language-wise, for them, but it is after all the learners who know directly what anxiety is all about. In addition to teaching learners, teachers should also let learners teach teachers to better teach learners—or rather, teachers should allow learners to help teachers learn how to better help learners learn!

In relation to anxiety, this means that we should strive to create learning conditions that will keep anxiety at reasonably low levels. It also means that we should encourage our learners to discuss anxiety openly and find creative ways of softening it. Only if anxiety is kept in check can language learners hope to reach their true potential.

NOTES

1. For discussions on this, see, e.g., Di Pietro (1987), Gaies (1985), Jones (1982), and Ur (1981). For further discussion and an annotated bibliography on simulation/gaming in language learning, see Crookall and Oxford (1990).

2. See Christopher and Smith (1990) for a discussion on convergent/divergent approaches. See Brown (1987) and Erhman and Oxford (1990) for discussions on extrovert/introvert differences in language learning.

3. Discussions on the teaching of learning strategies will be found in Chamot and Kupper (1989), Cohen (1990), Oxford (1990), and Wenden and Rubin (1986).

4. The term "Agony Aunt" may be considered by some as a little sexist, but it is the standard term in British English for this, and does refer concisely to this type of person (given the differential sex roles built into today's social institutions). Teachers may wish to adopt another term for use with their students, e.g., "Agony Uncle"—but isn't that sexist too?

5. A fuller discussion on the use of this activity will be found in Crookall (1990).

6. For discussions on the use of diaries (journals), see, e.g., Bailey (1983), Rubin (1981), and Schumann and Schumann (1977). For other activities, mainly related to language skills; see Ellis and Sinclair (1989); for other activities, related both to anxiety reduction and to learner strategies, see Oxford (1990). The authors of this article are compiling a compendium of activities for understanding and reducing anxiety and would be interested in hearing from you.

Part Six

Program Strategies: Institutional Responses to Language Anxiety

In Part Five, suggestions for coping with language anxiety on the classroom level were offered, but the task of providing learners with a nonthreatening language learning environment does not rest exclusively with teachers and students. In this section we consider ways that language programs may address the problem of language anxiety. Specifically, the papers consider: What can programs do to lessen language anxiety? How can students be better prepared to undertake language study? How can students be supported in their language learning efforts?

Campbell and Ortiz describe a workshop designed to prepare students for language learning; workshop leaders present effective language-learning strategies and dispel potentially harmful misconceptions about the language-learning process. The positive responses of students and instructors to the workshop suggest that students who are prepared to cope with the intellectual and emotional demands of language learning will be better and more relaxed learners, thus adding additional support for the concept of learner training proposed earlier by Crookall and Oxford.

In the second paper, Powell describes a number of approaches including support groups, informational talks, and strategy training to help students be more comfortable and effective in their language classes. In some cases, these strategies can be implemented in individual classrooms, but many—especially curricular modifications—must originate on the program level. In addition, Powell stresses the importance of developing positive and productive attitudes toward language learning. In the American context, where second-language learning is not commonplace, many students undertake language study with little confidence in their eventual success.

The papers in this section remind us that the safe and comfortable environment created by an individual teacher may well be counteracted by program expectations and requirements. Thus, any comprehensive approach to language anxiety must reach beyond the classroom to the institution and perhaps ultimately to society at large.

Chapter Thirteen

Helping Students Overcome Foreign Language Anxiety: A Foreign Language Anxiety Workshop

Christine M. Campbell   Defense Language Institute
and José A. Ortiz   Presidio of Monterey, California

INTRODUCTION

In varying degrees, foreign-language teachers have perceived anxiety reactions in their students. Although a number of studies in educational psychology have shown that some degree of anxiety can actually promote learning (Beeman, Martin, & Meyers, 1972; Spielberger, 1966a; Verma & Nijhawan, 1976), the same studies also demonstrate that too much anxiety can hinder academic performance at specific stages in the learning process and with certain types of activities.

Debilitating anxiety—the anxiety that impedes successful learning—has been the focus of a number of studies in math education (Richardson & Suinn, 1973; Betz, 1978; Hendel & Davis, 1978; Sepie & Keeling, 1978) and in science education (Torrance, 1963; Alvaro, 1978). In the 1970s, educators in these fields began to investigate instructional strategies to combat "math anxiety" and "science anxiety." Math/science anxiety workshops and clinics have been highly successful in reducing debilitating anxiety in participants. This paper describes a workshop designed to help students in an intensive foreign language program cope with "foreign language anxiety."

MATH AND SCIENCE ANXIETY WORKSHOPS AND CLINICS

Debilitating anxiety similar to that which foreign language teachers frequently see in their students has also been reported in other academic disciplines. In 1978, Sells, a California sociologist, reported her startling findings on the mathematics background of college freshmen at the University of California, Berkeley. She found that 57% of the males had taken four years of high school math, while only 8% of the females had done so. At Berkeley at that time, entering freshmen had to have four years of high school math in order to take the calculus sequence that formed a part of the core curriculum in subjects like chemistry, physics, intermediate statistics, and economics. Thus, 92% of the female students were effectively excluded from 10 of 12 colleges at Berkeley and 22 of 44 major fields of study.

Sells' report led to Tobias' (1978) well-known book *Overcoming Math Anxiety*, which discussed the nature of math anxiety, the relationship between gender and mathematics ability, and ways to overcome math anxiety. Tobias hoped "to convince women and men that their fear of mathematics is the result and not the cause of their negative experiences with mathematics, and to encourage them to give themselves one more chance" (p. 15). As a result of Tobias' work, a number of programs devoted to controlling math anxiety began to appear across the country.

These math anxiety workshops and clinics served as a model for later programs in other academic disciplines. The workshops and clinics included a number of innovative approaches including study skills presentations and math autobiographies and diaries. Although math anxiety workshops and clinics tend to be similar in format, some are more structured than others, and a variety of activities is offered. At Wesleyan University, Donady and Smith's Math Clinic begins with the sharing of math autobiographies and proceeds without a rigid schedule. The students talk about the reasons why they decided to overcome their handicap and eventually attempt mathematics problems. At the University of Minnesota's program for math-anxious people, Davis includes an interview, the tracking of subjects into one of three different math classes, and weekly support group sessions. In these sessions, students discuss their math anxiety, receive assertiveness training, and participate in desensitization exercises. At Mind over Math in New York City, Kogelman and Warren, two mathematicians, have a somewhat different approach to the problem of math anxiety; instead of helping students learn how to minimize math anxiety itself, they center on avoidance behaviors in general and include no mathematics whatsoever (Tobias, 1978).

Tobias (1978) also provides a step-by-step plan of a "math therapy" (p. 249) self-help program:

1. See an academic counselor or math anxiety clinic leader. She may ask you to take a math anxiety test and/or participate in an interview designed to produce your mathematics autobiography;

2. Attend a math anxiety clinic or course;

3. "[P]ractice math by increasing . . . awareness of numbers and playing with their relationships" (p. 263) through training in spatial skills, number play, and puzzle-solving;

4. Register for a math course such as algebra review;

5. Continue to do math exercises on one's own and to take math classes.[1]

The first Science Anxiety Clinic was conducted at Loyola University in 1976. Led by Mallow (1981), a science professor, and Grace, a Counseling Center staff psychologist, the clinic lasted seven weeks, beginning early in the semester and ending just before final exams. Today, the clinic is open to any student on a volunteer basis and consists of a series of 90-minute sessions in which the same small group of students discuss the roots of their science anxiety, learn science study skills, reflect on their self-image, and do relaxation and desensitization exercises. Alvaro (1978) found that the Science Anxiety Clinic significantly reduced the anxiety levels of almost all the participants when compared with a "waiting-list" control group.

One important premise of the anxiety workshops and clinics is a belief that students must develop a positive attitude toward the discipline in question. For example, Mallow (1981) maintains in *Science Anxiety: The Fear of Science and How to Overcome It:*

> From early childhood, most of us are taught that we cannot grasp science. That's for some-one else: the brain, the oddball, the misfit. As soon as we encounter science in school, we learn to tell one another that it is too difficult for us. We absorb the heritage of science anxi-ety even as we study the concepts of science. (p. 1)

The effect of this anxiety is alarming: It can act as a career filter that operates against all stu-dents, but most particularly against women and black and Hispanic minorities. As the per-centage of these groups in the scientific and quasi-scientific professions is relatively low, Mallow hypothesizes that society gives girls, black youth, and Hispanic youth both covert and overt messages that they cannot be successful science learners. According to Mallow (1981), some black and Hispanic students in his Science Anxiety Clinic have related that they were actually told by teachers, "You people can't do science" (p. 5). Mallow asserts: "If the first dogma of a science-anxious society is 'almost nobody can do science,' then the second is 'and certainly women and disadvantaged minorities can't' " (p. 5). In a similar vein, Tobias (1978) maintains that math anxiety has serious socioeconomic ramifications for society as a whole. Tobias insists: "[M]ath avoidance is extremely limiting for people at all levels of work. Com-petence in math is, as Sells puts it, truly a vocational filter" (p. 29).

THE FOREIGN LANGUAGE ANXIETY WORKSHOP AT THE DEFENSE LANGUAGE INSTITUTE

In 1987, the authors created a 3-hour (now 4-hour) Foreign Language Anxiety Workshop that all beginning students in the departments of German, Korean, Spanish, and Russian at the Defense Language Institute (DLI), San Francisco branch, attended before beginning lan-guage study.[2] Over a 12-month period, more than 300 students participated in the workshop. The workshop, which is not language specific, included students from one or more of the four languages. It attempted to prepare students psychologically for the experience of learning a foreign language in an intensive program by dispelling common myths about foreign lan-guage learning and by developing foreign language study skills. In addition to benefiting stu-dents in an intensive foreign language course, the workshop helped students develop a positive attitude toward foreign language study in any competitive environment in which lan-guage study is required. The workshop included the following activities:

1. An attitudinal survey constructed by the authors entitled *Survey of Attitudes Specific to the Foreign Language Classroom (SASFLC)* (Campbell & Ortiz, 1986) to assess students' anxiety levels pre- and post-workshop and to monitor student reactions throughout the language course (see Appendix A)[3]. The survey, which uses a 5-point Likert Scale rang-ing from 1 = strongly agree to 5 = strongly disagree, contains 11 items about foreign language anxiety and 5 items about the negative clichés associated with foreign language study, for example, "It is necessary to have a special aptitude [i.e., an inborn talent] in

order to learn a foreign language well." The *SASFLC* was distributed four times during the 6-month (Spanish), 8-month (German), or 10-month (Korean, Russian) program to monitor changes in student anxiety levels.

2. A discussion of a questionnaire based on Paul Pimsleur's (1980) renowned text *How to Learn a Foreign Language*. The questionnaire is entitled "The Myths and the Realities of Foreign Language Learning."

3. Information on learning strategies specific to foreign language study.

4. Exercises designed to sensitize participants to the importance of developing self-confidence, trust in the teacher, and a sense of camaraderie with the other students to make the learning of a foreign language an enjoyable experience.

5. An exercise in code deciphering aimed at teaching students how to cope with frustration in their learning.

6. A discussion of the characteristics of the ideal foreign language learner.

To help foreign language professionals who may be interested in offering their own anxiety workshops, the following activity descriptions are provided.

Icebreaker

The workshop begins with an icebreaker exercise, a game entitled "What I Want to Be When I Grow Up," which lasts 15 minutes. (The workshop leader may substitute any exercise designed to introduce people to one another in a nonthreatening way.) The students and teacher sit in a circle. The game helps students learn the names of the other students and thus facilitates verbal interaction during the group discussions, which are so critical to the success of the workshop. The workshop leader can begin by saying, "We are going to begin with a mnemonic game that will help you to learn the other students' names in record time. I will start by describing what I want to be when I grow up. When I grow up I want to be a. . . ." Going clockwise, one student after another makes a statement. After each student has made a statement, the workshop leader says to one of the students, "You are [name] and you want to be a [occupation or profession] when you grow up." With the teacher's encouragement, the other students verify whether or not they have remembered the names of the other students.

The Myths and the Realities of Foreign Language Learning

The second exercise, which lasts 60 minutes, includes a questionnaire entitled "The Myths and the Realities of Foreign Language Learning" followed by a discussion (see Appendix B). The questionnaire is based on Pimsleur's well-known text *How to Learn a Foreign Language* (1980) and examines a number of popular notions, both negative and positive, about the study of a foreign language. Students spend 10 minutes reading the questionnaire and answering the questions. Discussion follows, with the workshop leader acting as a facilitator. Although the workshop leader knows the correct responses, he or she gives the group the answer only after the group has thoroughly discussed the item. The workshop leader listens and guides the session.

Building Confidence, Trust, and Camaraderie

The third exercise, scheduled for 45 minutes, is designed to trigger class discussion in several areas: confidence in oneself, trust in the teacher, and class camaraderie. Here, confidence in oneself refers to the "can do," risk-taking attitude toward foreign language study that good language learners exhibit. Trust refers to the confidence students must have in their teacher, especially in a proficiency-oriented course that may differ greatly from their previous foreign language courses. A spirit of camaraderie among students is crucial in a foreign language classroom that promotes communicative activities in pairs and groups.

The workshop leader divides the class into groups of three and assigns one student from each trio as the "guide." The guide is asked to step outside the classroom and is given two blindfolds and written instructions for the exercise. The instructions are: "You are the guide for the other members of your group. You are to choose an itinerary for a 15-minute walk, meet with the other members, blindfold them, and guide them through the itinerary." When the groups return from their excursions, they discuss their reactions to the exercise. If the students fail to relate their walk to their upcoming foreign language study, the workshop leader suggests that they consider how the two might be similar.

Foreign Language Learning Strategies

The fourth exercise, which lasts 30 minutes, involves group discussion of a handout entitled "Foreign Language Learning Strategies" (Appendix C). During this time, workshop participants share with the class any foreign language learning strategies that they may have used and learn about others. The workshop leader provides a brief overview of the following list of strategies:

1. deduction based on observation
2. use of simple vs. complicated expression
3. use of context clues
4. risk-taking
5. brainstorming
6. cognate guessing
7. gist comprehension
8. clarifying meaning
9. circumlocution
10. use of idiomatic set phrases
11. negotiating meaning
12. paraphrasing and the use of fillers
13. dealing with uncertainty
14. topic expansion and the use of transitions
15. ability to differentiate between formal and informal expression
16. problem solving in groups
17. decision making.

Code Deciphering: Dealing with Frustration in the Foreign Language Classroom

The fifth exercise lasts 30 minutes and includes a code-identification game called "Crossed and Parallel," which helps students learn to deal with frustration related to foreign language learning. Before beginning the exercise, the workshop leader takes one student aside and tells him or her the code: In the exercise, the students will pass two pencils around the room, saying, "I pass them [the pencils] crossed" or "I pass them parallel." Although everyone will think that the words "crossed" and "parallel" refer to the pencils, they, in fact, refer to the position of the legs of the person who is passing the pencils.

The exercise begins with the workshop leader passing two pencils to the student next to her who knows the code. The student responds, "I received them crossed [or parallel, depending on the position of the workshop leader's legs] and I pass them crossed" [or parallel, depending on the position of the legs of the student who is passing the pencils on to the third person]. If the student does not know the code, he or she will most likely rely on the position of the pencils and state, "I received them . . . and I pass them. . . ." The workshop leader will then correct the student by making the correct observation: "No, you received them . . . and you passed them. . . . The students pass the pencils from one to another around the circle. Slowly, the participants discover the secret code, which they are told not to reveal to the others. Frustration builds for those who do not guess the code, as more and more students learn it. After all of the participants guess the code, students discuss their reactions with the workshop leader and relate the experience to learning a new code, namely the foreign language that they will soon study.

The Ideal Language Learner

The sixth exercise also lasts 30 minutes and involves group discussion of a handout entitled "The Ideal Language Learner" (Appendix D). Students spend 5 minutes studying a list of 20 behavioral characteristics before choosing the five that a good foreign language learner might exhibit. Although the participants do not know, all 20 characteristics promote successful foreign language learning. Group discussion follows.

The workshop helps the individual student cope with what he or she may perceive as a harrowing experience—learning a foreign language; it also acts as an icebreaker for the class as a whole as it slowly transforms a disparate group of individuals—who will be sharing both classrooms and housing for six months or more at DLI—into a cohesive community of language learners. As one professor who tried the workshop at his own university commented: "The workshop was really an exceptionally rewarding experience. There is a rare closeness among class members. There is some sort of a group-adhesion syndrome, as if there is a confidence that as long as an individual can cling to the class as a whole—not get too far from the others—the entire body will float the individual along with it" (T. Critchfield, personal communication, 4 September 1988).

The reactions of workshop participants to the workshop are similar to those of the professor. For example, after the workshop, many participants approach the workshop leaders to offer positive feedback about the workshop and to give personal testimony about bad experiences with foreign language study in the past. As one student revealed: "I now realize, for the first time, that I am not a weirdo or a wimp for being so nervous about studying a foreign language." Another exclaimed: "I am now ready to hit the course hard! I now know that I can do it!"

DISCUSSION

Evidence is increasing that significant numbers of post-secondary students are susceptible to debilitating foreign language anxiety. Horwitz, Horwitz, and Cope (1986, this volume) and Campbell and Ortiz (1988) found alarming levels of anxiety in post-secondary students enrolled in foreign language courses in competitive environments. According to these studies, we can estimate that anywhere from one-quarter to one-half of students in our institutions of higher education experience debilitating anxiety.

The percentages suggest that debilitating anxiety in the foreign language classroom is a concrete problem that merits the serious attention of foreign language educators. The anxiety workshops conducted at DLI, San Francisco, in 1987 and 1988 consistently received positive feedback from students. The previously mentioned professor who conducted a Foreign Language Anxiety Workshop at his university enthusiastically recommends it because of the exceptional camaraderie that it promotes among students. He asserts: "[There is] good humor and trust among members of the class as well as the lack of formal distance between students and instructor. Such is not unusual in my classes but [this] is a very, very early phenomenon, and one that I believe will result in a lower level of classroom frustration and consequent higher rate of student survival in the class" (T. Critchfield, personal communication, 4 September 1988).

The authors are convinced that further research will demonstrate the merit of the workshop as a viable tool for reducing foreign language anxiety. Anxiety workshops or clinics, which have been successfully implemented in the fields of math and science education since the 1970s, can help foreign language students cope with foreign language anxiety. Participant reaction compels us to continue this promising approach to helping anxious students. As the percentages in the surveys mentioned above demand, we educators must search out techniques and methods to help those students afflicted with debilitating foreign language anxiety become successful language learners. We cannot ignore our students who suffer from it.

NOTES

1. An excellent self-help exercise book in basic math is Hackworth's (1985) *Math Anxiety Reduction*.

2. DLI, San Francisco operations were transferred to DLI, Monterey, in 1988. The authors intend to continue their workshop activity at the Monterey site.

3. For an in-depth report of the study that attempted to determine workshop effect, see the 1988 article by Campbell and Ortiz, "Dispelling students' fears and misconceptions about foreign language study: The foreign language anxiety workshop at the Defense Language Institute," in T. B. Fryer and F. Medley, Jr., (Eds.), *New Challenges and Opportunities: Dimension—Languages '87* (pp. 29–40), published by the Southern Conference on Language Teaching, Columbia, South Carolina.

APPENDIX A

[For office use: WS— *Y/N*]
Course#_____Survey#_____1_____Date_____SS#_____Age_____
Location _____

SURVEY OF ATTITUDES SPECIFIC TO THE FOREIGN LANGUAGE CLASSROOM (SASFLC)

Please answer parts I and II below honestly and carefully. As the results will be used to better the current foreign language curriculum, it is very important that you spend time thinking about each answer. Your answers are anonymous.

I. Experience with the foreign language

1. Were any of your immediate family members (father, mother, brothers, or sisters) born in a foreign country? _____

   Which one(s)?   Where?

   _____   _____
   _____   _____
   _____   _____

2. Were you born in a foreign country? _____
   Where? _____

3. Do any of your immediate family members speak a foreign language *fluently* (*not* slightly)? _____

   Which family member(s)?   Which language(s)?

   _____   _____
   _____   _____

4. Do you speak a foreign language *fluently* (*not* slightly)? _____

   Which one(s)?   Did you learn it at home or in school?

   _____   _____
   _____   _____
   _____   _____

5. Below, fill in the number of years that you studied the foreign language(s) at school. *First, identify the language; then, place the number of years.*

	First foreign language (FL)	Second FL	Third FL
elementary school (grades 1–6)	_____	_____	_____
junior high school (grades 7–9)	_____	_____	_____
high school (grades 10–12)	_____	_____	_____
college	Number of semesters of the first FL	Second FL	Third FL
	_____	_____	_____

II. Attitudes Specific to the Foreign Language Classroom

Please respond to the statements below using the following scale:

1. strongly agree
2. agree
3. undecided
4. disagree
5. strongly disagree

Once again, please answer honestly and carefully. Spend time thinking about each answer. Your answers are anonymous.

1. It is necessary to have a special aptitude (i.e., an inborn talent) in order to learn a foreign language well.
   1. 2. 3. 4. 5.

2. It is necessary to have a special intelligence (i.e., a higher I.Q.) in order to learn a foreign language well.
   1. 2. 3. 4. 5.

3. It is necessary to have a special "ear" in order to learn a foreign language well.
   1. 2. 3. 4. 5.

4. I become anxious when I have to speak in a foreign language in a classroom setting.
   1. 2. 3. 4. 5.

5. I feel silly when I have to speak in a foreign language in a classroom setting.
   1. 2. 3. 4. 5.

6. I become anxious when I am being spoken to in a foreign language in a classroom setting.
   1. 2. 3. 4. 5.

7. I become anxious when I am asked to write in a foreign language in the classroom setting.
   1. 2. 3. 4. 5.

8. I become anxious when I have to read in a foreign language in a classroom setting.
   1. 2. 3. 4. 5.

9. I fear failing this course.
   1. 2. 3. 4. 5.

10. I fear receiving a low final grade (D or below) in this course.
    1. 2. 3. 4. 5.

11. I fear making a mistake when I speak in a foreign language in a classroom setting.
    1. 2. 3. 4. 5.

12. I fear not understanding what the teacher is saying in a foreign language when I am in a foreign language classroom.
    1. 2. 3. 4. 5.

13. I fear making a mistake in writing in a foreign language in a classroom setting.
    1. 2. 3. 4. 5.

14. I fear making a mistake in reading in a foreign language in a classroom setting.
    1. 2. 3. 4. 5.

Answer No. 15 only if you are a high school graduate:

15. I think that the standard foreign language high school course is more difficult than the standard "verbally oriented" high school course such as History.
1. 2. 3. 4. 5.

Answer No. 16 only if you are a high school graduate:

16. I think that the standard foreign language high school course is more difficult than the standard "numerically oriented" high school course such as Algebra I.
1. 2. 3. 4. 5.

APPENDIX B

LEARNING A FOREIGN LANGUAGE: THE MYTHS AND THE REALITY

1. We all accept as a principle that there is a correlation between individual intelligence and the degree of success attainable in a foreign language course. In my opinion, the percentage attributable to personal intelligence in successful language learning should be approximately:
   a. 80%
   b. 65%
   c. 50%
   d. 16%

2. It is widely believed that musical ability accounts for a certain percentage of the ability needed to learn a foreign language. I think that the percentage should be approximately:
   a. 25%
   b. 10%
   c. 75%
   d. 35%

3. One of the following items poses more of a learning challenge in language learning than the other two. The most difficult item is:
   a. vocabulary
   b. pronunciation
   c. grammar

4. The following four statements are about grammar. Only one of them is true. Circle the true statement.
   a. Even the most "primitive" of peoples possess a language with a grammar that is systematic, internally consistent, and well suited to their life needs.
   b. The grammar needed to become reasonably competent in the foreign language is unlimited in its scope and complexity.
   c. In order to learn a foreign language, the grammatical rules of the foreign language must be memorized.
   d. The grammatical systems of all languages are equally difficult to learn regardless of the learners' native language, i.e., An Englishman/woman or an American will have as much difficulty in learning Spanish as Russian.

5. The "basic" command* of a language requires that the speaker know at least:
   a. 10,000 words
   b. 6,000 words
   c. 1,500 words
   d. 400 words

6. Really fluent speakers† need to know approximately:
   a. 5,000 words
   b. 30,000 words
   c. 15,000 words
   d. 8,000 words

7. Read the list of languages below and circle the two that will pose the least amount of work for an English speaker to learn:
   a. Finnish
   b. Italian
   c. Arabic
   d. Korean
   e. German
   f. Greek

8. You are a language learner of average ability. You are learning one of the "easy" languages for your native linguistic group (e.g., You are an Englishman/woman or an American learning Spanish). In order to meet the first level of mastery in speaking (approximately survival level speech; able to *create* sentences orally in the foreign language or at the 1/1+ level according to the Foreign Service Institute scale), you will need approximately:
   a. 400 hours
   b. 220 hours
   c. 350 hours
   d. 90 hours

9. In order to meet a simple "courtesy and necessity" speaking level‡ as the Englishman/woman or American learning Spanish in No. 8 above, you will need approximately:
   a. 15 hours
   b. 90 hours
   c. less than 35 hours
   d. 60 hours

10. If your goal, as the Englishman/woman learning Spanish in No. 8 above, is to speak the foreign language comfortably (e.g., at the 2+ level on the Foreign Service Institute scale) you will need approximately:
    a. 2 months of full-time study (i.e., 6 hours a day, 5 days a week)
    b. 6 months of full-time study
    c. 1 year of full-time study
    d. 2 years of full-time study

11. Only one of the following statements is true. The true statement is made by Paul Pimsleur, the great foreign language educator, in his book *How to Learn a Foreign Language.*
    a. Foreign language learning requires a special talent that only a small percentage of the population possesses.
    b. A person without an especially good "ear" cannot learn a foreign language well.

   *i.e., minimal, but effective, command.
   †i.e., speakers who are able to speak with facility.
   ‡i.e., just well enough to exchange politenesses with people you meet, order food and drink, ask directions, get a taxi or take public transport, etc.

c. Anyone can learn a foreign language, but some people are quicker at it than others ("anyone" here refers to the majority of people).
d. The single best type of course for the learning of a foreign language is the intensive one (e.g., the DLI courses with 4 to 6 consecutive hours a day of class, 5 days a week).

Source: Pimsleur, P. (1980). *How to Learn a Foreign Language.* Boston: Heinle & Heinle Publishers.

KEY FOR "LEARNING A FOREIGN LANGUAGE: THE MYTHS AND THE REALITY"

1. d
2. b
3. a
4. a
5. c
6. a
7. b/e
8. b
9. d
10. b
11. c

APPENDIX C

FOREIGN LANGUAGE LEARNING STRATEGIES

Strategy 1—Deduction Based on Observation

As you will be exposed to a substantial amount of new information during the first week of the course, you should learn how to use *deduction based on observation* as a foreign language learning (FLL) strategy. *Deduction based on observation* is the ability to use observation skills to find coherence in what otherwise seems to be a chaotic collection of unrelated pieces of information.

Strategy 2—Use of Simple vs. Complicated Expression

You should learn the difference between *simple vs. complicated expression* in the target language and use simple expression at the beginning stages of FLL. At this initial stage in FLL, your language will be an interlanguage—a beginner's language made up of telegraphic messages consisting of words or very short phrases. Although you will want to speak in the target language at the same level and with the same eloquence as in English, you should not attempt to do so. You lack vocabulary and structures. For example, you might want to express yourself in the following way if you have a question for the teacher: *"Mr. Gomez, could you please explain a bit more about the instructions that you gave for the exercise that we are to do tonight?"* However, as you are limited in vocabulary and structures at this point in your language learning, simply recognize your limitations and state, "Mr. Gomez, I do not understand" or attempt to express yourself very simply using your own variety of interlanguage. As teachers are very familiar with the type of questions that students typically ask, they can usually understand your intentions even though they are expressed in an interlanguage. Do not worry about seeming infantile or Tarzan-like in your speech—Interlanguage is a normal part of language learning.

Strategy 3—Use of Context Clues

A *context clue* is a feature of the communicative situation that you can use to help you understand the target language when you are listening to it. You should exercise your power of observation and your common sense to deduce the meaning of words, expressions, body language, or descriptions that your teacher and fellow students may use. For example, if the instructor picks up a pen, points to it, and repeats a sentence that student *A* does not understand, student *A* can safely deduce, even though he or she might only understand a word or two, that the teacher is talking about the pen. The student may further deduce that the teacher is teaching the class an expression that in some way involves the pen.

Strategy 4—Risk-Taking

Risk-taking—making an attempt to communicate when you feel that your level in the target language is poor, or trying to react to a question addressed to you in the target language when you are unsure of what exactly you have understood—is an important language-learning strategy. You should develop a willingness to accept that making mistakes in speech is unavoidable during the early stages of an FLL course. In spite of your faulty vocabulary or grammar, you must be able to answer questions or react to comments that have not been thoroughly understood, to guess meanings, to *take risks.* You should also use *gist comprehension* and *context clues* to aid your understanding so that you can feel more confident when communicating with others in the target language.

Strategy 5—Brainstorming

Brainstorming—the free expression of innovative ideas, creative concepts, solutions to problems, etc. without critically evaluating the ideas, concepts, or solutions—is a learning strategy that can be successfully adapted to the foreign language setting.

Strategy 6—Cognate Guessing

A cognate is a word in the target language that looks similar to a word in English and is translated identically. For example, *organizacion* in Spanish is translated as *organization* in English. *Cognate guessing* is guessing the translation of a cognate. Use cognate guessing when speaking, listening, reading, and writing in the target language. Except for a few false cognates (e.g., *actual* in Spanish is not "actual" but "present" in English), Spanish is replete with cognates that English speakers can use to their advantage.

Strategy 7—Gist Comprehension

Gist comprehension is the understanding of the essence of what is being heard or read in the target language without accounting for every linguistic detail.

Strategy 8—Clarifying Meaning

As you will often feel that you have not adequately understood something that the teacher or your fellow students have said, it is critical that you ask them to *clarify the meaning* of what you have heard. You can ask for repetitions, ask them to speak more slowly, etc. Try to learn expressions such as "How do you say. . ." [in Spanish, French, etc.], "Please speak more slowly," "I am sorry, but I do not understand," etc., in the target language.

Strategy 9—Circumlocution

Circumlocution, which is the use of a roundabout or indirect way of speaking, allows the speaker to express the same idea in several different ways. It is an important FLL strategy.

Strategy 10—Use of Idiomatic Set Phrases

Idiomatic set phrases—colloquial phrases that are very typical in common conversation—exist in all languages. You should learn how and when to use the idiomatic set phrases in the target language that you will study.

Strategy 11—Negotiating Meaning

Negotiating meaning—a more sophisticated form of clarifying meaning—is an important FLL strategy. During the initial stages of FLL, you do not possess all the necessary vocabulary and structures to complete all of the tasks that you are assigned in class easily. However, you should learn how to negotiate meaning—to use whatever knowledge you currently have in the target language—to finish the exercises that your teacher gives you. Because real-life situations demand accuracy in speech, it is crucial that you practice negotiating meaning in the FLL classroom.

Strategy 12—Paraphrasing and the Use of Fillers

Paraphrasing—expressing the same idea in different ways—is particularly important when attempting to clarify or negotiate meaning in the target language. You should also be aware of *fillers*—meaningless words that people use in common conversation such as "You know. . .,"

"Well. . .," "So. . .," etc. Although native speakers tend to overuse fillers, they can be helpful communication tools if used sparingly.

Strategy 13—Dealing with Uncertainty

In your language-learning experience, you will constantly have to *deal with uncertainty*. The reality of the FLL classroom as well as that of the target culture makes it imperative for you to attempt to make sense out of information never before heard or read.

Strategy 14—Topic Expansion and the Use of Transitions

Topic expansion and the *use of transitions* (e.g., *sin embargo, a pesar de, respecto a, entonces, por consiguiente,* etc.) are important FLL strategies. The successful FL learner should be able to change the subject of a conversation in overt and subtle ways, to shift from one topic to another or from one topic to its subtopic with the appropriate transitional phrases, and to expand on a topic. For example, in a discussion about politics, one individual might say, "President Johnson got this country deeply in debt." Another individual might change the course of the conversation from commentary on individual presidents to discussion of the benefits or disadvantages of a particular social program that was instituted under President Johnson's administration. The teacher will support the flow of conversation by paraphrasing upon hearing a mistake.

Strategy 15—Ability to Differentiate Between Formal and Informal Expression

You should learn the *difference between formal and informal expression*. The written language tends to stress formality of expression. It is important that you become aware of register differences and learn when and how to use specific forms of register.

Strategy 16—Problem Solving in Groups

Problem solving in groups is a communication strategy that can be adapted to the FLL environment. You should develop sufficient linguistic dexterity to express yourself both at a concrete and at an abstract level while functioning as part of a team engaged in different problem-solving tasks.

Strategy 17—Decision Making

Decision making is a strategy that can be adapted to the FLL environment. In life, the ability to evaluate the different aspects of a given situation and to make valid decisions based on careful evaluation is basic to success in both the professional and personal arenas. You can practice the valuable skill of *decision making* in the FL classroom.

APPENDIX D

THE IDEAL LANGUAGE LEARNER

Using the list below, rank the five characteristics that, in your opinion, the ideal language learner displays:

_____ 1. intelligence

_____ 2. cooperative spirit

_____ 3. motivation

_____ 4. extroverted

_____ 5. perseverance (= firm or obstinate spirit of continuation; persistence)

_____ 6. fortitude (= courage in pain or adversity)

_____ 7. open-mindedness

_____ 8. mastery in the first language

_____ 9. self-discipline

_____ 10. good study skills (i.e., knowing how to study well)

_____ 11. risk-taking spirit

_____ 12. maturity

_____ 13. patience

_____ 14. curiosity

_____ 15. positive attitude toward required tasks (e.g., completion of a language program)

_____ 16. hard-working spirit

_____ 17. task-orientation (i.e., desire to finish the task once begun)

_____ 18. achievement-orientation (i.e., desire to achieve academic or physical heights)

_____ 19. competitive spirit

_____ 20. creativity

Chapter Fourteen

Foreign Language Classroom Anxiety: Institutional Responses

Jo Ann Cope Powell   The University of Texas at Austin

INTRODUCTION

University instructors in the foreign language classroom may not be alone, although they may feel so, in their efforts to enable students to master the curriculum.

Students in foreign language courses sometimes experience difficulties that are beyond the scope of the prescribed curriculum to alleviate. In particular, foreign language classroom anxiety (Horwitz, Horwitz, & Cope, 1986, this volume) may lead to difficulties in listening, comprehending speech, and speaking. Deficient study skills may cause a failure to organize time and efforts to adapt to the unique demands of a foreign language class. A poor background in English grammar may compound difficulties with grammar in a second language.[1]

Puzzled by motivated students who are doing poorly in coursework, the instructor usually turns to fellow instructors and teaching supervisors for shared wisdom and ideas that have worked. Professional journals occasionally offer practical as well as theoretical and research-based articles on teaching and learning foreign languages. Individual tutoring may be available through the foreign language department or the campus learning skills center. The range of resources may, however, be greater than one imagines.

Over the last decade at the University of Texas at Austin, three different administrative components—the College of Education's Department of Curriculum and Instruction, the Student Affairs Division's Learning Skills Center, and the College of Liberal Arts' Department of Germanic Languages—have sponsored innovative support programs for foreign language learning. These three programs have extended the campus response to foreign language learning problems.

First, a faculty member of the Department of Curriculum and Instruction and a learning specialist from the Learning Skills Center co-facilitated a *foreign language support group.*

This group shares some features with supplemental instruction (SI) groups that have been implemented nationwide during the past decade by college developmental education programs and by academic departments to support other content-area courses.

Second, every semester for several years the Learning Skills Center sponsored an *informal talk* on foreign language study skills. Such a program provides an example of outreach services by a college developmental learning center. The same information is available in a self-help format in the Learning Skills Center's Independent Study Lab.

Third, the Department of Germanic Languages, in a *modification of the curriculum* for lower division classes, included instruction in study skills and effective attitudes toward foreign language learning. This curriculum represents the efforts of a traditional program to acknowledge and cope with study skills deficiencies and foreign language classroom anxiety via an alternative to acquisition strategies approaches.

All these programs share a commitment to eliminating as many artificial barriers to learning as possible and an acknowledgment that knowing how to learn contributes significantly to retention and success. Each embodies these values through the procedures and outcomes described in the following pages.

A FOREIGN LANGUAGE SUPPORT GROUP

An Experimental Program

Students enrolled in freshman and sophomore foreign language classes during a first-summer session were invited to participate in an optional "Foreign Language Skills Group." This group, an adjunct to their foreign language class, was scheduled to meet two extra hours a week throughout the 6-week semester. The purpose of the group was to provide study skills instruction, anxiety management, and group support for students who were having difficulties studying a foreign language. The group was developed, promoted, implemented, and evaluated by Dr. Elaine Horwitz of the Department of Curriculum and Instruction in the College of Education and by the author, a learning specialist with the Learning Skills Center, part of the Counseling, Learning and Career Services of the Division of Student Affairs.

Advertising for the group consisted mostly of 5-minute visits on the first day of class to every section of lower division French, German, and Spanish, the three languages with the largest enrollments. (Letters were sent to instructors of lower division classes in other languages requesting that they inform their students of the group.) Contact with the lower division coordinators garnered permission for these visits. During the visits, the purpose of the group was explained and a descriptive flyer was distributed to the students. As a motivational device, students were offered information concerning time management during the condensed summer semester. Also, the flyers contained provocative questions:

> Do you have a phobia about foreign languages?
>
> Do you think you were born without foreign language aptitude?
>
> Have foreign language classes always been a problem for you?
>
> Do language classes scare you?

In addition to the goals of the group described above, the flyer proposed that a group participant would develop his or her individual successful learning style. About 225 students were contacted through these visits.

Response to the advertising was strong: Some 35% of the students expressed their interest in the group by returning the flyer with their names, phone numbers, and schedules. The large demand led to the scheduling of a second adjunct group, but time constraints limited each group to 15 members.

The foreign language support group provided the students information via lecture on study skills for foreign language learning: time management, task definition, and particular activities to accomplish each of the four language skills. In addition, relaxation exercises were taught. On the first day of class, the instructors collected from the students demographic data, the students' histories of foreign language learning, a questionnaire concerning beliefs about foreign language learning (Horwitz, 1984), and a foreign language anxiety questionnaire (Horwitz, 1983). Students were encouraged to discuss their past and current frustrations in foreign language classes. (See Horwitz, Horwitz, & Cope, 1986, this volume for a presentation of the data from this group.)

Evaluations of the support group were collected via structured telephone interviews (N = 10) after the semester was completed. Half of those contacted reported doing well in their classes (although they didn't yet know their grades, students anticipated A's or B's); most of the rest withdrew. The primary benefit to all from the support group was the study skills instruction, although several also cited the relaxation exercises and the value of knowing that other students shared their discomfort with language study. Attrition in the support group was very high: Many students dropped their foreign language course, while others discovered that they could handle it on their own and could not afford the extra time for the support group. Those who withdrew said that the summer pace was too fast for their tastes and planned to register again in the fall semester. These results suggest that the summer is a difficult time to add more hours, even helpful ones, to a student's language-learning activities. Several said that they would seek help from the support group instructors when they registered again.

Perhaps the most important outcome of the foreign language support group was a better understanding of students' felt needs in foreign language study. When asked what they were hoping for when they enrolled in the support group, students were usually vague: They hoped for *any* help with their studies. However, most discovered in the process—and a couple were clear from the start—that what they really wanted was help in their *particular* language: additional explanations, conversation practice, individual tutoring.

The needs expressed by these anxious foreign language students are characteristic of those students taking courses in a variety of content areas on university campuses.

> Students typically perceive their need as largely content-centered. Experience shows, however, that the most common need is for the prerequisite learning and thinking skills which are basic to content mastery.... Recent research ... indicates that substantial gains in the level of these skills can be achieved through appropriate strategies and techniques.... (Martin, Blanc, & DeBuhr, 1983, pp. 2–3)

The Model: Supplemental Instruction

Over the last decade, learning centers at a number of campuses nationwide have developed modes of student academic assistance known as *adjunct classes* and *supplemental instruction* (Martin, Blanc, & DeBuhr, 1983). They evolved out of the perceived need to integrate study skills with content area learning; their development was fed by a nationwide need to address high attrition rates. The concept of the adjunct class, for example, was based on the philosophy that a university has the responsibility to support those it admits and that study skills training contributes to the exercise of a student's true abilities (Tomlinson & Green, 1976).

The foreign language support group reported above is very similar in concept to an adjunct class, an antecedent of supplemental instruction. In an adjunct class, a learning specialist teaches study skills pertinent to a particular class in a small-group parallel to the class. Study skills training is different from the tutoring provided by a faculty member, a teaching assistant, or even an individual tutor: Its focus is on process rather than product (Tomlinson & Green, 1976).

Supplemental instruction (SI) evolved from adjunct classes as more of an interaction developed between teaching content-area study skills and providing weekly out-of-class reviews of content being taught in the university class. A supplemental instruction group is a small voluntary group of students, all of whom are taking the same university class, which meets one or two times a week throughout the semester. Students may attend as frequently or as seldom as they choose; six or seven times a semester is an average (Blanc, DeBuhr, & Martin, 1983).

The SI class is conducted by a learning specialist competent in the subject area or by a graduate or upper division undergraduate student who has received training in conducting such a group. The SI leader attends the content-area class. His or her role is to serve as a model for the procedures and activities that promote the thinking, reasoning, and questioning skills necessary for success in the class. The SI leader clarifies and reinforces course content while integrating appropriate study techniques for the course. Skills such as note-taking, reading, writing, and test-taking are introduced as they become relevant and when there is a perceived need for them.

Supplemental instruction forms a bridge between what happens in the lecture and the students' out-of-class study experiences. Because the SI leader also attends the class, students can raise questions about what has happened in class—something the instructor has said or done, for example. The SI leader is in a position to formulate and recommend effective study responses for particular problems or assignments. The SI leader fosters independence in students. For example, early in the semester he or she may provide a practice test before the first exam; later in the semester this same individual will teach the students how to make up their own practice tests. Essentially, the person serves as a guide (rather than a tutor) to learning the content of the particular class.

Supplemental instruction is particularly powerful in reducing attrition. It was developed to address high-risk courses—those in which 30% or more of the students enrolled typically withdraw or receive semester grades of D or F. Evaluation research (Martin, Blanc, & DeBuhr, 1983) indicates that SI students (when compared to students in control groups matched for motivation, high school rank, and college entrance exam scores) earned higher grades in the target course, higher total semester GPA's, and lower percentages of D and F grades and withdrawals; more SI students reenrolled the following semester than did non-SI students. Note that SI works for students in both the highest and lowest quartiles on college entrance examination scores: Both groups earned higher grades than their counterparts in the control groups. At the University of Texas at Austin, supplemental instruction has been piloted and researched by the Learning Skills Center through a summer "Preview" program for selected minority incoming freshmen. Over three years of study, "Preview" students with supplemental instruction have consistently earned higher grades and continued university enrollment at a significantly higher level than carefully matched control groups (Learning Skills Center, 1988).

A foreign language department that is considering instituting supplemental instruction needs to consider several issues. One issue is whether foreign language classes are high-risk: It may be that a substantial percentage of students in foreign language classes do not regularly drop out or make D's or F's.

Another issue is staffing. Supplemental instruction programs are usually outreach efforts of learning assistance centers; but some academic departments have set them up, hiring learning specialists to staff them (Harding, 1981). As the technique has been modified, difficulties (Herlin, 1978) have been resolved and guidelines are now available for funding, staffing, and implementing (Martin, Blanc, & DeBuhr, 1983).

The adjunct class with one instructor who teaches students from several sections of a foreign language course without attending all the classes is an alternative to supplemental instruction. Most foreign language classes are quite small, and supplemental instruction, for reasons of economy and service, is usually offered to large sections of dozens or even hundreds of students: The SI leader would not be able to be present in every section of the foreign language.

An interesting direction is the possibility of training the department's own teaching assistants to be SI leaders. In a dissertation study in math education (Kinney, 1988), one math teaching assistance taught four sections of calculus, two in a traditional TA role and two as an SI leader. Both the mean course grade and the mean semester GPA were significantly higher for students in the SI sections than for students matched on several predictive academic measures in the traditional sections.

A rare application of supplemental instruction to foreign language classes at the University of Missouri–Kansas City[2] offers us three interesting generalizations that need to be compared to experiences in other foreign language departments. The staff of the Student Learning Center there provided support services to students in beginning Spanish sections for three semesters (Fall 1979; Fall 1980; Winter 1981). The first point to observe is that, during these semesters, the number of students in beginning Spanish who withdrew or made D's or F's ranged from 23% to 29.7%. Spanish, then, at the University of Missouri–Kansas City at that time approached the status of a high-risk course.

A second observation is that more students made A's and B's who did *not* use supplemental instruction than those who did take advantage of it. This fact seems to imply that students who are rightly confident of their language learning ability know who they are and opt to master the material on their own.

The third observation is that, among students who made lower grades, students who chose to seek help through supplemental instruction made C's but *no* D's or F's (although a few withdrew), while those who did not take SI made fewer C's, more D's and F's, and more frequently withdrew. It appears that a critical dichotomy exists among language students: those who are skilled and confident in language learning, and those who have difficulty mastering foreign languages. For those in the latter group at Missouri who were motivated, supplemental instruction may have contributed to the significant difference in their performance.

A MODIFICATION IN CURRICULUM

At the University of Texas, the Department of Germanic Languages instituted in 1977 a lower division German program that incorporated learning skills into its classroom curriculum (Donahue, 1980). Such a program represents a second major institutional response to students who have concerns regarding learning foreign languages. It successfully interfaced effective learning skills with course content without the use of supplemental classes. Moreover, it addressed specifically the issue of classroom anxiety both by providing suggestions and attitudes for the students and by training instructors and teaching assistants in classroom teaching techniques designed to calm rather than heighten classroom anxiety. This curriculum (a four-skills program employing conventional textbooks and teaching methods) functioned effectively for a decade before it was significantly revised in 1986 to focus on proficiency goals; however, the study skills and anxiety management components have been retained in the new curriculum.

The innovation in this program was a *Supplement* that students purchased along with their textbooks. The *Supplement* outlined daily class topics, homework assignments, and test dates, and it taught study techniques to accomplish these tasks. The study skills suggestions and daily study plans in the *Supplement* told students what to do, when and how to do it: It organized the students' study goals and tasks for them. It told students explicitly what was expected of them both daily and throughout the course. For a particular learning task, it told the student how to accomplish it: to separate from each other, for example, the tasks of vocabulary, grammar, and reading mastery. For a particular task, it explained how to go about it: to distribute practice, for example, when memorizing. It offered extremely important time-management principles and information on how many hours of daily practice are necessary for a particular grade (based on the experience of past German-language students). It motivated the student to good practices, warning them, for example, not to skip a review before a test and citing past students' experiences that such reviews improved grades. The *Supplement* offered study aids such as useful classroom expressions and practice tests.

A particular strength of the *Supplement* was its advice concerning foreign language classroom anxiety. It anticipated and acknowledged the feelings that might arise in students who must listen and speak a foreign language in a group. It pointed out that, when learning to pronounce a foreign language, people often feel embarrassed when uttering "strange" sounds. The *Supplement* assured the students that such feelings are normal, that they should accept them and trust that such feelings will pass as experience in the language develops. It acknowledged individual difference in the ability to imitate sounds. Such simple information relieves the minds of students who catch on more slowly than others. The *Supplement* advocated competence, not perfection, as an expectation of the student: Anxious students are often already perfectionists! It pointed out that a person can't make progress in learning without making mistakes, so it is important to expect and accept one's mistakes and also to accept correction. It encouraged the learner to be active in class and to take risks, because both traits characterize good students.

German instructors were trained also in classroom techniques that reduce anxiety. Teacher training is an issue of absolute importance in the management of classroom anxiety, for teachers may be primary contributors to the problem. Instructors were reminded not to criticize someone in front of the entire class; to reinforce and reward effort whether it is successful or not; to encourage students to help each other so that their peers are resources and supports. Instructors still exercise the prerogative of offering a "free space" to their students where they may sit and not be called on if such is their need on a particular day, though of course a regular claiming of such a privilege would lead to an individual conference with the student to diagnose his or her difficulty.

The *Supplement* embodied the principle that learning is the consequence of a process of specific activities. Learning is easier and faster if these activities are selected and organized. They should be selected to enable the accomplishment of specific learning goals, and they need to be organized in sequences that lead experientially to these goals. Moreover, it cannot be assumed that students know these learning principles; rather, most people stumble along through trial and error, especially when faced with an esoteric task such as foreign language study.

AN "INFORMAL TALK"

Learning Center Outreach

As part of a comprehensive campus-wide outreach program, the Learning Skills Center (LSC) at the University of Texas for several years offered once each semester a one-hour lecture entitled "Tips on Studying Foreign Languages." This lecture was advertised through a notice in the campus newspaper as well as through individual letters mailed to all instructors of lower division foreign language classes. These letters outlined the content of the lecture, provided a copy of the handout to be delivered at the lecture, and requested the instructors to announce the lecture to their classes. The lecture was scheduled relatively early in the semester yet late enough for the students to appreciate the difficulties of their language studies.

Occasionally, a foreign language faculty member was invited to co-present the lecture. The faculty member who was invited was someone who had come to the attention of the LSC because of his or her interest in foreign language learning methods.

The content of the lecture included time-management and suggestions to students for the most efficient uses of their time for the separate tasks of vocabulary development, grammar learning, reading, and listening and speaking skills.

A number of specific suggestions regarding student management of foreign language classroom anxiety were included in the lecture. Regular and well-designed preparation and rehearsal of the lesson a few minutes before class begins were recommended as the surest ways to prevent classroom anxiety. Making friends in the class, mental rehearsal of classroom conversation and drill, physical relaxation, and asking the instructor for "time out" from classroom participation were all suggested. Risk-taking was encouraged, since mistakes are by and large unavoidable. Moreover, it appeared particularly valuable to students to assure them that different people learn different ways. Those who are by nature more careful and detailed are likely to be more tense in the ambiguous flow of class participation; those who are more gregarious and spontaneous may feel more relaxed there.

These presentations usually attracted a substantial audience and were generally evaluated as valuable by those who attended. Sometimes instructors sent their entire classes and came themselves, contributing their recommendations as well. Students at times regretted that help in their particular language was not provided; students in exotic languages (those with non-Roman alphabets) were not always satisfied with a presentation that was directed predominantly at French, Spanish, and German.

Independent Study

Although informal talks are no longer offered because of changing staff priorities, University of Texas students who are experiencing difficulty with their foreign language classes may come to the Learning Skills Center for help. Such students may either make an appointment with a learning specialist to talk over language-learning problems or arrange to visit the Independent Study Lab. In the lab they will find an Independent Study Guide that directs them to several books, videotapes, and slide-tape presentations. These media offer information on how to study foreign languages and also grammar assistance. The audiovisual media were developed by LSC staff using campus media facilities.

CONCLUSION

Rarely does an academic department include in its mandate the responsibility to teach its students how to learn. Yet, as campuses become more sensitive to the need to retain those students they admit, the importance of learning skills assistance, including anxiety-management methods, surfaces as a central means of enabling students to do their best. The more academic departments develop their own student-learning supports, the greater the economy of time and effort for students and the greater returns in retention and success for the departments. However, developmental learning skills centers at the college and university levels currently provide and for many years will probably continue to provide most of the alternative support resources for academic departments in contradistinction to the ones that departments can develop for themselves.

NOTES

1. Learning specialists on the staff of the Learning Skills Center at the University of Texas at Austin have observed that these three problems predominate among students who over the years have sought help for learning problems in foreign language classes.

2. M. Garland, Center for Academic Development, personal communication, September 24, 1986.

Afterword

We are only beginning to understand language anxiety and its functioning in the development and performance of second languages. Indeed, in many ways, this volume raises more questions than it answers. Of primary importance is the fundamental source of language anxiety. How much anxiety is inherent in language learning and how much is due to the classroom practices that language teachers choose to employ? The papers in this volume begin to identify those classroom activities that learners find most stressful and suggest ways that instruction can be modified. Further investigation is needed to determine other classroom sources of anxiety.

To date, anxiety has most often been associated with oral activities, but anxieties related to listening, reading, and writing have also been reported. We look forward to a better understanding of how and under what circumstances particular activities or linguistic tasks are anxiety-provoking for particular individuals. On the other hand, it is likely that some amount of anxiety emanates from the intrinsic nature of the language-learning process, making the complete elimination of debilitating language anxiety an impossibility. We must, therefore, continue to develop approaches to help learners cope with the built-in demands of language learning. We look to future investigations to help clarify the boundaries between inherent and instruction-induced language anxiety.

Exactly how anxiety impedes language learning has not been resolved. Several theorists assert that anxiety interferes directly with the development of second language fluency. For example, Krashen maintains that anxiety inhibits the learner's ability to process incoming language, short-circuiting what he calls the language acquisition process. It is also possible that anxiety does not hinder the development of language ability directly but rather that it acts as a kind of gate, preventing students from adopting effective learning practices. It would seem, then, that the discourse on language anxiety has implications for the emerging literature on learner strategies and that future empirical efforts should explore relationships between anxiety and the choice of specific learning and communication strategies.

We also need to know more about the incidence of language anxiety. Horwitz, Horwitz, and Cope, and Campbell and Ortiz found that anxiety is experienced by many students —perhaps one third—in response to at least some aspects of classroom language learning. In addition, Mejías, Applbaum, Applbaum, and Trotter reported significant levels of communication apprehension in Mexican-American high school and college students. From these studies, it seems reasonable to conclude that many people experience at least some anxiety in the course of learning or speaking a second language.

On the other hand, the prevalence of severe anxiety reactions as well as the number of students who drop-out prematurely or avoid language study entirely is open to speculation. In such individuals, language anxiety, like mathematics and science anxiety, may act as a job filter influencing the choice of a major and even a career. An understanding of how language anxiety varies by cultural group is crucial to the development of effective responses for all student populations.

Finally, many definitional and investigative issues related to language anxiety remain unresolved. We expect the debate concerning the nature of language anxiety to continue for some time; some researchers will explore the relationship between language anxiety and related situational anxieties especially test anxiety, communication apprehension, and fear of negative evaluation, while others consider the unique nature of language anxiety. This dual line of investigation should help refine our understanding of language anxiety and eventually lead to improved research approaches and a better model of how anxiety functions in second language learning and performance.

Although many questions about language anxiety remain, teachers and students look to the literature on anxiety for prompt answers to their problems. A number of promising suggestions for alleviating and coping with language anxiety have been offered throughout this volume. Many of the papers emphasized the development of learner autonomy. By encouraging students to take control of their own language learning and helping them develop effective learning strategies and reasonable expectations, it is hoped that debilitating language anxiety can be minimized. As many anxious learners feel that they are the only ones experiencing such distress, simply recognizing the problem and talking with affected individuals may be helpful for some students. Teachers should be mindful of signs of severe anxiety whenever their students perform.

We hope that in the future language anxiety receives greater attention both from language-teaching professionals and researchers. If, however, this volume serves to heighten consciousness about an important factor in the development of second language competence, our purpose has been served.

References

ALLEN, J. L. (1984). *Gender, communication, competence, apprehension and the Basic Skills Course.* Paper presented at the Seventh Annual Communication, Language and Gender Conference, Miami University, Oxford, OH.

ALLEN, J. L., O'MARA, J., & ANDRIATE, G. S. (1984a, December). *Communicating in a second language: Importance, competency, and apprehension.* Paper presented at the meeting of the Speech Communication Association of Puerto Rico.

ALLEN, J. L., O'MARA, J., & ANDRIATE, G. S. (1984b, December). *Second language experience, and communication apprehension in functional contexts.* Paper presented at the meeting of the Speech Communication Association of Puerto Rico.

ALPERT, R., & HABER, R. (1960). Anxiety in academic achievement situations. *Journal of Abnormal and Social Psychology, 61,* 207–215.

ALVARO, R. A. (1978). *The effectiveness of a science therapy program upon science-anxious undergraduates.* Unpublished doctoral dissertation, Loyola University of Chicago.

AMMANN, R. (1970). The influence of psychological stress on test results. *Psychologie und ihre Anwendung, 29,* 471–491.

ANDERSEN, P., ANDERSEN, J. F., & GARRISON, J. P. (1978). Singing apprehension and talking apprehension: The development of two constructs. *Sign Language Studies, 19,* 155–186.

ANDERSEN, P., & LEIBOWITZ, K. (1978). The development and nature of the construct touch avoidance. *Environmental Psychology and Nonverbal Behavior, 3,* 89–106.

ASHER, J. (1977). *Learning another language through actions: The complete teacher's guide.* Los Gatos, CA: Sky Oaks.

ASTIN, A. W. (1982). *Minorities in American higher education.* San Francisco: Jossey-Bass.

BACHELLER, F. (1980). Communicative effectiveness as predicted by judgments of the severity of learner errors in dictations. In J. W. Oller & K. Perkins (Eds.), *Research in language testing.* Rowley, MA: Newbury House.

BACKMAN, N. (1976). Two measures of affective factors as they relate to progress in adult second language learning. *Working Papers in Bilingualism, 10,* 100–122.

BAILEY, K. M. (1983). Competitiveness and anxiety in adult second language learning: Looking at and through the diary studies. In H. W. Seliger & M. H. Long (Eds.), *Classroom oriented research in second language acquisition.* Rowley, MA: Newbury House.

BARABASZ, A. F. (1970). Galvanic skin response and test anxiety among Negroes and Caucasians. *Child Study Journal, 1,* 33–35.

BARTZ, W. H. (1974). *A study of the relationship of certain factors with the ability to communicate in a second language (German) for the development of communicative competence.* Unpublished doctoral dissertation, The Ohio State University.

BEEMAN, P., MARTIN, R., & MEYERS, J. (1972). Interventions in relation to anxiety in school. In C. Spielberger (Ed.), *Anxiety: Current trends in theory and research* (pp. 40–50). New York: Academic Press.

BENSON. H., (1973). *The relaxation response.* New York: Morrow.

BENTON, A. L., HARTMAN, C. H., & SARASON, I. G. (1955). Some relations between speech behavior and anxiety level. *Journal of Abnormal Psychology, 51,* 295–297.

BETZ, N. E. (1978). Prevalence, distribution and correlates of math anxiety in college students. *Journal of Counseling Psychology, 25,* 441–448.

BLANC, R. B., DeBUHR, L. E., & MARTIN, D. C. (1983). Breaking the attrition cycle: The effects of supplemental instruction on undergraduate performance and attrition. *Journal of Higher Education, 54*(1), 80–90.

BLATCHFORD, C. (1976). *My silent way experience—one model for training teachers and students.* Paper presented to the Tenth Annual TESOL Convention, New York.

BOSTRUM, R. N. (ED.). (1984). *Competence in communication.* Beverly Hills, CA: Sage.

BREWSTER, E. S. (1971). *Personality factors relevant to intensive audiolingual foreign language learning.* Unpublished doctoral dissertation, University of Texas, Austin.

BRIÈRE, E. J. (1973). Cross-cultural biases in language testing. In J. W. Oller, Jr. & J. C. Richards (Eds.), *Focus on the learner: Pragmatic perspectives for the language teacher.* Rowley, MA: Newbury House.

BRONZAFT, A. L., MURGATROYD, D., & McNEILLY, R. A. (1974). Test anxiety among black college students: A cross-cultural study. *Journal of Negro Education, 43,* 190–193.

BRONZAFT, A. L., & STUART, I. R. (1971). Test anxiety, GSR and academic achievement. *Perceptual and Motor Skills, 33,* 535–538.

BROWN, B. L., & RENCHER, A. C. (1990). *The DataMax User's Guide.* Orem, UT: Echo Solutions.

BROWN, H. D. (1973). Affective variables in second language acquisition. *Language Learning, 23,* 231–244.

BROWN, H. D. (1977). Some limitations of Counseling-Learning/Community Language Learning models of second language teaching. *TESOL Quarterly, 11,* 365–372.

BROWN, H. D. (1987). *Principles of language learning and teaching* (2nd ed.). Englewood Cliffs, NJ: Prentice-Hall.

BROWNELL, W. W., & KATULA, R. A. (1984). The communication anxiety graph: A classroom tool for managing speech anxiety. *Communication Quarterly, 32,* 243–249.

BRYCE, G. R. (1982). *Data analysis in RUMMAGE: A user's guide.* Provo, UT: Brigham Young University, Statistics Department.

BUSS, A. (1988). *Personality: Evolutionary heritage and human distinctiveness.* Hillsdale, NJ: Erlbaum.

CAMPBELL, C., & ORTIZ, J. (1986). *Survey of attitudes specific to the foreign language classroom.* Presidio of Monterey, CA: The Defense Language Institute.

CAMPBELL, C., & ORTIZ, J. (1988). Dispelling students' fears and misconceptions about foreign language study: The foreign language anxiety workshop at the Defense Language Institute. In T. B. Fryer & F. Medley, Jr. (Eds.), *New challenges and opportunities: Dimension—Languages '87* (pp. 29–40). Columbia, SC: Southern Conference on Language Teaching.

CATTELL, R. B. (1966). The screen test for the number of factors. *Multivariate Behavioral Research, 1,* 245–276.

CHAMOT, A. U., & KUPPER, L. (1989). Learning strategies in foreign language instruction. *Foreign Language Annals, 22,* 13–24.

CHASTAIN, K. (1975). Affective and ability factors in second language acquisition. *Language Learning, 25,* 153–161.

CHASTAIN, K. (1976). *Developing second language skills: Theory to practice.* Chicago: Rand McNally.

CHRISJOHN, R. D. (1981). *A substantive approach to the state-trait distinction in anxiety.* Unpublished doctoral dissertation, University of Western Ontario, London.

CHRISTOPHER, L., & SMITH, E. (1990). Shaping the content of simulation. In D. Crookall & R. Oxford (Eds.), *Simulation, gaming, and language learning.* New York: Newbury House/Harper & Row.

CLÉMENT, R. (1987). Second language proficiency and acculturation: An investigation of the effects of language status and individual characteristics. *Journal of Language and Social Psychology, 5,* 271–290.

CLÉMENT, R., & KRUIDENIER, B. G. (1985). Aptitude, attitude, and motivation in second language proficiency: A test of Clement's model. *Journal of Language and Social Psychology, 4,* 21–37.

CLEVENGER, T. (1959). A synthesis of experimental research in stage fright. *Quarterly Journal of Speech, 45,* 134–145.

COHEN, A. (1990). *Second language learning: Insights for learners, teachers, researchers.* New York: Newbury House/Harper & Row.

COHEN, R. M. (1971). *Effects of feedback on test anxiety and performance as a function of certain personal characteristics.* Unpublished doctoral dissertation, New York University.

CONZE, E. (1967). *Buddhist thought in India: Three phases of Buddhist philosophy.* Ann Arbor: University of Michigan Press.

COOPER, P. J. (1984). *Speech communication for the classroom teacher* (2nd ed.). Scottsdale, AZ: Gorsuch Scarisbrick.

CROFT, K. (1980). *Readings on English as a second language.* Boston: Little, Brown.

CROOKALL, D. (1983). Learner training: A neglected strategy. Parts 1 & 2. *Modern English Teacher, 11*(1), 31–33; *11*(2), 41–42.

CROOKALL, D. (1990). Helping learners deal with anxiety: An essential component in learner training. *Simulation/Games for Learning, 20,* 2.

CROOKALL, D., & OXFORD, R. (EDS.). (1990). *Language learning through simulation/gaming.* New York: Newbury House/Harper & Row.

CROOKALL, D., & SAUNDERS, D. (EDS.). (1989). *Communication and simulation: From two fields to one theme.* Clevedon, Avon: Multilingual Matters.

CUÉLLAR, I., HARRIS, L., & JASSO, R. (1980) An acculturation scale for Mexican American normal and clinical populations. *Hispanic Journal of Behavioral Science, 2,* 199–211.

CURRAN, C. A. (1976). *Counseling-learning in second languages.* Apple River, IL: Apple River Press.

CZIKO, G. A. (1980). The development of a criterion-referenced test of ESL dictation. In J. E. Redden (Ed.), *Proceedings of the Southern Illinois Language Testing Conference.* Carbondale: Southern Illinois University.

DALY, J. A. (1977). The effects of writing apprehension on message encoding. *Journalism Quarterly, 27,* 566–572.

DALY, J. A. (1985). Writing apprehension. In M. Rose (Ed.), *When a writer can't write: Studies in writer's block and other composing process problems* (pp. 43–82). New York: Guilford.

DALY, J. A. (1987). Personality and interpersonal communication: Issues and directions. In J. C. McCroskey & J. A. Daly (Eds.), *Personality and interpersonal communication* (pp. 13–41). Newbury Park, CA: Sage.

DALY, J. A., & BUSS, A. (1984). The transitory causes of audience anxiety. In J. A. Daly & J. C. McCroskey (Eds.), *Avoiding communication* (pp. 67–80). Beverly Hills, CA: Sage.

DALY, J. A., & MCCROSKEY, J. C. (1975). Occupational choice and desirability as a function of communication apprehension. *Journal of Counseling Psychology, 22,* 309–313.

DALY, J. A., & MCCROSKEY, J. C. (EDS.). (1984). *Avoiding communication: Shyness, reticence, and communication apprehension.* Beverly Hills, CA: Sage.

DALY, J. A., MCCROSKEY, J. C., & RICHMOND, V. P. (1977). The relationship between vocal activity and perceptions of communicators in small groups. *Western Journal of Speech Communication, 41,* 175–187.

DALY, J. A., & MILLER, M. D. (1975a). Apprehension of writing as a predictor of message intensity. *Journal of Psychology, 89,* 175–177.

DALY, J. A., & MILLER, M. D. (1975b). The empirical development of an instrument to measure writing apprehension. *Research in the Teaching of English, 9,* 242–256.

DALY, J. A., RICHMOND, V. P., & LETH, S. (1979). Social communicative anxiety and the personnel selection process: Testing the similarity effect in selection decisions. *Human Communication Research, 6,* 18–32.

DALY, J. A., & SHAMO, W. (1977). *Academic decisions as a function of written and oral communication apprehension.* Paper presented at the Annual Conference of the International Communication Association, West Berlin, West Germany.

DALY, J. A., & STAFFORD, L. (1984). Correlates and consequences of social communicative anxiety. In J. A. Daly & J. C. McCroskey (Eds.), *Avoiding communication: Shyness, reticence, and communication apprehension* (pp. 125–144). Beverly Hills, CA: Sage.

DARLEY, S. A., & KATZ, I. (1973). Heart rate changes in children as a function of test versus game instructions and test anxiety. *Child Development, 44,* 784–789.

DESROCHERS, A. M. (1980). *Imagery elaboration and the acquisition of French vocabulary.* Unpublished doctoral dissertation, University of Western Ontario, London.

DI PIETRO, R. J. (1987). *Strategic interaction: Learning languages through scenarios.* Cambridge: Cambridge University Press.

DISICK, R., & BARBANEL, L. (1974). Affective education and foreign language learning. *ACTFL Review, the Challenge of Communication, 6,* 185–222.

DODD, C. (1982). *Dynamics of intercultural communication.* Dubuque, IA: Wm. C. Brown.

DONAHUE, F. E. (1980). *Lower Division German Supplement IV—Skills Program.* Minneapolis: Burgess Publishing Company.

DULAY, H., BURT, M., & KRASHEN, S. (1982). *Language Two.* New York: Oxford University Press.

DUNKEL, H. B. (1947). The effect of personality on language achievement. *Journal of Education Psychology, 38,* 177–182.

DURÁN, R. P. (1983). *Hispanics' education and background.* New York: College Entrance Board.

EHRMAN, M., & OXFORD, R. (1990). Effects of sex differences, career choice, and psychological type on adult language learning strategies. *Modern Language Journal, 73*(1), 1–13.

ELLIS, G., & SINCLAIR, B. (1989). *Learning to learn English: A course in learner training.* Cambridge: Cambridge University Press.

ELY, C. M. (1986). An analysis of discomfort, risktaking, sociability, and motivation in the L_2 classroom. *Language Learning, 36,* 1–25.

ENDLER, N. S. (1980). Person-situation interaction and anxiety. In I. L. Kutash (Ed.), *Handbook on stress and anxiety.* San Francisco: Jossey-Bass.

FAYER, J., MCCROSKEY, J. C., & RICHMOND, V. P. (1984, May). *Communication apprehension in Puerto Rico and the United States. I: Initial comparisons.* Paper presented at the meeting of the International Communication Association, San Francisco.

FARHADY, H. (1979). Test bias in language placement examinations. In C. A. Yorio, K. Perkins, & J. Schachter (Eds.), *On TESOL '79.* Washington, DC: TESOL.

FLIGSTEIN, N., & FERNÁNDEZ, R. M. (1982). *The causes of Hispanic educational attainment, patterns and analysis.* Chicago: National Opinion Research Center.

FORD FOUNDATION. (1984). *Hispanics' challenges and opportunities.* New York: Office of Reports.

Foss, K. A. (1982). Communication apprehension: Resources for the instructor. *Communication Education, 31,* 195–203.

Fremouw, W. J. (1984). Cognitive-behavioral therapies for modification of communication apprehension. In J. A. Daly & J. C. McCroskey (Eds.), *Avoiding communication: Shyness, reticence, and communication apprehension* (pp. 209–218). Beverly Hills, CA: Sage.

Fremouw, W. J., & Zitter, R. E. (1978). A comparison of skills training and cognitive restructuring-relaxation for the treatment of speech anxiety. *Behavior Therapy, 9,* 248–259.

Friedman, P. G. (1980). *Shyness and reticence in students.* Washington, DC: National Education Association.

Friedrich, G., & Goss, B. (1984). Systematic desensitization. In J. A. Daly & J. C. McCroskey (Eds.), *Avoiding communication: Shyness, reticence, and communication apprehension* (pp. 173–188). Beverly Hills, CA: Sage.

Gaies, S. J. (1985). *Peer involvement in language learning.* New York: Harcourt Brace Jovanovich.

Gardner, R. C. (1985). *Social psychology and second language learning: The role of attitudes and motivation.* London: Edward Arnold.

Gardner, R. C., Clément, R., Smythe, P. C., & Smythe, C. C. (1979). *Attitudes and motivation test battery, Revised manual* (Research Bulletin No. 15). London: University of Western Ontario.

Gardner, R. C., Lalonde, R. N., Moorcroft, R., & Evers, F. T. (1987). Second language attrition: The role of motivation and use. *Journal of Language and Social Psychology, 6,* 29–47.

Gardner, R. C., Moorcroft, R., & MacIntyre, P. D. (1987). *The role of anxiety in second language performance of language dropouts* (Research Bulletin No. 657). London: University of Western Ontario.

Gardner, R. C., Smythe, P. C., Clément, R., & Gliksman, L. (1976). Second language learning: A social and psychological perspective. *Canadian Modern Language Review, 32,* 198–213.

Gardner, R. C., Smythe, P. C., & Lalonde, R. N. (1984). *The nature and replicability of factors in second language acquisition* (Research Bulletin No. 605). London: University of Western Ontario.

Gary, C. F. (1973). *Effect of unannounced examinations on achievement, test anxiety, and attitude in certain junior college mathematics courses.* Unpublished doctoral dissertation, University of Oklahoma.

Gattegno, C. (1972). *Teaching foreign languages in school: The silent way.* New York: Educational Solutions.

Gaudry, E., & Fitzgerald, D. (1971). Test anxiety, intelligence, and academic achievement. In E. Gaudry & C. Spielberger (Eds.), *Anxiety and educational achievement.* Sydney: John Wiley.

Glaser, S. (1981). Oral communication apprehension and avoidance: The current status of treatment research. *Communication Education, 30,* 321–341.

Gliksman, L. (1981). *Improving the prediction of behaviors associated with second language acquisition.* Unpublished doctoral dissertation, University of Western Ontario, London.

Gordon, E. M., & Sarason, S. B. (1955). The relationship between "test anxiety" and "other anxieties." *Journal of Personality, 23,* 317–323.

Grieger, R., & Boyd, J. (1980). *Rational-emotive therapy: A skills-based approach.* San Francisco: Van Nostrand Reinhold.

Groot, P. J. M. (1976). Luistervaardigheid, Frans, Duits, Engels. In *Doelstelling entoetsing.* Amsterdam: Muelenhoff.

Guiora, A. Z. (1983). The dialectic of language acquisition. In A. Z. Guiora (Ed.), *An epistemology for the language sciences. Language Learning, 33,* 8.

Guiora, A. Z., Beit-Hallahmi, B., Brannon, R. C. I., Dull, C. Y., & Scovel, T. (1972). The effects of experimentally induced changes in ego status on pronunciation ability in a second language: An exploratory study. *Comprehensive Psychiatry, 13,* 421–428.

Gulliksen, H. (1950). *Theory of mental tests.* New York: John Wiley.

Gynther, R. A. (1957). The effects of anxiety and of situational stress on communicative efficiency. *Journal of Abnormal and Social Psychology, 54,* 274–276.

Hackworth, R. D. (1985). *Math anxiety reduction.* Clearwater, FL: H & H Publishing.

HANSEN, L. (1984). The ESL noise test: Cultural differences in affect and performance. In P. Larson, E. L. Judd, & D. S. Messerschmitt (Eds.), *On TESOL '84: A brave new world*. Washington, DC: TESOL.

HARDING, I. B. (1981). Adjunct courses: Integrating study skills into content courses. *Proceedings of the Fourteenth Annual Conference of the Western College Reading Association, 14,* 110–116.

HEMBREE, R. (1988). Correlates, causes, effects, and treatment of test anxiety. *Review of Educational Research, 58,* 47–77.

HENDEL, D. D., & DAVIS, S. O. (1978). Effectiveness of an intervention strategy for reducing mathematics anxiety. *Journal of Counseling Psychology, 25,* 429–434.

HERLIN, W. (1978). An attempt to teach reading and writing skills in conjunction with a beginning biology course for majors. *Proceedings of the Eleventh Annual Western College Reading Association Conference, 9,* 134–136.

HIGHNAM, S., & GEIST, P. (1981). Value systems: A prescriptive journal assignment. *Communication Education, 30,* 54–56.

HILGARD, E., ATKINSON, J., & ATKINSON, L. (1971). *Introduction to Psychology.* New York: Harcourt, Brace, & World.

HODGES, W., & SPIELBERGER, C. (1969). Digit span: An indirect indicant of trait or state anxiety? *Journal of Consulting and Clinical Psychology, 33,* 430–434.

HOLMES, C. C. (1972). Specific effects of test anxiety on reading comprehension as measured by the cloze procedure. Unpublished doctoral dissertation, University of Chicago.

HOPF, T. S. (1970). Reticence and the oral interpretation teacher. *Speech Teacher, 19,* 268–271.

HORWITZ, E. K. (1983). *Foreign language classroom anxiety scale.* Unpublished manuscript.

HORWITZ, E. K. (1984, March). *What ESL students believe about language learning.* Paper presented at the annual meeting of TESOL, Houston.

HORWITZ, E. K. (1985). *Scale of reactions to foreign language class.* Unpublished instrument. Austin: The University of Texas.

HORWITZ, E. K. (1986). Preliminary evidence for the reliability and validity of a foreign language anxiety scale. (This volume, pp. 37–39.)

HORWITZ, E. K., HORWITZ, M. B., & COPE, J. (1986). Foreign language classroom anxiety. (This volume, pp. 27–36.)

HULIN, C. L., DRASGOW, F., & PARSONS, C. I. (1983). *Item response theory: Applications to psychological measurement.* Homewood, IL: Dow Jones-Irwin.

HUMMEL, T. J., & SLIGO, J. R. (1971). Empirical comparison of univariate and multivariate analysis of variance procedures. *Psychological Bulletin, 76,* 49–57.

HUNSLEY, J. (1985). Test anxiety, academic performance, and cognitive appraisals. *Journal of Educational Psychology, 77,* 678–682.

HUNT, P. C. (1979). An interpersonal communication journal model. *Communication Education, 28,* 208–210.

HURT, H. T., & PREISS, R. (1978). Silence isn't necessarily golden: Communication apprehension, desired social choice, and academic success among middle-school students. *Human Communication Research, 4,* 315–328.

HURT, H. T., PREISS, R., & DAVIS, B. (1976). *The effects of communication apprehension of middle-school children of sociometric choice, affective and cognitive learning.* Paper presented at the meeting of the International Communication Association.

HURT, H. T., SCOTT, M. D., & McCROSKEY, J. C. (1978). *Communication in the classroom.* Reading, MA: Addison-Wesley.

JACKSON, D. N. (1978). Interpreter's guide to the Jackson Personality Inventory. In P. McReynolds (Ed.), *Advances in psychological assessment.* San Francisco: Jossey-Bass.

JACOBSON, E. (1938). *Progressive relaxation.* Chicago: University of Chicago Press.

JONES, K. (1982). *Simulations in language teaching.* Cambridge: Cambridge University Press.

JONES, R. L. (1976). Achieving objectivity in subjective foreign language tests. *Proceedings of the Fourth International Congress of Applied Linguistics.* Stuttgart: Hochschul Verlag.

JONES, R. L. (1985a). Second language performance testing: An overview. In P. C. Hautpman, R. LeBlanc, & M. B. Wesche (Eds.), *Second language performance testing.* Ottawa: University of Ottawa Press.

JONES, R. L. (1985b). Some basic considerations in testing oral proficiency. In *New Directions in Language Testing.* London: Pergamon Press.

JONES, R. L., & MADSEN, H. S. (1980). State affect questionnaire. Provo, UT: Brigham Young University.

JORSTAD, H. L. (1974). Testing as communication. *ACTFL Review: The Challenge of Communication, 6,* 223–268.

KANTER, N. J., & GOLDFRIED, M. R. (1979). Relative effectiveness of rational restructuring and self-control desensitization in the reduction of interpersonal anxiety. *Behavior Therapy, 10,* 472–490.

KENNEY, D. A. (1975). Cross-legged panel correlation: A test for spuriousness. *Psychological Bulletin, 82,* 887–903.

KESTENBAUM, J. M., & WEINER, B. (1970). Achievement performance related to achievement motivation and test anxiety. *Journal of Consulting and Clinical Psychology, 34,* 343–344.

KINNEY, P. (1988). *Effects of supplemental instruction on student performance in a college-level mathematics course.* Unpublished doctoral dissertation, University of Texas, Austin.

KLEINMANN, H. H. (1977). Avoidance behavior in adult second language acquisition. *Language Learning, 27,* 93–107.

KOCH, A. (1984). *The effects of the natural approach on the affective filter.* Unpublished master's thesis, University of California, Irvine.

KRASHEN, S. D. (1976). Formal and informal linguistic environments in language acquisition and language learning. *TESOL Quarterly, 10,* 157–168.

KRASHEN, S. D. (1980). The input hypothesis. In J. E. Alatis (Ed.), *Current issues in bilingual education, Georgetown University round table on languages and linguistics* (pp. 168–180). Washington, DC: Georgetown University Press.

KRASHEN, S. D. (1981). *Second language acquisition and second language learning.* Oxford: Pergamon.

KRASHEN, S. D. (1982). *Principles and practice in second language acquisition.* New York: Pergamon.

KRASHEN, S. D., & TERRELL, T. D. (1983). *The natural approach: Language acquisition in the classroom.* Heyward, CA: Alemany/Janus Press.

LABOV, W. (1972). Academic ignorance and black intelligence. *Atlantic Monthly, 229,* 59–67.

LALONDE, R. N., & GARDNER, R. C. (1984). Investigating a causal model of second language acquisition: Where does personality fit? *Canadian Journal of Behavioral Science, 15,* 224–237.

LAMENDELLA, J. (1977). The limbic system in human communication. In H. Whitaker & H. Whitaker (Eds.), *Studies in Neurolinguistics* (Vol. 3). New York: Academic Press.

LAMENDELLA, J. (1977). General principles of neurofunctional organization and their manifestation in primary and nonprimary language acquisition. *Language Learning, 27,* 155–196.

LANTOLF, J. P., & FRAWLEY, W. (1985). Oral proficiency testing: A critical analysis. *Modern Language Journal, 69,* 337–345.

LAOSA, L. (1977). Inequality in the classroom: Observational research on teacher–student interactions. *Aztlan International Journal of Chicano Studies Research, 8,* 51–67.

LEACH, J. N. (1979). *Bias in standardized testing: An update.* Paper presented at the 13th annual TESOL convention, Boston.

LEARNING SKILLS CENTER. (1988). *Annual Report 1987–1988.* Austin: The University of Texas.

LEVITT, E. E. (1981). *The psychology of anxiety.* Hillsdale, NJ: Erlbaum.

LITTLEWOOD, W. (1984). *Foreign and second language learning: Language acquisition research and its implications for the classroom.* Cambridge: Cambridge University Press.

LOZANOV, G. (1973). *Suggestology.* Nauka I. Izkistvo. Sofia (in Bulgarian; English translation pending with Gordon & Breach Science Publishers, New York).

LOZANOV, G. (1979). *Suggestology and outlines of suggestopedia*. New York: Gordon & Breach.

LUCAS, J. (1984). Communication apprehension in the ESL classroom: Getting our students to talk. *Foreign Language Annals, 17,* 593–598.

MACINTYRE, P. D. (1988). *The effect of anxiety on foreign language learning and production*. Unpublished master's thesis, University of Western Ontario, London.

MACINTYRE, P. D., & GARDNER, R. C. (1988). *The measurement of anxiety and applications to second language learning: An annotated bibliography* (Research Bulletin No. 672). London: University of Western Ontario.

MADSEN, H. S. (1982). Determining the debilitative impact of test anxiety. *Language Learning, 32,* 133–143.

MADSEN, H. S. (1987). Utilizing Rasch analysis to detect cheating on language examinations. In K. M. Bailey, T. L. Dale, & R. T. Clifford (Eds.), *Language Testing Research*. Monterey, CA: Defense Language Institute.

MADSEN, H. S., & MURRAY, N. N. (1984, MARCH). *Achieving a research synthesis through triangulation: A test affect application*. Paper presented at the 18th annual TESOL convention, Houston.

MALEY, A., & DUFF, A. (1982). *Drama techniques in language learning: A resource book of communication activities for language teachers*. Cambridge: Cambridge University Press.

MALLOW, J. V. (1981). *Science anxiety: The fear of science and how to overcome it*. New York: Thomond Press.

MALUF, S. (1979). *The use of native language cues: Evaluating foreign language listening skills of low proficiency students*. Unpublished master's thesis, Brigham Young University, Provo, UT.

MANLEY, M. J., & ROSEMEIR, R. A. (1972). Developmental trends in general and test anxiety among junior and senior high school students. *Journal of Genetic Psychology, 120,* 219–226.

MANSELL, M. (1981). Transcultural experience and expressive response. *Communication Education, 30,* 93–108.

MARASCUILO, L. A., & LEVIN, J. R. (1983). *Multivariate statistics in the social sciences: A researcher's guide*. Monterey, CA: Brooks/Cole.

MARTIN, D. C., BLANC, R., & DEBUHR, L. (1983). *Supplemental instruction: A model for student academic support*. Kansas City: University of Missouri Student Learning Center.

MAURER, E. D. (1973). *The effects of locus-of-control and test anxiety on children's response to social reinforcement in an evaluative situation*. Unpublished doctoral dissertation, University of Illinois, Urbana–Champaign.

MCCOY, I. R. (1979). Means to overcome the anxieties of second language learners.

MCCROSKEY, J. C. (1970). Measures of communication-bound anxiety. *Speech Monographs, 37,* 269–277.

MCCROSKEY, J. C. (1977a). Classroom consequences of communication apprehension. *Communication Education, 26,* 27–33.

MCCROSKEY, J. C. (1977b). Measures of communication-bound anxiety. *Speech Monographs, 37,* 269–277.

MCCROSKEY, J. C. (1977c). Oral communication apprehension: A summary of recent theory and research. *Human Communication Research, 4,* 78–96.

MCCROSKEY, J. C. (1978). Validity of the PRCA as an index of oral communication apprehension. *Communication Monographs, 45,* 192–203.

MCCROSKEY, J. C. (1982a). *An introduction to rhetorical communication*. Englewood Cliffs, NJ: Prentice-Hall.

MCCROSKEY, J. C. (1982b). Oral communication apprehension: A reconceptualization. In M. Burgoon (Ed.), *Communication Yearbook 6* (pp. 136–170). Beverly Hills, CA: Sage.

MCCROSKEY, J. C. (1984a). The communication apprehension perspective. In J. Daly & J. McCroskey (Eds.), *Avoiding communication: Shyness, reticence, and communication apprehension*. Beverly Hills, CA: Sage.

MCCROSKEY, J. C. (1984b). *An introduction to rhetorical communication*. Englewood Cliffs, NJ: Prentice-Hall.

McCroskey, J. C. (1987). Willingness to communication. In J. C. McCroskey & J. A. Daly (Eds.), *Personality and interpersonal communication* (pp. 129–156). Newbury Park, CA: Sage.

McCroskey, J. C., & Andersen, J. (1976). The relationship between communication apprehension and academic achievement among college students. *Human Communication Research, 3,* 73–81.

McCroskey, J. C., Andersen, J., Richmond, V., & Wheeless, L. (1981). Communication apprehension of elementary and secondary students and teachers. *Communication Education, 30,* 122–132.

McCroskey, J. C., & Beatty, M. J. (1984). Communication apprehension as a function of communication state anxiety experiences. *Communication Monographs, 51,* 79–84.

McCroskey, J. C., & Daly, J. A. (1976). Teachers' expectations of the communicative apprehensive child in the elementary school. *Human Communication Research, 3,* 67–72.

McCroskey, J. C., Daly, J. A., Richmond, V. P., & Falcione, R. L. (1977). Studies of the relationship between communication apprehension and self-esteem. *Human Communication Research, 3,* 269–277.

McCroskey, J. C., Fayer, J. M., & Richmond, V. P. (1983, December). *Don't speak to me in English: Communication apprehension in Puerto Rico.* Paper presented at the meeting of the Speech Communication Association of Puerto Rico.

McCroskey, J. C., & Richmond, V. P. (1980). *The quiet ones: Communication apprehension and shyness.* Dubuque, IA: Gorsuch Scarisbrick.

McCroskey, J. C., & Richmond, V. P. (1981). *The etiology and effects of communication apprehension: Cross-cultural implications.* Paper presented at the meeting of the Speech Communication Association of Puerto Rico.

Mier, D. R. (1983). Learning the art of management through the art of oral reading. *Communication Education, 32,* 293–301.

Morris, L. W., & Liebert, R. M. (1970). Relationship of cognitive and emotional components of text anxiety to physiological arousal and academic performance. *Journal of Consulting and Clinical Psychology, 35,* 332–337.

Morris, L. W. et al. (1976). Components of school anxiety: Developmental trends and sex difference. *Journal of Genetic Psychology, 128,* 49–57.

Moskowitz, G. (1978). *Caring and sharing in the foreign language class.* Rowley, MA: Newbury House.

Mullen, K. A. (1979). An alternative to the cloze test. In C. A. Yorio, K. Perkins, & J. Schacter (Eds.), *On TESOL '79.* Washington, DC: TESOL.

Murray, N. N. (1985). *A qualitative study of text anxiety among non-university ESL students.* Unpublished master's thesis, Brigham Young University, Provo, UT.

Murray, N. N., & Madsen, H. S. (1984). Retrospective evaluation of testing. In A. Melby (Ed.), *Deseret Language and Linguistic Society Proceedings.* Provo, UT: Brigham Young University.

Naimon, N., Fröhlich, M., Stern, D., & Todesco, A. (1978). *The good language learner.* Toronto: Ontario Institute for Studies in Education.

Nideffer, R., & Yock, T. (1976). The relationship between a measure of palmar sweat and swimming performance. *Journal of Applied Psychology, 61,* 376–378.

Ohlenkamp, E. A. (1976). *The relationship among test anxiety, self-esteem, and achievement for cooperative career education students in grades eleven and twelve.* Unpublished doctoral dissertation, Northern Illinois University.

Oller, J. W. Jr., & Perkins, K. (1978). Intelligence and language proficiency as sources of variance in self-reported affective variables. *Language Learning, 28,* 85–97.

Oller, J. W., & Streiff, V. (1975). Dictation: A test of grammar-based expectancies. In R. Jones & B. Spolsky (Eds.), *Testing language proficiency.* n.p.: Center for Applied Linguistics.

Omaggio, A. C. (1986). *Teaching language in context.* Boston: Heinle & Heinle.

Osterhouse, R. A. (1975). Classroom anxiety and the examination performance of test-anxious students. *Journal of Educational Research, 68,* 247–249.

Oxford, R. (1990). *Language learning strategies: What every teacher should know.* New York: Newbury House/Harper & Row.

PAIVIO, A. (1965). Personality and audience influence. In *Progress in experimental personality research: Vol. 2.* New York: Academic Press.

PAUL, G. L. (1966). *Insight vs. desensitization in psychotherapy.* Stanford, CA: Stanford University Press.

PASSEL, J. S., & WARREN, R. (1983). *Population division, U.S. Bureau of the Census from Mexico Counted in the United States.*

PELIAS, R. J. (1984). Oral interpretation as a training method for increasing perspective-taking abilities. *Communication Education, 33,* 143–151.

PIMSLEUR, P. (1970). New approaches to old problems through testing. *Wisconsin Association of Foreign Language Teachers Bulletin, 56,* 2–9.

PIMSLEUR, P. (1980). *How to learn a foreign language.* Boston: Heinle & Heinle.

PIMSLEUR, P., MOSBERG, L., & MORRISON, A. L. (1962). Student factors in foreign language learning. *Modern Language Journal, 46,* 160–170.

PIMSLEUR, P., SUNDLAND, D. M., & McINTYRE, R. D. (1964). Underachievement in foreign language learning. *IRAL, 2,* 113–150.

POPKIN, D. (1985). Dialogue journals: A way to personalize communication in a foreign language. *Foreign Language Annals, 18,* 153–156.

POWERS, W., & SMYTHE, M. J. (1980). Communication apprehension and achievement in a performance-oriented basic communication course. *Human Communication Research, 6,* 146–152.

PRESTWOOD, J. S., & WEISS, D. J. 1978). *The effects of knowledge of results and test difficulty on ability test performance and psychological reactions to testing* (Research Report No. 78–2). Resources in Education. Minneapolis: Minnesota University. ERIC Document Reproduction Service No. ED 166 232.

PRICE, M. L. (1988). *Anxiety and the foreign language learner: Correlates of foreign language anxiety.* Unpublished doctoral dissertation, University of Texas, Austin.

RAMIREZ, A. (1981). Language attitudes and the speech of Spanish-English bilingual pupils. In R. P. Duran (Ed.), *Latino language and communicative behavior* (pp. 217–232). Norwood, NJ: Ablex.

RENCHER, A. C., & CHEN PAN, FU. (1990). Assessing the contribution of individual variables following rejection of a multivariate hypothesis. Unpublished manuscript, Brigham Young University, Provo, UT.

RICHARDS, J. C. (1983). Communicative needs in foreign language learning. In N. Wolfson & E. Judd (Eds.), *Sociolinguistics and language acquisition* (pp. 242–252). Rowley, MA: Newbury House.

RICHARDSON, F. C., & SUINN, R. M. (1973). A comparison of traditional systematic desensitization, accelerated massed desensitization, and anxiety management training in the treatment of mathematics anxiety. *Behavior Therapy, 4,* 212–218.

RICHARDSON, F. C., & WOOLFOLK, R. L. (1980). Mathematics anxiety. In I. G. Sarason (Ed.), *Test anxiety: Theory, research and application* (pp. 271–288). Hillsdale, NJ: Erlbaum.

RICHMOND, V. P. (1984). Implications of quietness. In J. A. Daly & J. C. McCroskey (Eds.), *Avoiding communication: Shyness, reticence, and communication apprehension* (pp. 145–156). Beverly Hills, CA: Sage.

RICHMOND, V. P., & McCROSKEY, J. C. (1988). *Communication: Apprehension, avoidance, and effectiveness.* Scottsdale, AZ: Gorsuch Scarisbrick.

ROSE, M. (ED.) (1985). When a writer can't write. New York: Guilford.

ROSENZWEIG, S. J. (1974). *The effects of examiner anxiety level, student test anxiety level, and examiner-student sex interacting on student performance in a group test-taking situation.* Unpublished doctoral dissertation, Boston University School of Education.

RUBIN, J. (1981). Study cognitive processes in second language learning. *Applied Linguistics, 11* (2), 118–131.

SARASON, I. G. (1958). Interrelationships among individual difference variables, behavior in psychotherapy, and verbal conditioning. *Journal of Abnormal and Social Psychology and Verbal Conditioning, 56,* 330–334.

SARASON, I. G. (1952). Some correlates of test anxiety. *Journal of Abnormal and Social Psychology, 47,* 810–817.

SARASON, I. G. (1978). The test anxiety scale: Concept and research. In C. D. Spielberger & I. G. Sarason (Eds.), *Stress and anxiety: Vol. 5* (pp. 193–216). Washington, DC: Hemisphere.

SARASON, I. G. (1980a). Introduction to the study of test anxiety. In I. G. Sarason (Ed.), *Text anxiety: Theory, research and applications.* Hillsdale, NJ: Erlbaum.

SARASON, I. G. (ED.). (1980b). *Text anxiety: Theory, research and applications.* Hillsdale, NJ: Erlbaum.

SARASON, I. G. (1983). Understanding and modifying test anxiety. In S. B. Anderson & J. S. Helmich (Eds.), *On educational testing.* San Francisco: Jossey-Bass.

SARASON, I. G. (1986). Test anxiety, worry, and cognitive interference. In R. Schwarzer (Ed.), *Self-related cognition in anxiety and motivation.* Hillsdale, NJ: Erlbaum.

SARASON, I. G., & GANZER, V. J. (1962). Anxiety, reinforcement, and experimental instructions in a free verbalization situation. *Journal of Abnormal and Social Psychology, 65,* 300–307.

SARASON, I. G., & GANZER, V. J. (1963). Effects of test anxiety and reinforcement history on verbal behavior. *Journal of Abnormal and Social Psychology, 67,* 513–519.

SAVIGNON, S. J. (1972). *Communicative competence: An experiment in foreign language teaching.* Philadelphia: Center for Curriculum Development.

SAVIGNON, S. J. (1982). Dictation as a measure of communicative competence in French as a second language. *Language Learning, 32,* 33–51.

SAVIGNON, S. J. (1985). The ACTFL provisional proficiency guidelines. *The Modern Language Journal, 69,* 129–134.

SCHAFFER, L. (1947). Fear and courage in serial combat. *Journal of Consulting Psychology, 11,* 137–143.

SCHMITT, C. (1975). Oral interpretation as a catalyst for the reticent. *Pennsylvania Speech Communication Annual, 31,* 47–56.

SCHNORE, M. (1959). Individual patterns of physiological activity as a function of task differences and degree of arousal. *Journal of Experimental Psychology, 58,* 117–128.

SCHUMANN, F. E., & SCHUMANN, J. N. (1977). Diary of a language learner: An introspective study of second language learning. In H. D. Brown, C. A. Yorio, & R. Crymes (Eds.), *On TESOL '77: Teaching and learning ESL.* Washington, DC: TESOL.

SCHUMANN, J. (1976a). Second language acquisition research: Getting a more global look at the learner. In H. D. Brown, (Ed.), *Papers in second language acquisition.* Ann Arbor, MI: n.p.

SCHUMANN, J. (1976b). Second language acquisition: The pidginization hypothesis. *Language Learning, 26,* 391–407.

SCHWARTZ, L. (1972). *Educational psychology: Focus on the learner.* Boston: Holbrook Press.

SCHWARZER, R., VAN DER PLOEG, H. M., & SPIELBERGER, C. (1982). *Advances in test anxiety research, Vol. 1.* Hillsdale, NJ: Erlbaum.

SCOON, A. (1971). Affective influences on English language learning among Indian students. *TESOL Quarterly, 5,* 285–291.

SCOTT, D. T., CARTER, M. W., BRYCE, G. R., & JOINER, B. L. (1974). *RUMMAGE: A general data analysis system.* Paper presented at the joint meetings of ASQC and the American Statistical Association's section on physical and engineering sciences, Richmond, VA.

SCOTT, M. L. (1980). *The effect of multiple retesting on affect and test performance.* Unpublished master's thesis, Brigham Young University, Provo, UT.

SCOTT, M. L. (1986). Student affective reactions to oral language tests. *Language testing, 3* (1), 99–118.

SCOTT, M. L., & MADSEN, H. S. (1983). The influence of retesting on test affect. In J. W. Oller, Jr. (Ed.), *Issues in language testing research.* Rowley, MA: Newbury House.

SCOVEL, T. (1973). Language learning as a sport. *Education, 93,* 84–87.

SCOVEL, T. (1978). The effect of affect on foreign language learning: A review of the anxiety research. *Language Learning, 28,* 129–142.

SELLS, L. (1978). Mathematics as a critical filter. *The Science Teacher, 45,* 28–29.

SEPIE, A. C., & KEELING, B. (1978). Relationships between types of anxiety and underachievement in mathematics. *Journal of Educational Research, 72,* 15–19.

SHOHAMY, E. (1980). *Students' attitudes toward tests: Affective considerations in testing.* Paper presented at the 14th annual TESOL convention, San Francisco.

SHOHAMY, E. (1982). Affective considerations in language testing. *Modern Language Journal, 66,* 13–17.

SMITH, R. E., ASCOUGH, J., ETTINGER, R., & NELSON, D., (1971). Humor, anxiety, and task performance. *Journal of Personality and Social Psychology, 19,* 243–246.

SNYDER, C. R., & RAY, W. J. (1971). Observed body movement in the college test-taking situation and scores on the Scholastic Aptitude Test. *Perceptual and Motor Skills, 32,* 265–266.

SPENCE, K. (1958). A theory of emotionally based drive (D) and its relation to performance in simple learning situations. *American Psychologist, 13,* 131–141.

SPIELBERGER, C. (1966a). The effects of anxiety on performance in complex learning tasks. In C. Spielberger (Ed.), *Anxiety and behavior.* New York: Academic Press.

SPIELBERGER, C. (ED.). (1966b). *Anxiety and behavior.* New York: Academic Press.

SPIELBERGER, C. (1972). *Anxiety: Current trends in theory and research.* New York: Academic Press.

SPIELBERGER, C. (1980). *Test anxiety inventory: Preliminary professional manual.* Palo Alto, CA: Consulting Psychologists Press.

SPIELBERGER, C. (1983). *Manual for the state-trait anxiety inventory (STAI-Form Y).* Palo Alto, CA: Consulting Psychologists Press.

SPIELBERGER, C., & DÍAZ-GUERRERO, R. (1976). *Cross-cultural anxiety.* New York: John Wiley.

SPIELBERGER, C., GONZALEZ, H., TAYLOR, C. J., ALGAZE, B., & ANTON, W. D. (1978). Examination stress and test anxiety. In C. Spielberger & I. Sarason (Eds.), *Stress and Anxiety (Vol. 5)* (pp. 167–192). Washington, DC: Hemisphere Publishing.

SPIELBERGER, C., GORSUCH, R. L., & LUSHENE, R. E. (1970). *State-trait anxiety inventory.* Palo Alto: Consulting Psychologist Press.

SPITZBERG, B. H., & CUPACH, W. R. (1984). *Interpersonal communication competence.* Beverly Hills, CA: Sage.

SPITZBERG, B. H., & HURT, H. T. (1987). The measurement of interpersonal skills in instructional contexts. *Communication Education, 36,* 28–45.

STANSFIELD, C. W. (1985). A history of dictation in foreign language teaching and testing. *Modern Language Journal, 69,* 122–128.

STANTON, H. E. (1973). The effect of music on test anxiety. *Australian Psychologist, 8,* 220–228.

STATON, J. (1983). Dialogue journals: A new tool for teaching communication. *ERIC/Clearinghouse on Languages and Linguistics, 6,* 1–6.

STEINBERG, F. S. (1982). *The relationship between anxiety and oral performance in a foreign language.* Unpublished master's thesis, University of Texas, Austin.

STEINBERG, F. S., & HORWITZ, E. K. (1986). The effect of induced anxiety on the denotative and interpretive content of second language speech. *TESOL Quarterly, 20,* 131–136.

STEVENSON, D. G. (1979). *The experimental evaluation of test affect.* Unpublished master's thesis, Brigham Young University, Provo, UT.

STEVICK, E. (1976). *Memory, meaning and method: Some psychological perspectives on language learning.* Rowley, MA: Newbury House.

STEVICK, E. (1980). *Language teaching: A way and ways.* Rowley, MA: Newbury House.

STRAATMEYER, A. J., & WATKINS, J. T. (1974). Rational-emotive therapy and the reduction of speech anxiety. *Rational Living, 9,* 33–37.

SWAIN, M. (1977). Future directions in second language research. *Proceedings of the L. A. Second Language Research Forum.* UCLA: Department of English, ESL Section.

SWAIN, M., & BURNABY, B. (1976). Personality characteristics and second language learning in young children: A pilot study. *Working Papers in Bilingualism, 11,* 115–128.

SWAIN, M., & NAIMAN, N. (1976). Discussion of Schumann's paper. In Brown (Ed.), *Papers in Second Language Acquisition.* Ann Arbor, MI: n.p.

TAYLOR, B. (1974). Toward a theory of language acquisition. *Language Learning, 24,* 23–35.

TAYLOR, J. A. (1953). A personality scale of manifest anxiety. *Journal of Abnormal and Social Psychology, 48,* 285–290.

TAYLOR, J. A. (1956). Drive theory and manifest anxiety. *Psychological Bulletin, 53,* 303–320.

TAYLOR, J. W. (1971). Problems of educational testing in Pacific Island Territories. South Pacific Commission. Noumea, New Caledonia. *New Guinea Psychologist, 3,* 13–19.

TERRELL, T. D. (1977). A natural approach to the acquisition and learning of a language. *Modern Language Journal, 61,* 325–336.

TERRELL, T. D. (1981). The natural approach in bilingual education. In *Schooling and language minority students: A theoretical framework* (pp. 117–145). California State University, Los Angeles: Office of Bilingual Education, California State Department of Education.

TERRELL, T. D. (1982). The natural approach to language teaching: An update. *Modern Language Journal, 66,* 121–131.

TERRELL, T. D. (1986). Acquisition in the natural approach: The binding/access framework. *Modern Language Journal, 70,* 213–227.

TERRELL, T. D., ANDRADE, M., EGASSE, J., & MUNOZ, E. M. (1986). *Dos mundos: A communicative approach.* New York: Random House.

THORPE, G., AMATU, H., BLAKEY, R., & BURNS, L. (1976). Contributions of overt instructional rehearsal and specific insight to effectiveness of self-instructional training: A preliminary study. *Behavior Therapy, 7,* 504–511.

TOBIAS, S. (1978). *Overcoming math anxiety.* New York: W. W. Norton & Co., Inc.

TOBIAS, S. (1979). Anxiety research in educational psychology. *Journal of Educational Psychology, 71,* 573–582.

TOBIAS, S. (1980). Anxiety and instruction. In I. G. Sarason (Ed.), *Test anxiety: Theory, research and applications.* Hillsdale, NJ: Erlbaum.

TOBIAS, S. (1986). Anxiety and cognitive processing of instruction. In R. Schwarzer (Ed.), *Self-related cognition in anxiety and motivation.* Hillsdale, NJ: Erlbaum.

TOMLINSON, B. M., & GREEN, T. (1976). Integrating adjunct reading and study classes with the content areas. *Proceedings of the Ninth Annual Conference of the Western College Reading Association, 9,* 199–203.

TORRANCE, E. P. (1963). Changing reactions of preadolescent girls to tasks requiring creative scientific thinking. *Journal of Genetic Psychology, 102,* 217–223.

TOWLE, N. J., & MERRILL, P. F. (1972). *Effects of anxiety type and item difficulty sequencing on mathematics aptitude test performance* (Tech. Memo No. 46). (ERIC Document Reproduction Service No. ED 070 284.)

TRYLONG, V. L. (1987). *Aptitude, attitudes, and anxiety: A study of their relationships to achievement in the foreign language classroom.* Unpublished doctoral dissertation, Purdue University, West Lafayette, IN.

TRYON, W. W., LEIB, W., & SHIEK TRYON, G., (1973). *Test anxiety as a function of academic achievement, grade level, and sex in ghetto elementary school children.* Proceedings, 81st annual convention. American Psychological Association, Montreal, 1973.

TUCKER, R., HAMAYAN, E., & GENESEE, F. H. (1976). Affective, cognitive, and social factors in second language acquisition. *Canadian Modern Language Review, 32,* 214–226.

U.S. BUREAU OF THE CENSUS (1981). *Persons of Spanish origin by state: 1980* (Supplementary Report No. PC 80–81–7).

U.S. DEPARTMENT OF EDUCATION (1982). Commission on Higher Education of Minorities.

UPSHUR, J. A., ACTON, W., ARTHUR, B., & GUIORA, A. Z. (1978). Causation or correlation: A reply to Oller and Perkins. *Language Learning, 28,* 99–104.

UR, P. (1981). *Discussions that work: Task-centered fluency practice.* Cambridge: Cambridge University Press.

VAN KLEECK, A., & DALY, J. A. (1982). Human development and instructional communication. In M. Burgoon (Ed.), *Communication Yearbook V* (pp. 685–716). New Brunswick, NJ: Transaction Books.

VERMA, P., & NIJHAWAN, H. K. (1976). The effect of anxiety reinforcement and intelligence on the learning of a difficult task. *Journal of Experimental Child Psychology, 22,* 302–308.

WARNER, R. S., & KAUFFMAN, J. M. (1972). Effect of prearrangement of testing on anxiety and performance of second- and sixth-grade boys. *Psychology in the Schools, 9,* 75–78.

WASHINGTON, E. M. (1983). Choral reading: An aid to teaching novice oral interpretation students. *Communication Education, 32,* 117–122.

WATSON, D., & FRIEND, R. (1969). Measurement of social-evaluative anxiety. *Journal of Consulting and Clinical Psychology, 33,* 448–451.

WEISS, D. J. (ED.) (1983). *New horizons in testing: Latent trait test theory and computerized adaptive testing.* New York: Academic Press.

WENDEN, A. L., & RUBIN, J. (EDS.). (1986). *Learner strategies in language learning.* Englewood Cliffs, NJ. Prentice-Hall.

WESTCOTT, D. B. (1973). *Personality factors affecting high school students learning a second language.* Unpublished doctoral dissertation, University of Texas, Austin.

WHEELESS, L. R. (1975). An investigation of receiver apprehension and social context dimensions of communication apprehension. *Speech Teacher, 24,* 261–268.

WILD, C. (1975). The oral interview test. In R. L. Jones & B. Spolsky (Eds.), *Testing Language Proficiency* (pp. 29–44). Arlington, Virginia: Center for Applied Linguistics.

WILDEMUTH, B. (1977). (Introduction) *Test anxiety: An extensive bibliography* (TM Report No. 64). (ERIC Document Reproduction Service No. ED 152 860.)

WINE, J. D. (1980). Cognitive-attentional theory of test anxiety. In I. G. Sarason (Ed.), *Test anxiety: Theory, research and applications* (pp. 349–385). Hillsdale, NJ: Erlbaum.

WITTENBORN, J. R., LARSEN, R. P., & MOGIL, R. L. (1945). An empirical evaluation of study habits for college courses in French and Spanish. *Journal of Educational Psychology, 36,* 449–474.

YOUNG, D. J. (1986). The relationship between anxiety and foreign language oral proficiency ratings. (This volume, pp. 57–63.)

ZEIDNER, M., & BENSOUSSAN, M. (1988). College students' attitudes towards written versus oral tests of English as a foreign language. *Language Testing, 5,* (1), 100–114.